MW00617542

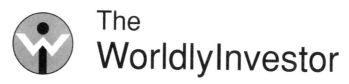

The
WorldlyInvestor

Guide to
BEATING
the
MARKET

The WorldlyInvestor

Guide to

BEATING

the

MARKET

Beat the Pros at Their Own Game

Ben Warwick

John Wiley & Sons, Inc.

New York • Chichester • Weinheim • Brisbane • Singapore • Toronto

This book is printed on acid-free paper. ∞

Copyright © 2001 by Worldly Information Network Inc.

Published by John Wiley & Sons, Inc.
Published simultaneously in Canada.

No part of this publication may be reproduced, stored in a retrieval system, or
transmitted in any form or by any means, electronic, mechanical, photocopying,
recording, scanning, or otherwise, except as permitted under Section 107 or 108 of
the 1976 United States Copyright Act, without either the prior written permission
of the Publisher, or authorization through payment of the appropriate per-copy fee
to the Copyright Clearance Center, 222 Rosewood Drive, Danvers, MA 01923,
(978) 750-8400, fax (978) 750-4744. Requests to the Publisher for permission should
be addressed to the Permissions Department, John Wiley & Sons, Inc., 605 Third
Avenue, New York, NY 10158-0012, (212) 850-6011, fax (212) 850-6008,
E-Mail: PERMREQ@WILEY.COM.

This publication is designed to provide accurate and authoritative information in
regard to the subject matter covered. It is sold with the understanding that the
publisher is not engaged in rendering professional services. If professional advice or
other expert assistance is required, the services of a competent professional person
should be sought.

CFA® and Chartered Financial Analyst™ are trademarks owned by the Association
for Investment Management and Research (AIMR®). The Association for
Investment Management and Research does not endorse, promote, review, or
warrant the accuracy of the products or services offered by John Wiley & Sons.

Library of Congress Cataloging-in-Publication Data:
Worldly Information Network Inc.
    The worldlyinvestor guide to beating the market / Worldly Information
Network Inc. ; Ben Warwick.
        p.   cm.
Includes bibliographical references.
    ISBN 0-471-39426-2 (cloth : alk. paper)
    1. Investment analysis.   I. Title
HG4529 .W37 2001
332.6–dc21   00-046262

Printed in the United States of America

10 9 8 7 6 5 4 3 2 1

Foreword

When I was asked to write the Foreword to Ben Warwick's newest book—*The WorldlyInvestor Guide to Beating the Market*—I jumped at the chance for two reasons.

First, Worldly Information Network and TD Waterhouse, the company I lead as president, share a vision and mission: to serve the individual investor. At TD Waterhouse we help our customers—self-directed investors—manage their money successfully. Worldly Information Network is one of the Internet's leading providers of financial information about financial markets, stocks, bonds, and mutual funds, and delivers thoughtful, fresh investing ideas. Our ultimate goals are strikingly similar.

The second reason I'm delighted to be contributing to Ben's latest work is simply that I've always enjoyed reading Ben's column on worldlyinvestor.com. I think he's at the head of the class when it comes to communicating market-related ideas in a very intelligent, refreshing, and accessible manner. He has a great knack for being in touch with both investor and market psychology, and delivering his perceptions in a way we can all readily understand. Just two examples, if I may:

> On a failed market rally in May 2000: "... it was as if your football team came within a field goal of winning a crucial game, only to fumble the ball on the opponent's 5 yard line...."

On mutual fund managers in October 2000: ". . . after all, mutual fund pros generally hold stocks of 'good' companies, yet the S&P 500 outperforms the bulk of active managers, year in and year out. The predilection of fund managers to pick already established, well-performing stocks is similar to a baseball team paying millions of dollars for a superstar third baseman—while ignoring potential superstars in the minor leagues. . . ."

What I also admire in Ben is his ability to entertain while educating. In his first book, *Event Trading—Profiting from Economic Reports and Short Term Market Inefficiencies* (June 1996), Ben's style was more serious. Even so, he managed a few down-to-earth, humorous analogies (e.g., Michael Jordan versus the Welder). Then, in a subsequent work, *Searching for Alpha* (May 2000), he loosened up through great usage of cartoons to illustrate his points (imagine a cartoon depicting "searching for alpha"—I think you get it).

His ability to call on the work and best thinking of the giants of the investing world (Harry Markowitz, John Maynard Keynes, John Burr Williams, Benjamin Graham, Warren Buffett, and so on) earns my respect and admiration. In 1986, I completed my studies for the Chartered Financial Analyst (CFA) designation after studying for three years and learning about Modern Portfolio Theory, the Capital Asset Pricing Model, as well as the other investment tenets that a professional must master. Nevertheless, after having read all of Ben's books I now understand these concepts more clearly than ever.

Both Ben and I are very fortunate to be involved in the great individual investor revolution that has taken place over the past quarter century, beginning with the "Big Bang" on May Day 1975, when the SEC abolished fixed commission rates. This helped level the capital markets playing field so that retail investors could participate and benefit in a way that previously had been available only to institutions and the very wealthy.

From 1975 to 1995, discount brokerage firms grew to approximately 15 percent of total stock trading volumes by attracting self-directed investors who were tired of paying high commissions to their brokers. With the advent of online trading in 1996, investing became a whole new ball game. Over the past four years, online investors have taken control of their financial lives and have become a significant force. Today, more than half of the retail stock trading volume is from online investors.

The Internet was the great equalizer. Retail investors now have access to the markets and to real-time research information and tools, a development that allows them to make more timely and better-informed decisions about their investments.

This is where the book you are about to read comes in. Ben has presented a plethora of easy-to-execute strategies the individual investor can use to outperform the investment management professionals.

He begins with a persuasive overview of exactly where we are at the present moment, and why the individual investor in this brave new millennium holds high cards. With reduced transaction costs, enhanced research tools, and the ever-expanding wealth of information available over the Internet, today's investor has a better-than-ever chance of beating the market. What's more, Ben unequivocally claims, savvy investors can understand and apply the strategies used by professional investment managers to increase the performance of their own portfolios. His contagious enthusiasm for the market-beating possibilities this offers individual investors is backed up so convincingly with chapter after chapter of stock and mutual fund strategies that you'll become equally enthusiastic.

The WorldlyInvestor Guide to Beating the Market is especially useful to individual investors who can track the methodologies by using the stock screening tools found on worldlyinvestor.com. Chapters in this book offer lists of online screens that make the theoretical material not only accessible but, more importantly, *applicable*—and the site's "Quant View" portfolio keeps you constantly updated on how the strategies are actually performing.

In Part One you'll find a range of strategies for trading individual stocks. The author first explores momentum stocks: why what goes up continues to do so—and why it must come down. He looks at the differences between "news watcher" traders and momentum traders, how the two influence price movements, and how to trade momentum stocks. Chapter 2, "A New Paradigm for Growth Stocks," offers an analysis of why the old-school method of picking tech stocks doesn't work any more, why you should maintain a large-cap bias, diversify ruthlessly with the help of the stock screening tools and information found on worldlyinvestor.com, and beware of trying to catch growth industries too early.

In Chapter 3, "Uncovering the Value in Value Stocks," the author looks at the art of buying stocks that are trading below their true value and then selling them after a price run-up, the emotional versus the logical side of value investing, and how to identify value stocks with the greatest potential for appreciation. And in Chapter 4, "Distressed Stocks, the Dregs of the Market," he tells you why the so-called experts shun them, what you need to know to enter this arena, and how to identify good "unexcellent" companies ready to revert to the mean and rise toward the average return of the market.

In Part Two, Warwick tackles index trading with exchange-traded funds and mutual funds, offering insight into how to profit hand-somely by trading broad market indexes instead of individual stocks. He explains the various investment vehicles you can use to trade the market as a whole, how investors can profit from market movements associated with the release of economic information, what savvy traders need to know to profitably exploit the market's tendency to rise around specific times of the year—and when to sit on the side-lines. And, finally, he reveals one of investment management's most guarded secrets: how to exploit the pricing errors in mutual funds.

If you're eager to learn Warwick's tips for online investors, Part Three teaches you how to use the Internet to build a portfolio that closely mimics—and in many cases surpasses—the performance of any stock index. You'll also get a solid overview of how this approach gives you more control over taxes and their impact on your overall return. Chapter 10 takes you through the darker side of Internet trading, the many poorly designed trading systems touted by unscrupulous operators, and the evaluative techniques you can use to determine whether a given strategy is likely to hold up in the future. The chapter also examines penny stocks and why there are still a number of pitfalls to watch out for in this area, and the serious impediments to success in day trading.

In Part Four, Warwick provides a thorough guide to selecting mutual funds and an incisive overview of the market timing strategies most frequently used by mutual fund and exchange-traded fund investors.

While my opinion of the strategies in *The WorldlyInvestor Guide to Beating the Market* varies from strategy to strategy, I find Ben Warwick's presentation of them to be superb throughout, and rich with fresh perspective. I believe any investor stands to benefit from Warwick's advice, regardless of one's particular investing style. There are, however, several keys to success that are worth bearing in mind no matter which strategy you follow:

- Clearly identify your investing goals.
- Create a plan that will help you accomplish those goals.
- Know what your risk/return tolerance boundary is, and stay within it—there are no free lunches.
- Stay disciplined and focused on your investing goals.
- Remember your partner, Uncle Sam—the only rich uncle who never dies.
- Never confuse any company with its stock, or the stock with the company—and never fall forever in love with either.
- Always Do Your Homework!

Best of luck in all your investing endeavors.

Frank Petrilli
President & Chief Operating Officer
TD Waterhouse

Contents

not work any longer. The stock screening tools and information found on the worldlyinvestor.com web site will greatly simplify the task of finding the next Dell Computer or America Online.

A mountain of evidence suggests that, over the long run, investing in value stocks is a superior strategy. So why have these issues underperformed virtually every market index for the past five years? A new way to look at the value investing concept.

Distressed companies–those so far gone that virtually no one will touch them–can transform an amateur stock picker into a well-known market pundit. But how do you separate the wheat from the chaff? This simple stock-screening method will give you a leg up on the competition.

Due to the tendency of macroeconomic data to trend, it is often easier to trade broad market indexes rather than individual stocks. Here's how to cash in.

These simple strategies will show the enormous profit potential of trading with government reports and stock-specific information.

Contents

The Individual Investor of the Next Millennium

I am convinced that an individual investor with sound principles, and soundly advised, can do distinctly better over the long pull than a large institution.
    –Benjamin Graham, "Security Analysis"

Everyone knows that technological innovation has changed our lives in innumerable ways. And one of the most recent and dramatic changes will alter the way people invest their money for the next century.

Individual investors have a better chance at generating market-beating returns than either professional investment managers or mutual funds.

And the size of the edge enjoyed by savvy private investors over institutional-sized professional traders? An astonishing 4 to 7 percent per year.

As we shall see, the bulk of this advantage comes largely from the reduced transaction costs and the enhanced research tools now available on the Internet.

What allowed for this tremendous shift in power from the hands of Wall Street insiders to the technologically savvy private trader–liquidity, deregulation, and the advent of the Internet–will transform the investment landscape for years to come.

1

THE ADVENT OF MUTUAL FUNDS

Stock investing entered the modern age in 1951, with the development of Modern Portfolio Theory (MPT). Among other lessons, MPT showed the world that diversification could enhance returns while simultaneously decreasing overall risk. Although initially shunned by the investment community as a fruitless academic exercise, the theory was wholeheartedly embraced by the bull market of the 1960s and the new revolution of investment–the mutual fund.

The mutual fund industry was in the process of transforming Wall Street both economically and socially. As recently as the end of World War II, the funds had been at best a trivial element in the securities industry, with just over $1 billion of assets under management. By the early 1960s, that figure was $35 billion and rising at a rate of nearly $2.5 billion per year. The fund industry was already accounting for a quarter of the value of all stock exchange transactions. And with such momentum, it was clear that this was no more than the beginning.

Mutual funds seemed to be the ideal investment vehicle. Through funds, small investors could get the expert advice that their limited resources otherwise denied them. And with MPT and the advent of more powerful computers, vital investment data could be analyzed in a fraction of the time it would take for an individual to do the analysis. But perhaps the most persuasive argument in favor of the mutual fund industry harkened back to the law of supply and demand. With such an astonishing influx of new capital into mutual funds, wasn't the market bound to go up and up, to everyone's benefit? Weren't the funds, so long as they thrived, a sort of guarantee of a permanent bull market?

This mind-set quickly dissipated after the devastating bear market of the 1970s left many investors holding onto stock worth less than one-half of their purchase price. Clearly, mutual funds were not the savior of the investment industry.

Even so, the mutual fund has become the most important financial device of the twentieth century. The bulk of assets dedicated to capital markets today are managed by a cadre of investment professionals whose job is to put the nation's savings to work in the best way possible.

If they were always successful at doing so, our story would be over. But as we shall see, this is certainly not the case.

LUCKY FELICITY FORESIGHT

A February 2000 article in the venerable British publication *The Economist* tells the tale of a little-known but brilliant lady who used her clever investment strategy to become the world's richest person. Her secret? Perfect foresight.

Starting with one dollar on January 1, 1900, she would predict at the beginning of each year the asset that would experience the highest total dollar return over the following 12 months. She would then put all of her wealth in that asset and not touch it for a year. By the 100th year Ms. Foresight had turned her meager beginnings into an after-tax windfall of $1.3 quadrillion—enough to buy the estate of Bill Gates roughly 15,000 times.

Along comes Henry Hindsight, an old flame of Felicity's. Lacking Felicity's extrasensory powers, Henry is more the typical investor who tends to follow a similar but less robust approach: Henry fastidiously invests each January in the *previous* year's best-performing asset. Yet, all too often last year's highflier turns out to be this year's tunnel dweller. During the past 50 years he has suffered a loss, on average, every other year. These were offset by one or two spectacular gains, but over the past century his initial $1 stake grew to a modest after-tax $283.

No wonder Felicity refused to marry poor Henry! One of the best of all her predictions was that the marriage would never work. Henry was last seen investing his little sum in Internet stocks.

Felicity and Henry represent the two extremes of investing. Most would compare Henry's well-intentioned but futile attempt at playing the market to the mass of mutual fund investors who tend to chase last year's most spectacularly returning fund featured on the cover of *Money* magazine. Unfortunately for these throngs of investors, markets have a tendency to be *mean reverting*—a fancy way of saying that yesterday's winner is often today's has-been. For these investors, the shattered dreams of future potential bonanzas are often lost in the spectacular scene in the rearview mirror—*if only I'd gotten in last year*, they all seem to say.

But what of Felicity? Many view mutual fund managers and other market professionals in the same light as our fictional protagonist. Armed with unlimited research budgets, expert advice from the world's largest brokerage firms, and up-to-the minute news and stock prices, these titans of the stock market are virtually unbeatable—according to the perceptions of many.

It is at this point in our story that perception and reality travel down different paths. Virtually all of the studies of the performance of professionally managed stock portfolios have determined the same thing: that *the average mutual fund cannot beat the market consistently*. In fact, many mutual fund pros are not even motivated to deliver exceptional returns. Consider the following:

The bulk of mutual fund managers are compensated based on fund assets—and not on the success of their investment strategies. Shockingly, a well-placed sound bite is often more valuable to a mutual fund manager than an exceptional market call. As long as the stock market rises, mutual fund managers need only produce positive returns to maintain their client base. In fact, a recent study showed that fund buyers weigh intangibles like customer service and the availability of 800-number phone lines more important than performance in choosing their investments. Bowing to the demands of their client base, mutual fund operators have become service organizations for those satiated with comfortable mediocrity.

Even if a mutual fund professional had sufficient skill to beat the market, the fund's swollen asset base would work against them, increasing his or her transaction costs to an appreciable extent. For fund managers intent on maximizing their personal bottom lines—a rational objective, I might add—even those with market-beating abilities will have serious problems delivering exceptional performance to their clients. Why? Because great returns require more than savvy stock selection—investment managers must also be able to trade their picks effectively.

Transaction costs consist of four components. The first, commissions, represents the fee paid to a broker for buying and selling stock. Commissions represent the only component of transaction costs that have gone down over time. In many instances, commissions are negligible compared to the other three components.

The second component, market impact, represents the change in the stock's price caused by the execution of a trade. Often, buying a large block of stock causes its price to move upward, which adds significantly to the cost of trading.

Delay costs are incurred when an investment manager decides to wait for the "best time to trade" (either a better price or more liquidity). Many times, stock prices fall when managers wait to sell stock, and rise while they wait to buy. Delay costs are often referred to as market timing costs.

Finally, opportunity costs represent the costs of not trading or only partially completing a transaction. This cost is generally associated with issues of limited liquidity.

Figure I.1 shows typical transaction costs for two types of mutual funds for the purchase or sale of one share of $100 stock. As you can see, transaction costs vary among fund types. Small-cap growth funds, for instance, have higher costs simply because the stocks that they buy and sell are more illiquid than their large-cap counterparts. Another factor is trade size—as mutual funds get larger, they are forced to trade stocks in larger and larger blocks. These block orders can be quite costly to trade. This factor largely explains why mutual funds with relatively small amounts of client assets tend to perform better than larger funds.

Transaction Costs for Mutual Fund Managers—Total Cost for Trading One Share of a $100 Stock

Fund Type	Commissions	Market Impact	Delay Costs	Opportunity Costs	Total
Large-cap growth fund	$0.10	$0.21	$1.14	$0.14	$1.59
Small-cap growth fund	$0.18	$0.57	$2.08	$0.29	$3.12

FIGURE I.1 Transaction costs for mutual fund managers are often large enough to impede their performance.
Source: Adapted from Wayne Wagner and Steven Glass, "Analyzing Transaction Costs: Part I," *Journal of Investment Consulting* 1, No. 2 (June 1999), p. 7.

Now, let's analyze the transaction costs for an individual investor. Of course, individuals still have to pay commissions. But commission rates have gone down dramatically, even for the smallest investor. Internet trading firms like E*Trade and Ameritrade offer flat rates for orders of any size.

The next three areas of cost, though, are where the individual trader has the real advantage. Since market impact, delay costs, and opportunity costs all increase as order size gets larger, private traders are not affected by these costs as much as the average mutual fund manager. *Savvy private investors can expect to pay about 75 percent less to execute a trade than the typical investment professional.*

This edge translates surprisingly well to the bottom line. Over the past 10 years, the average actively managed large-cap stock mutual fund has underperformed its benchmark, the Standard & Poor's 500 index, by about 1.7 percent per year. Let's suppose that the execution edge enjoyed by private traders amounts to 3.4 percent per year (a rather conservative estimate, since most investors would not charge themselves the hefty management fees levied by the mutual funds). If that is the case, if both entities execute the same trades in a given year, the private trader should outperform the mutual fund by 3.4 percent, and the S&P 500 by 1.7 percent.

And as Figure I.2 shows, that slight edge can radically change the size of one's nest egg. A passive investment in the S&P 500 index grew from $10,000 on the first day of 1990 to $53,287 on the last day of 1999–for an impressive average annual return of 20.3 percent. If one had chosen an actively managed large-cap mutual fund, the money would have grown to $46,055. But if the private investor had, using his or her own investing acumen, implemented the same strategies as the fund manager, the account would boast a value of $61,524–*over 33 percent more than the value of the mutual fund at the end of 10 years.*

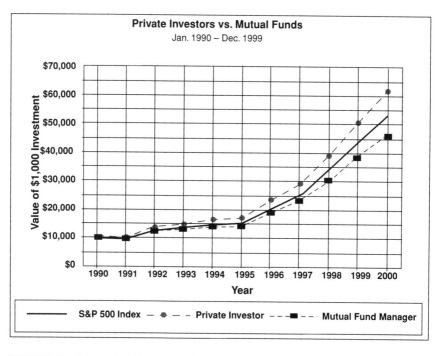

FIGURE I.2   Due to their lesser trading costs, private traders have significant advantages over mutual fund managers.

Small-cap investors have an even bigger advantage over small-cap funds. Considering the difficulty in trading small stocks, I would conservatively estimate that active private trades using the same strategy as professional managers should outperform funds by 7 percent per year.

THE INDIVIDUAL INVESTOR OF THE NEXT MILLENNIUM

That leads to an obvious question: *Can an individual investor understand and apply the strategies used by professional investment managers?* The answer is an unqualified *yes*.

In the past 10 years, the investment management business has witnessed the largest paradigm shift in its history–the transfer of market power from the professional manager to the individual investor. As commissions have plummeted and financial information has become more accessible, a diligent private investor may find it easier to generate market-beating returns than a seasoned mutual fund operator.

The increasing size and utility of the Internet have allowed individual investors to access the same fundamental and technical information as mutual fund managers, thus bridging the gap between the haves and the have-nots. The only data not available to private investors is that produced by Wall Street analysts–and virtually all studies have shown that their information is useless in predicting the future direction of stock prices.

That is where this book, and the worldlyinvestor.com web site, enters the fray.

The purpose of *The WorldlyInvestor Guide to Beating the Market* is to present a potpourri of strategies that can be used by savvy investors to increase the performance of their portfolios. There are strategies for stock and mutual fund investors, as well as useful information on how to combine the ideas presented into a cogent, all-weather portfolio for virtually any market condition.

In addition, the book is designed to work in concert with the worldlyinvestor.com site in presenting these investing ideas. For example, the many stock screening methodologies presented in the book can be easily performed on the Investor Tools section of the web site, along with useful tools for picking growth stocks, choosing mutual funds, and obtaining useful information on the stock market as a whole.

On a broader note, worldlyinvestor.com contains over two dozen completely original stories every day on everything from technology stocks to emerging markets. Our editors come from some of the top financial publications and television networks in the world, including the *Wall Street Journal* and CNN. Our reporters adhere to strict journalistic standards and report stories in an accurate, fair, and unbiased manner. Our columnists, whose job it is to deliver their opinions on the markets, always disclose whether or not they own a stock that they are writing about.

The site is one of the Internet's largest providers of free investing newsletters, with over five million e-mailed each month. One of these newsletters is based on the site's "Market View" column, which updates readers on the performance of the strategies contained in this book.

And if you are smart enough to have accumulated enough money to consider investing, you are probably smart enough to invest it on your own volition. Congratulations—and welcome to the world of investing, the greatest game of them all!

PART ONE

Strategies for Individual Stocks

The market is made of many types of stocks. Some enjoy superstar status, are followed by a large number of Wall Street analysts, and boast earnings that exceed Wall Street expectations. Computer maker Cisco Systems (CSCO), for example, falls into this growth stock category. The company has an enviable record of earnings growth, and its large market capitalization has made it a favorite of many professional investors. The stock has handily exceeded the return of the S&P 500 index (see graph on page 12).

At the other end of the spectrum are stocks in out-of-favor industries that, because of their lack of potential, are virtually shunned by mutual fund managers and most private traders. For example, few investors would go near Lehman Brothers (LEH) a few years ago. Concerns over the brokerage firm's losses surrounding the failure of Long-Term Capital Management scared away many large investors, and the stock fell dramatically in the summer of 1998. But as the graph shows, the company was able to regain profitability and has maintained an impressive lead over the broad market indexes, the S&P 500.

Although these two companies have little in common, the result was the same: *true market-beating performance.*

Part One shows how private traders, armed with the democratizing power of the Internet, can identify these stocks before the large

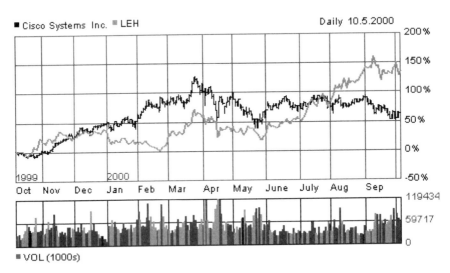

Growth stock Cisco Systems (CSCO) and value stock Lehman Brothers (LEH) managed to exceed the return of the S&P 500 in 1999–2000.
Copyright © Stockpoint, Inc.

institutional traders and mutual fund managers notice them and ramp up their price.

In examining our four distinct investing styles (see table on page 13), we will use a tool called a *stock screen*. Simply, a stock screen is a tool that is used by many professional money managers to identify those stocks that have certain characteristics that have been deemed desirable. To allow users to highlight the information that matters most to them, screening engines let one apply software "filters" against the contents of a large stock database. For example, one can sort all stocks listed on U.S. exchanges for those with earnings that have increased 20 percent per annum and boast a market capitalization of at least $1 billion. The features in many of the better search engines allow users to sort by virtually any stock market measurement, from recent trading volume to quarterly sales revisions.

Using screening tools, we will search through every stock that trades in the U.S. markets to cull those that best suit our criteria. But instead of your having to procure and utilize a screening tool,

Stock Strategies Discussed in Part One

Chapter	Stock Strategy	Stock Type	Market Capitalization	Dividends
1	Momentum	Growth	Small	No
2	Pure growth	Growth	Large	No
3	Pure value	Value	Large	Yes
4	Distressed	Value	Small	Yes

worldlyinvestor.com has done the work for you. Investors need only log on to the site, print out the list of the screened stocks, and then click over to the Internet brokerage of your choice and make the purchase recommendations.

Chapter 1 examines momentum trading. This strategy looks to make big returns by trading stocks that have had the most price appreciation. The mantra of the typical momentum investor is "what goes up keeps going up." In a bull market, the momentum style of investing can produce incredible returns.

Chapter 2 looks at growth investing, which involves buying stocks that are a bit more established than momentum issues. Growth strategies dominated the investment scene in the 1990s, and using these criteria will enable savvy private investors to have the opportunity to cash in on this dynamic and time-tested style.

Chapter 3 focuses on value investing. Investing in value stocks–those companies that trade close to their book values–has been proven to be a superior investment style over the past 50 years. We will examine some new ways of looking at value investing, and some of the companies that fall into this category.

Finally, Chapter 4 examines distressed stocks–those that have been beaten down so far that few investors will touch them. As we shall see, the returns of these stocks are often superior to those companies that have established track records of profitability.

A WELL-BALANCED PORTFOLIO

Growth investing and value investing are like oil and water. On one hand, growth investors have enjoyed incredible returns in the last decade. In 1999, for example, growth mutual funds returned an average 38.8 percent. In contrast, value funds increased a modest 6.3 percent for the year.

Value investors shine, however, when one examines returns over the past several decades. In fact, value investing would have produced gains 75 percent larger than growth investing over the last 25 years. But by combining these two styles (and the stocks from our four categories), investors can create a portfolio that can exceed the

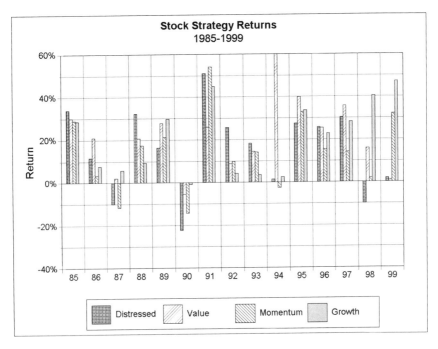

The returns of the stock strategies covered in Part One vary with economic conditions. To minimize volatility and maximize returns, it is best to own stocks from each category.

return of the stock markets during the good times and avoid calamity in the bad times.

Growth stocks tend to do better in raging bull markets. Value stocks are superior in flat or downtrending markets, when large investors become selective and tend to concentrate on stocks that pay dividends and are priced relatively cheaply by traditional valuation standards.

The bar graph on page 14 shows how returns can vary among the four categories.

Will distressed stocks start to outperform after five years of modest returns? Will growth stocks lose their status to value issues? These are questions often submitted by readers of the worldlyinvestor.com web site.

Unfortunately, the answers to these queries are unattainable by mere mortals. But that doesn't mean that private investors must settle for mediocre returns. By using the screens in Part One of *The WorldlyInvestor Guide to Beating the Market,* and selecting stocks from all of these categories, individual investors have an excellent chance of beating the performance of the largest mutual fund managers and the broad market indexes.

1

Momentum Stocks for the Short Run

Be courageous and steady to the Laws and you cannot fail.
−Sir Isaac Newton

Sir Isaac Newton is universally regarded as one of the most influential scientist who ever lived. Among his better-known accomplishments are the discovery of gravity, the invention of calculus, and the construction of the first reflecting telescope. Little did he know that one of his most famous discoveries−now referred to as Newton's Laws of Motion−would someday become the basis for a popular investment strategy.

DEFINING MOMENTUM

Newton's First Law of Motion is commonly known as the Law of Inertia (or momentum):

I. An object [stock] in motion [in an uptrend] tends to remain in motion [in an uptrend], and an object [stock] at rest [underperforming] tends to remain at rest [underperforming], unless an external force is applied to it.

Momentum is certainly a familiar concept to many. Political candidates, for example, are said to have momentum if they are able to leverage one victory into a string of successes. The term is also common to sport aficionados. And perhaps no other sport captures the true definition of momentum as well as football.

The Denver Broncos are a case in point. After losing at home against the Jacksonville Jaguars in a 1996 play-off game, the Broncos were determined the following year to bring Super Bowl glory to their much-beleaguered hometown. After cruising through the 1997 regular season with an 12–4 record, the team went onto beat the Green Bay Packers 31–24 in Super Bowl XXXII. At this point, the Broncos had a head of steam—real momentum—on their side.

Before the 1998 regular season, the Broncos were heavily favored to repeat as world champions. True to form, the Broncos won their first 13 regular-season games—again, serious momentum. After a few close losses (notably against the New York Giants and Miami Dolphins late in the season), the Broncos did what every good team with momentum is able to do—get back on a winning streak. After avenging their loss against the Jaguars in Denver two years before, the Broncos came to Super Bowl XXXIII with one goal in mind—to beat the Atlanta Falcons and keep the crown in Cow Town. Thus, the Broncos became the seventh team in National Football League history to win back-to-back championships.

Considering the implicit logic of momentum—a concept that is readily observed not only in the natural world but also in the realms of politics and sports—it should come as no surprise that the idea has filtered its way into the field of investment management. Similar to a fan's attraction to a winning team, traders are captivated by stocks whose prices rise more than other stocks around them. And considering the rather selective market rallies of the past few years, what might seem to work in theory actually has some merit in practice.

The year 1999 is a case in point. Although the S&P 500 index gained an impressive 21 percent, nearly one-half of the stocks in the index registered a loss for the year. Those who found themselves invested in the wrong sector underperformed the broad market indexes or even lost money for the year. Yet, if one had invested in the seven stocks with the most price momentum in early 1999, one would have earned over 180 percent. As Figure 1.1 shows, these seven issues contributed almost 50 percent of the entire return of the S&P 500 index in 1999.

Considering the computing power of the average private stock trader, the accessibility of price information on the Internet, and the seemingly endless rhetoric about momentum stocks on cable television, it is no wonder that the momentum concept is a sizzling-hot investment craze. Giddy day traders and desperate mutual fund managers are not the only ones interested in the momentum approach. Academic researchers, who have been forced to admit that the method has some merit, have also entered the fray. Numerous studies have shown that issues that exhibit price momentum tend to do well in future periods–better than the stock market as a whole, and better than stocks in similar industry groups.

While the existence of momentum in stock returns does not seem

Biggest Contributors to Performance in the S&P 500 Index, 1999

Company	Ticker Symbol	1999 Return	Contribution to S&P 500 Index Return
1 Microsoft	MSFT	68.4%	11.3%
2 Cisco Systems	CSCO	130.8%	9.3%
3 General Electric	GE	53.6%	8.4%
4 Wal-Mart	WM	70.4%	6.0%
5 Oracle Corporation	ORCL	289.8%	5.7%
6 Nortel Networks	NT	305.5%	4.8%
7 Qualcomm*	QCOM	349.8%	4.1%
Totals		181.2%	49.6%

*Qualcomm's return is from its inclusion in the S&P 500 index (July 22, 1999).

FIGURE 1.1 The biggest gainers in the S&P 500 index for 1999. Not surprisingly, six of the seven companies are technology-related stocks.

The Growing Popularity of the Internet

The U.S. Internet population was estimated at 100 million in 1999. International Data Corp. forecasts that number will grow to 180 million over the next four years.

---

to be too controversial, it is much less clear what might be driving it. Many believe that the effect is due to the relatively slow dissemination of firm-specific news to the investing public. If this is the case, stocks with low analyst coverage (i.e., stocks that are not readily followed by Wall Street analysts) should exhibit more price momentum than, say, IBM or Philip Morris (i.e., companies that are heavily followed by the Street). Indeed, this seems to be the case–profits derived from momemtum-based strategies have been shown to be roughly 60 percent greater among the one-third of stocks with the lowest analyst coverage, compared to the one-third of stocks with the highest analyst coverage (Figure 1.2).

But it takes more than a string of unappreciated good news on a company to make it a momentum stock. That is where Newton's Second Law comes into play.

VOLUME AND PRICE

II. There is a clear relationship between an object's mass [a stock's price], its acceleration [its price momentum], and the force applied to it [a stocks trading volume].

Analyst Coverage Varies Widely by Firm

Computer juggernaut IBM has 24 analysts covering it, while B2B (business-to-business) firm IntraNet, Inc. is followed by only five analysts.

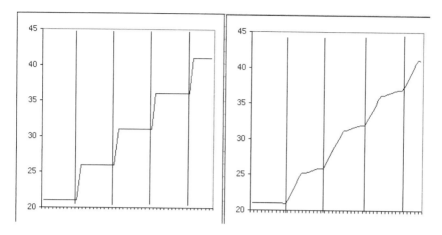

FIGURE 1.2 A stock with significant analyst coverage, shown at left, rapidly responds to inputs of new information. Less widely covered issues often underreact to news, creating a *price trend* (the vertical lines on the graphs correspond to bullish earnings announcements).

In order for a stock to exhibit serious price momentum, it has to attract heavy trading volume. As an example, we will examine the stock of Qualcomm as it slowly morphed from an underfollowed value stock to a momentum stock.

Qualcomm (QCOM: Nasdaq), the wireless telecommunications company, might well be remembered as one of the greatest technology stocks of the 1990s. But this was not always the case. In fact, there were times in October 1998 when the stock was trading below its levels of 1993.

But a lot can happen in a year. QCOM posted an astounding 2,619 percent gain for 1999. Seemingly overnight, Qualcomm was a $100 billion company. The rally was even more stunning when one considers that the stock was not a red-hot IPO (initial public offering), and had not even introduced a breakthrough technology during the year. But when one studies the rise to fame of the company, it will become apparent that it shares many of the characteristics of other great momentum stocks.

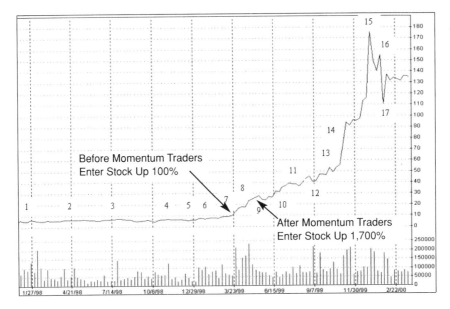

FIGURE 1.3 Qualcomm Corporation (QCOM: Nasdaq) stock price (split-adjusted) from January 1998 to March 2000.
Source: Chart created using Zacks' Integrated Company Analysis software.

As Figure 1.3 shows, Qualcomm was no overnight success. In fact, the company had been a player in the communications technology industry since 1985. The following are some of the milestones and other corporate events that transformed QCOM from a sleepy issue into the best-performing stock in the S&P 500 index.

1. 1/98–Qualcomm announces earnings that exceed Wall Street expectations.

2. 4/98–Company again reports surprisingly strong earnings.

3. 7/98–QCOM reports record earnings.

4. 11/98–QCOM forms WirelessKnowledge with Microsoft; reports record earnings.

5. 12/98–QCOM again reports record earnings. The company boasts a five-year growth rate of 30 percent per year, yet the company's price-to-earnings ratio (23) and price-to-sales ratio (1.0) remain at the bottom of the telecommunications industry. QCOM announces layoff of 700 employees. *The company's stock price is below its intrinsic value, making QCOM a value stock.*

6. 1/99–QCOM reports earnings that exceed Wall Street estimates.

7. 3/99–European giant Ericsson agrees to support QCOM's CDMA (code division multiple access), a cellular communications standard. Stock rises from $6.41 at the beginning of 1999 to $10.27.

8. 4/99–Stock now trading at $21.77. Trading volume peaks at 250,000 shares per day from less than 100,000 shares. *QCOM begins to attract momentum traders; stock is now up 240 percent for 1999.*

9. 6/99–QCOM announces that it will top earnings expectations.

10. 7/99–CDMA takes the lead as the dominant digital wireless standard for the first time.

11. 7/99–QCOM stock added to the S&P 500 index; company reports earnings that exceed Wall Street estimates.

12. 9/99–Wall Street analysts lower rating on QCOM, citing "pinched" margins due to competition from Nokia and Motorola.

13. 10/99–QCOM stock shakes off lowered ratings, reaches all-time high.

14. 11/99–QCOM CEO Irwin Jacobs announces that the company will top earnings estimates for the sixth consecutive quarter; stock splits 4:1.

15. 12/99–QCOM ends the year up 2,619 percent; is best-performing stock in the S&P 500 index.

16. 1/00–QCOM earnings exceed Wall Street estimates.

17. 2/00–QCOM stock drops 35 percent from high in 1999. Price-earnings ratio of QCOM is now 126, up from 23 in late 1998.

As we can see from this list, the most obvious attribute of Qualcomm is its consistent earnings history. In the two-year period shown on Figure 1.3, the company reported record profits 10 times!

This is a crucial element of a momentum stock. Eventually, Wall Street analysts are forced to put companies like these on their radar screens. As analyst coverage increases for these stocks, consistent earnings performance garners more and more attention from large institutional investors and sophisticated private traders. The result is frequently a marked increase in trading volume and a spectacular run-up in share price.

This can even happen before the company actually earns a profit. A distinguishing characteristic of momentum stocks is not record earnings, but earnings that are consistently better than consensus estimates.

One example of this is Domtar, a Canadian forest products company. Domtar management embarked on a plan of adding shareholder value and dumped some unsuccessful business lines. The company then positioned itself to be the low-cost producer in its industry. Although these changes were made in a negative operating environment, they precipitated a number of positive earnings surprises (Wall Street parlance for earnings releases that exceed analysts' expectations). Analysts became increasingly comfortable with Domtar's growth and revised their estimates higher.

Because Domtar (DTC) does not boast a long-term track record of earnings growth or profitability, strict growth investors may not have selected it for their portfolios. But it seems to have been a good choice for momentum investors (Figure 1.4).

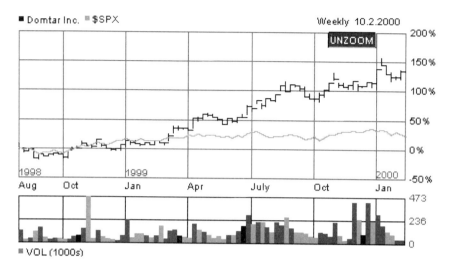

■ Domtar Inc. ■ $SPX   Weekly 10.2.2000

FIGURE 1.4 Momentum traders drove up the price of Domtar (DTC) on the expectation of better financial performance.
Copyright © Stockpoint, Inc.

TWO KINDS OF TRADERS

In order for QCOM to evolve from unloved value issue to hot momentum stock, two distinct types of market participants were involved—the *news watchers* and the *momentum traders*.

The first movers of the market are the news watchers. These traders typically use a fundamental approach to stock picking—meaning that they primarily consider a company's revenue growth, market share, and other financial data in deciding what to buy and sell. News watchers continuously scan the Internet, Wall Street analyst reports, and other media in order to assimilate as much company-specific data as possible. One of their most important considerations is a company's quarterly earnings announcement. When a company reports earnings that are much higher than Wall Street expects, news watchers act quickly and buy those issues, because higher earnings usually translate into higher stock prices.

The ability to gather breaking news varies among news watchers. Although some are quick to gather and assimilate news, others require more time to analyze the implications of such information. *As a result, when only news watchers are active, prices adjust slowly to new information—that is, stock prices underreact.*

This gradual diffusion of information is a key component in the role of the news watchers. In the case of Qualcomm stock, a string of strong earnings reports was met with a collective yawn on Wall Street. Even after six positive earnings surprises, QCOM barely budged. In order for a stock to really surge, momentum traders must get into the action.

The most distinguishing characteristic of momentum traders is the type of information they use to make their investment decisions. Whereas the news watchers consider only fundamental information in their decision-making process, momentum traders buy basal on price action. Fundamental information is typically not considered by momentum traders.

Momentum traders became a factor in QCOM's rise at about Point 7 on Figure 1.3. It was the stock's rise from $6.41 to $10.27 that got the momentum traders' attention, and not the fundamental reason why that occurred. This group of traders buys stocks simply because they are rising; they feel that the rising stock price must be occurring because the prospects for the company are improving.

And, as Point 7 on Figure 1.3 attests, there are a lot of momentum traders. When they pounce on a stock, its average trading volume can easily double or triple in just a matter of months. This increased volume is the fuel that propels momentum stocks higher.

Ideally, one would use a momentum strategy because a price increase signals that there is good news about fundamentals that is not yet fully incorporated into prices. Sometimes, though, a price increase is not because of good news—but simply the result of more and more momentum traders climbing on the bandwagon, sending the stock's price higher and higher. And because momentum traders consider only a stock's price action when making their trading decisions, there is no way for them to know whether they are early or late in the cycle. Hence, they must accept the fact that sometimes they buy when earlier rounds of momentum trading have pushed prices past long-run equilibrium values—and not because of new information.

As a result, momentum traders have a tendency to push a stock's price grossly above its true value—which brings us to Newton's Third Law.

BEAR TRACKS

III. For every action [stock that goes up], there is an equal and opposite reaction [stock comes down].

If only Newton's first two laws applied to momentum stocks, the strategy would be simple to implement and infinitely profitable. One would merely pick the best-performing stocks for a given period, and hold onto them as they continued into the stratosphere.

But, unfortunately, all traders have to live with the Third Law—that stocks that are traded way above their fair value have the tendency to fall from grace rapidly. Sometimes these issues drop because earnings are slightly lower than estimates. Other times, there is no explanation for why they drop.

As Figure 1.3 shows, Qualcomm is no exception to the law of gravity. The stock dropped 35 percent in a seven-week period—for no fundamental reason.

Even with an IQ of 190, Sir Isaac had problems with the Third Law. "I can calculate the motions of the heavenly bodies," he wrote, "but not the madness of people." Neither Newton's intellect nor his scientific thinking could prevent him from losing £13,000 in the South Sea Bubble. The South Sea Company was formed in 1711 by a group of English merchants, who paid off the British national debt of £10 million in return for a 6 percent interest rate and exclusive trade rights with South America. Although the company never profited from its monopoly (and, indeed, failed to transact any business whatsoever), the prospects of such a scheme were so tempting that people fell over themselves to invest. By 1720, the expectation of immense profits drove the company's stock up 1,000 percent in just a few months. The ensuing collapse of the stock's price nearly brought down the English government.

Often the first sign of an overheated market is the insistence of market participants to invest in stocks not because of their intrinsic value, but in fear of missing a potential rally. These types of investors are commonly known as the "weak hands" in the market, because their lack of conviction usually results in them fleeing their positions at the first sign of trouble. When that occurs, the sell-off in the market is sometimes large enough to affect other traders. This vicious circle can cause a protracted market drop. Nowhere is this phenomenon more apparent than in the world of momentum investing.

Market professionals use the term *mean reversion* when describing the tendency of stocks to reverse after a long run-up. What really occurs is not prices adjusting to new information, but rather investor expectations adjusting to the harsh reality that stocks simply cannot increase in perpetuity.

Consider the stock of Lucent Technologies (LU: NYSE), a bellwether of the technology and communications industries. Since it was spun off from AT&T, the company has had an enviable record

Momentum Investing and Emerging Industries

Emerging industries are often populated by large numbers of momentum players. Auto and radio stocks were immensely popular in the early 1900s, and witnessed huge price appreciation. But in the end, only a few selected market leaders from each industry were able to survive.

of earnings growth and expanding market share. But LU's stunning announcement on January 6, 2000, that business had weakened during the previous quarter sent the stock reeling (Figure 1.5).

As it turned out, earnings decreased by about 30 percent over quarter-ago levels. But the stock's price fell by a much greater amount—in other words, *the market overreacted to the announcement.*

Thus is the pattern for momentum stocks. News watchers readily buy into the stock as good fundamental information is released, but because they do not trade as a cohesive group, the price does not fully reflect all the information.

As the stock price increase is noticed by the momentum traders—a more uniform group, since they condition their buy patterns solely on the basis of price action—they tend to bid up the price of a stock quite aggressively. Eventually, the price is so far above fair value that even the tiniest bit of bad news can send the stock's price to the cellar (Figure 1.6).

FIGURE 1.5 Lucent Technologies (LU) was slammed when it reported lower-than-expected earnings in January 2000.
Copyright © Stockpoint, Inc.

FIGURE 1.6 Growth stock Pinnacle Systems (PCLE) was a darling of the growth stock crowd—until an earnings warning issued by the company caused the share price to tumble by 50 percent in one day.
Copyright © Stockpoint, Inc.

NEWTON'S LAWS: A HOLISTIC VIEW

In order to profitably exploit Newton's three laws in the trading of equities, one must consider that stocks often exhibit the following characteristics:

- *Stocks often trend in the short term.* For those issues with low analyst coverage, earnings surprises and other firm-specific news are only gradually reflected in the stock's price. As a result, stock prices should drift upward in the presence of bullish news, allowing traders to establish profitable positions in high-performance stocks.

- *Stock prices mean revert over longer time horizons.* Stocks that trend in the short run show a tendency for extreme price reversals over longer time periods. Indeed, stocks that have had the highest returns for any given five-year period tend to have low returns over the subsequent period.

"Wow," some readers might be exclaiming. "Is this all there is to it?" Armed with a powerful personal computer, a discount brokerage account, up-to-the-minute news, and Internet quotes, some readers might think it a relatively easy task to make money from these simple concepts. But a cursory examination of the behavior of individual traders might cast considerable light on this view.

A recent series of studies performed by Terrance Odean at the University of California sought to determine the profitability of the average retail trader with a discount brokerage account. The research examined over 10,000 brokerage accounts and nearly 200,000 transactions between 1987 and 1993, and revealed a number of broad psychological tendencies shared by many market participants.

These tendencies underscore the difficulty of generating market-beating returns. Traders might not be able to control market volatility, order entry problems, or the inability to get a decent number of shares of the hottest initial public offering—but they can definitely control themselves.

Problem I: Disregarding Transaction Costs

Individuals tend to buy and sell without regard to transaction costs. Profitable traders realize that one should buy a stock only if one's profit objective exceeds transaction costs. Generally, transaction costs are composed of commissions, which vary depending on your choice of brokerage firm, and the bid-ask spread, which ranges from a quarter to half a tick (i.e., 25 to 50 cents) per share. In Odean's study, the average cost for buying and selling a stock position was 5.9 percent. Unfortunately, the average trader was not willing to hold a stock until it appreciated that much, preferring to sell it as soon as its price registered a smaller gain. As a result, the accounts that traded the most were the least profitable.

Odean also found that women were consistently more profitable than men. It seems that the predilection of males to be trigger-happy also applies to the world of investing, as they consistently trade more often than their feminine counterparts. The higher commission bills generated by these extra transactions handicap men's accounts, allowing women to earn more profits.

Problem II: Buying Momentum Stock Too Late

Retail traders often like momentum stocks, but wait too long to buy them. Odean found that investors are indeed attracted to momentum stocks. However, they tend to wait until these stocks have run for a number of years before they are willing to initiate a position. By this time, the price of the stock is so far away from the fair value of the company that they sharply underperform the market at the first sign of trouble. According to Odean, it is likely that these investors are often the last ones to buy these stocks and among the first to suffer losses when the trend reverses to the downside.

Momentum investing is a viable strategy in the stock market. Many studies have documented momentum patterns in stock returns. However, these stocks establish reliable trends for only 12 months or so, and afterward tend to reverse.

The bottom line: If you are going to trade momentum stocks, remember that trends don't last forever!

Problem III: Selling Winning Positions

Traders may sell winning positions but hold losing positions. The transactions studied by Odean clearly showed that the average retail investor is quick at taking profits, and is especially fond of selling

---

Transaction Costs

Watch out—there is a lot more to transaction costs than just commissions! In fact, commissions can be the smallest component. The biggest expense is generally the difference between the buy and the sell price, which is often called the bid-ask spread.

---

those stocks that have appreciated significantly in the two weeks following purchase. However, if a purchased stock goes down, the typical investor is more willing to keep it in the hope that its price will rebound. As a result, the average stock position maintained in an investor's account registers below-market returns, while the positions that were exited actually beat the market.

This puzzling result has an equally puzzling interpretation. According to the study, *individual investors possess valuable information with which to trade.* This information takes a number of forms, including recent price history, industry or company fundamentals, and order flow. However, instead of using this information to their advantage, retail investors misinterpret it to the extent that they consistently exit the stocks they should hold, and hold the stocks that they are better off dumping.

One of the oldest trading adages is "Let your profits ride, and cut your losses short." Why is this advice so hard to follow? Chalk it up to human nature. In all probability, we are probably wired to fail in the markets. The only way to succeed is to refuse to follow our instincts, which constantly bombard us with "A bird in the hand is worth two in the bush."

THE WORLDLYINVESTOR.COM MOMENTUM STOCK SCREEN

Having been confronted with the reasons why individuals are so often disappointed with their performances in the stock market, it is wise to consider the ways that such behavior can be avoided.

Discretionary versus Quantitative Trading

Many professional traders are discretionary—they make their buy and sell decisions based on experience and gut instinct. Quantitative traders, however, follow rigorously developed models in making their investment decisions.

The screens in *The WorldlyInvestor Guide to Beating the Market* are all quantitative, and can be used by all investors, regardless of experience level.

The best way to avoid these issues is by utilizing a systematic approach to the markets, free of emotion and the human tendency we all have to tinker, second-guess, and delay our decision-making processes. And the best way to achieve these objectives is by using a stock screening methodology.

The core of the stock screening approach is in developing a quantitative method of choosing investments. Based on the general characteristics of momentum stocks described earlier, and the tendency for them rapidly to fall out of favor, a stock screen can easily be constructed to take all of these factors into account.

The worldlyinvestor.com momentum stock screen has the following criteria:

- **Small Cap Bias.** To limit ourselves to those firms that have yet to be identified by a large number of Wall Street analysts, we will screen for companies that have a market capitalization below $3 billion.
- **Zacks Rank.** We will focus on those stocks that have a Zacks rank (a proprietary measure of financial performance designed by Zacks Investment Research) in the top 25 percent of all listed stocks.
- **Short-Term Relative Strength.** To ensure that our stocks have been noticed by other momentum traders, we will screen for those issues that have outperformed their peers in the most recent four-week period.
- **String of Earnings Surprises.** Finally, our screen will focus on those stocks that have exceeded expectations in earnings growth.

The result of this screen is shown as Figure 1.7.

A cursory glance at our potential momentum screen stocks shows that most of the selections are not well known. For our purpose, that is good–we aren't interested in buying what is known now, but rather what might become well known in the future!

Company	Ticker Symbol	Market Cap ($mil)	% Price Change 4 Weeks
APPAREL			
Fila Hldgs Spa	FLH	$290	34.1
MEDIA			
Saga Comms-ClA	SGA	$332	9.64
NONFOOD RETAIL-WHOLESALE			
1-800 Contacts	CTAC	$280	35.24
Ac Moore Arts	ACMR	$ 56	21
Brauns Fashions	BFCI	$254	33.48
Coldwater Creek	CWTR	$294	47.4
Gadzooks Inc	GADZ	$121	66.15
Movado Grp Inc	MOVA	$148	17.04
Sharper Image	SHRP	$188	23.15
Sport Chalet	SPCH	$ 32	9.72
DRUGS			
Axys Pharm Inc	AXPH	$238	31.71
Draxis Health	DRAX	$ 89	16.67
Gliatech Inc	GLIA	$215	13.12
Immune Response	IMNR	$310	46.56
Warmer Chlt-Adr	WCRX	$303	23.91
MEDICAL CARE			
Prww Ltd	PRWW	$ 92	16.48
MEDICAL PRODUCTS			
Ats Medical Inc	ATSI	$262	20.21
METALS-NONFERROUS			
Hawk Corp	HWK	$ 68	8.55
INDUSTRIAL PRODUCTS-SERVICES			
Cone Mills	COE	$161	18.82
Galey & Lord	GNL	$ 37	32.43
BUILDING PRODUCTS			
Us Timberlands	TIMBZ	$ 92	11.77
COMPUTER-OFFICE EQUIPMENT			
3d Systems Corp	TDSC	$213	23.73
Breezecom Ltd	BRZE	$282	31.76
Ikos System Inc	IKOS	$101	19.75
Info Res Engr	IREG	$167	37.93
Planar Systems	PLNR	$155	38.1
Zapme! Corp	IZAP	$140	10.87

(Continued)

FIGURE 1.7 The worldlyinvestor.com Momentum Stock Screen.

Company	Ticker Symbol	Market Cap ($mil)	% Price Change 4 Weeks
COMPUTER SOFTWARE-SERVICES			
Asd Systems Inc	ASDS	$ 56	9.09
Avid Tech Inc	AVID	$278	13.56
Coda Music Tech	COMT	$ 26	8.33
Done Onesource Info	ONES	$122	50.67
Private Bus Inc	PBIZ	$ 59	21.05
Software Spectr	SSPE	$ 61	8.71
ELECTRONIC-SEMICONDUCTORS			
Calif Micro Dev	CAMD	$290	23.89
ELECTRONICS			
Appld Firms Cp	AFCO	$280	45.32
Bmc Inds Inc-Mn	BMC	$140	24.24
Jaco Electronic	JACO	$101	12.6
Microtest Inc	MTST	$ 95	12.82
Nu Horizons Ele	NUHC	$321	58.51
Xetel Corp	XTEL	$ 28	38.24
TELECOMMUNICATIONS EQUIPMENT			
Dset Corp	DSET	$339	12.67
AEROSPACE-DEFENSE			
Be Aerospace	BEAV	$222	34.29
OIL MACHINERY-SERVICES-DRILLING			
Natco Group Inc	NTG	$151	22.46
OIL-EXPLORATION & PRODUCTION			
Comstock Resources	CRK	$219	15.97
Eex Corp	EEX	$236	8.64
Remington Oil	ROIL	$153	10.68
TRANSPORTATION			
Ambassador Intl	AMIE	$154	13.22
Conrad Indus	CNRD	$ 44	14.94
Omi Corp	OMM	$331	17.95
BUSINESS SERVICE			
Rmh Teleservice	RMHT	$124	96.67
Average		$175	25.48

FIGURE 1.7   *(Continued)*

Further, our screen should result in stocks that have already begun to rise—like Point 7 on Figure 1.3.

Let's examine a few of the more exceptional stocks on our list for those criteria we have described.

Comstock Resources (CRK, Figure 1.8), an independent oil and gas producer, is a $219 million company with an impressive string of earnings surprises. The company has managed to exceed Wall Street expectations for the past six quarters. What makes the stock even more intriguing is its minimal analyst coverage. As of mid-2000, only seven Wall Street firms follow the company. If Comstock can continue its earnings growth, more analysts will inevitably follow the stock—which will drive institutional investor interest, and hopefully cause the stock to continue rising.

Shoppers may be more familiar with Sharper Image (SHRP, Figure 1.9) than investors are. With $300 million in annual sales and a market capitalization of less than $200 million, the company may be too small for the radar screen of many mutual fund managers.

But if the company continues to impress Wall Street with its earnings growth—and its six consecutive positive earnings surprises—that may become a thing of the past. And with only six analysts monitoring the company's progress, there's still plenty of room on the upside.

1-800 Contacts Inc. (CTAC, Figure 1.10) is a direct marketer of replacement contact lenses. The name of this company's game is volume, and it continues dramatically to increase its sales growth and profit margins through its proprietary management systems and well-known brand name.

Even though CTAC has experienced dramatic stock appreciation and rapidly growing earnings, only three Wall Street firms follow the stock. But the steadily increasing volume of CTAC shows that momentum traders have noticed its strong stock price performance.

Figure 1.11 shows the three most promising momentum stocks from our screen. To get a more updated list, please refer to the worldlyinvestor.com web site.

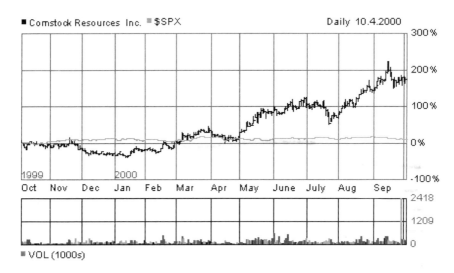

FIGURE 1.8 Comstock Resources (CRK), October 1999–September 2000. Note the increased volume in June 2000—a sure sign of interest from momentum traders.

Copyright © Stockpoint, Inc.

FIGURE 1.9 Sharper Image (SHRP), January–July 2000.

Copyright © Stockpoint, Inc.

FIGURE 1.10   1-800 Contacts (CTAC), October 1999–July 2000.
Copyright © Stockpoint, Inc.

Stock	Ticker Symbol	Number of Consecutive Earnings Surprises	Number of Analysts Coverage
Comstock Resources	CRK	6	7
Sharper Image	SHRP	6	6
1-800 Contacts	CTAC	4	3

FIGURE 1.11   The worldlyinvestor.com Momentum Stock Focus List.

WorldlyInvestor Quick Summary

1. Momentum: What goes up keeps going up.
2. What is behind the momentum in momentum stocks?
   - Low analyst coverage is critical. Returns in the one-third of momentum stocks with the lowest analyst coverage have been shown to be 60 percent greater than the returns for the one-third with the highest coverage.
   - "News watchers" initially process positive fundamental information on the company and cause the price to increase slowly. The dissemination of information is so slow that prices tend to underreact. Many companies at this stage regularly exceed quarterly earnings expectations with little change in their stock prices.
   - "Momentum traders" base their buy and sell decisions on past price action. They buy simply because the price is rising and have no interest in fundamentals. They initially act on the price increase caused by the news watchers and then on the feeding frenzy that they cause as their buying drives prices higher. Ultimately, prices overreact as more momentum traders enter the fray. Trading volume typically spikes as the number of momentum players dramatically increases the total number of market participants interested in the stock.
3. What goes up must come down.
   - As a result of significant stock price appreciation, momentum stocks tend to suffer violent reactions to the downside once the stock has peaked. Often the slightest bit of bad news will have a dramatic effect.
4. How to trade momentum stocks:
   - Look for stocks with low analyst coverage that appreciate slowly after bullish news.
   - Get in early. Momentum traders typically lose if they enter late due to the short-lived nature of the opportunity. Few momentum trends last longer than 12 months.
   - Go against the crowd and be willing to take your losses quickly, and let your profits ride. Take into account your transaction costs, and be sure that your profits will more than exceed your costs. Trade infrequently on higher-probability trades to keep your transaction costs low.
   - Use the WorldlyInvestor stock screen to identify potential high-performance momentum stocks.

2

A New Paradigm for Growth Stocks

A s its name suggests, growth investing involves the purchase of stock in fast-growing businesses. Many of these firms have become household names–not only because of the products that they make, but also because of their consistent record of earnings and stock price appreciation.

With the raging bull market of the 1990s, growth stocks do not need much of a cheerleading section. The returns of growth issues have been nothing short of astounding. From December 1989 to the end of 1999, the growth-laden Nasdaq index surged nearly eightfold, versus a gain of less than fourfold in the Dow Jones Industrial Average, an index of more established companies. *And the six stocks that boasted the greatest returns for the latter half of the 1990s were all technology-related* (Figure 2.1).

Growth stocks are those issues whose sales and earnings have grown faster than the norm and are expected to do so in the future. These stocks occasionally pay dividends, but it is much more common to see any profits be plowed back into the companies.

As opposed to momentum stocks, which are typically much smaller in capitalization and relatively unknown to Wall Street analysts, growth stocks typically represent large corporations that have been around long enough to generate an impressive record of earnings growth and expanding market share. A great example of a typical growth stock is

Stock	Ticker Symbol	Gain
Xcelera.com	XLA	77,800%
CMGI	CMGI	22,220%
JDS Uniphase	JDSU	19,800%
Veritas Software	VRTS	17,200%
QLogic	QLGC	13,100%
ImClone Systems	IMCL	13,010%

FIGURE 2.1 Top-Performing Stocks, 1995–1999.

McDonald's Corporation (MCD). Regardless of the direction of interest rates or the rate of unemployment, people will always eat burgers and fries (and children like mine will always go for the toys).

Growth investing is a matter of expectations. Besides buying the stock of leading companies in established industries, growth investors also buy stock in the companies that have the greatest chance of transforming society through technological innovation. Considering the impact of such products as the personal computer and the cellular telephone, it is little wonder that these companies are viewed by many as exhilarating investment vehicles.

Since the prices of growth stocks are usually much higher than their book values would indicate, they are rarely regarded as bargains. But growth investors reason that a stock that might appear insanely overpriced based on its current earnings will look cheap at today's price a year or two down the road.

THE TENACITY OF GROWTH STOCKS

The 1990s were not the only time that growth stocks were in vogue. Growth investing was also tremendously popular in the early 1970s. The hottest growth issues in those days—frequently referred to as the *Nifty Fifty* stocks—commanded sky-high *P/E ratios*.

The P/E or price-to-earnings ratio is one of the most often used financial metrics. Quite simply, the P/E measures how many times current earnings the market will pay for a stock. For instance, if a company earns one dollar per share of stock outstanding, and it trades at a P/E of 12, its stock would sell for $12 per share.

Growth stocks are generally defined as those with a P/E higher than average. The reason is that investors have gained more confidence in the earnings growth of the company, and are thus willing to pay a higher earnings multiple for the stock. Today's growth stocks include high-tech firms like Intel (INTC) or Microsoft (MSFT); established conglomerates like General Electric (GE); and consumer companies like Coca-Cola (KO). Regardless of the business they are in, growth stocks usually possess a technological edge or a sustainable niche in an established market. In either case, growth stocks must boast a competitive advantage that is meaningful enough to give the market a high degree of comfort to justify its higher than normal P/E ratio.

Investors in the 1970s were certainly in a state of extreme comfort when it came to the prospects of a handful of blue-chip growth stocks. In this period, the traditional rule that stocks should sell for 10 to 15 times current-year earnings had been supplanted by multiples of 25 or even 100 times earnings for the most glamorous issues. As growth took on an almost mystical significance, questioning the propriety of such valuations became highly suspect. The Nifty Fifty were often called one-decision stocks—buy and never sell. Because their prospects were so bright, the only logical direction their price could go was higher.

And there was another, more obvious reason that these stocks were so highly thought of by investors: Their share prices had appreciated dramatically over the previous decade. Investment professionals who were not overweighted in the Nifty Fifty lagged their competitors by a wide margin, since the stocks of other well-known industrial concerns failed to reach new highs during the market advance. As a result, investment firms began to mimic each other's portfolios of Nifty Fifty stocks. This only served to boost the share prices of the Nifty Fifty companies even higher.

Eastman Kodak was the group's star performer, and an excellent example of the period's stock market euphoria. In 1972, Kodak's sales were $3.5 billion and the company was valued in the market at $24 billion—the same as General Motors, which at the time had sales of over $30 billion.

It is hard to overstate the drama experienced by growth investors during the early 1970s. In the first few years of the decade, the performance of the Nifty Fifty stocks was nothing short of spectacular, as these stocks outperformed the S&P 500 index by a stunning 71 percent. But the OPEC-related bear market of 1973–1974 brought a quick end to the party. When the bear market finally bottomed out in late 1973, a portfolio of Nifty Fifty stocks was worth only 20 cents on the dollar. After 10 years of market-beating returns, many investors vowed never again to pay an outrageous multiple for a stock, no matter how promising its prospects.

Did the Nifty Fifty stocks become overvalued during the buying spree of 1972? The answer, according to author and academician Jeremy Siegel, is a surprising *no*! In his book *Stocks for the Long Run*, Siegel found that as a group the Nifty Fifty actually *outperformed* the S&P 500 index from 1971 to 1993. He even showed how some of the Nifty Fifty stocks—including Philip Morris, Coca-Cola, and Disney— were actually worth quite a bit more than what the market had priced the stocks at in 1972.

Amazingly, the Nifty Fifty gained fourfold in the 12-month period following the market bottom—and never looked back. Its lead over the S&P 500 index was never seriously challenged. Twenty years after the market drop, every dollar invested in the Nifty Fifty portfolio was worth $16.10, compared to $12.20 if placed in the S&P 500 index (Figure 2.2).

There are three valuable lessons that can be learned from the stock market of the 1970s. First, growth stocks are often excellent investments for the long run—as long as investors remain focused on

Company	Ticker Symbol	Annual Return	P/E Ratio
Philip Morris	MO	19.5%	21.0
Gillette	GS	16.2%	19.7
PepsiCo Inc.	PEP	16.2%	27.0
Heublein Inc.	HBL	14.8%	26.7
Merck	MRK	14.5%	25.9
Coca-Cola	KO	14.3%	42.3
McDonald's	MCD	14.0%	59.8
Bristol-Myers	BMY	14.0%	24.4
Schlumberger	SLB	13.4%	35.7
Walt Disney Co.	DIS	13.1%	55.3
General Electric	GE	12.8%	22.6
Pfizer	PFE	12.6%	27.9
Squibb	SQB	12.5%	30.2
Chesebrough Pond's	CBM	12.1%	34.0
Schering Plough	SGP	11.9%	39.3
AMP Inc.	AMP	11.8%	36.4
Am. Home Products	AHP	11.7%	32.9
Revlon	REV	11.6%	25.5
Dow Chemical	DOW	11.5%	22.3
Procter & Gamble	PG	11.3%	24.0
Anheuser-Busch	BUD	11.0%	36.7
Upjohn	UPJ	10.9%	32.8
Inter. Flavors	IFF	10.4%	57.9
Am. Hospital Supply	AHS	10.3%	47.9
Johnson & Johnson	JNJ	10.2%	55.5
3M	MMM	9.7%	35.7

(Continued)

FIGURE 2.2 Nifty Fifty Stocks versus Standard & Poor's 500 Index, January 1972 to May 1993.

Source: Adapted from Jeremy J. Siegel, *Stocks for the Long Run* (Chicago: Irwin Professional, 1994), pp. 98–99.

Company	Ticker Symbol	Annual Return	P/E Ratio
LA Land & Exploration	LLX	9.2%	27.0
Citicorp	C	8.9%	17.5
J.C. Penney	JCP	8.9%	28.7
American Express	AXP	8.8%	28.4
Halliburton	HAL	8.8%	27.7
Baxter International	BAX	7.9%	59.5
Lubrizol	LZ	7.7%	34.9
Texas Instruments	TXN	7.4%	36.8
ITT	ITT	7.0%	14.8
Kmart	KM	6.7%	42.5
Jos. Schlitz Brewing	SLZ	6.1%	32.2
Digital Equipment	DEC	5.9%	53.2
Sears, Roebuck	S	5.0%	28.6
Eastman Kodak	EK	4.9%	37.7
Eli Lilly	LLY	4.4%	37.7
IBM	IBM	2.9%	35.5
Avon Products	AVP	2.9%	55.4
Xerox Corp.	XRX	2.1%	46.9
Black & Decker	BDK	1.7%	40.9
Polaroid	PRD	1.2%	93.5
Simplicity Patterns	SYP	0.2%	45.0
Burroughs	BGH	−0.8%	41.0
Emery Air Freight	EAF	−4.4%	49.6
MGIC Inv. Corp.	MGI	−8.7%	53.0
Nifty Fifty average		12.0%	37.3
S&P 500 Index		11.7%	18.2

FIGURE 2.2 *(Continued)*

long-term results and can ignore the gut-wrenching volatility that accompanies them. After all, an 80 percent drop in valuation is hard for even the most die-hard investor to stomach.

A second lesson from the Nifty Fifty study is the importance of diversification. Several of the Nifty Fifty stocks had negative total returns, and one resulted in a total loss of capital. A perennial investor favorite, IBM, yielded less than a risk-free Treasury bill over the 20-year period. Portfolio diversification is a simple cure for the danger of a few bad apples spoiling the whole bushel.

The third lesson from our example is the democracy of bear markets. There are few places to hide when stocks are dropping. Often, the highest-flying issues are the ones that are hurt the most when prices head south. But even though the Nifty Fifty took it on the chin during 1973 and 1974, when the market bottomed out they came roaring back with a vengeance.

Established, large-cap stocks like the Nifty Fifty are not the only type of growth issues available to investors. Many market participants are biased toward the stocks of newer companies in emerging industries. Good examples are America Online, Yahoo!, and the myriad of other companies that seek to exploit what has been referred to as the biggest business opportunity of our generation—the Internet. And considering the incredible price appreciation of these issues, it should come as no surprise that many investors have committed a substantial amount of their risk capital (that portion of their total portfolio committed to high-risk, high-profit strategies) to Internet stocks.

GRAVITY BUSTERS

Of all the emerging technologies that have affected our lives, air travel ranks as one of the twentieth century's enduring legacies. The aviation industry allows us to travel huge distances in a relatively short amount of time, and has done more to promote trade between

countries than any other innovation. It also allows companies to expand operations beyond their sovereign borders, which makes for much more efficient global enterprises. One might imagine that the first investors in the modern airline industry were fabulously successful, just as the first venture capitalists that backed such Internet visionaries as Jeff Bezos's Amazon.com garnered spectacular returns.

But as we shall see, buying stock in fast-growing companies is not always a surefire way to riches.

Aviation's origins can be traced to the lighter-than-air dirigible craft, especially those made famous by the German Count Ferdinand von Zeppelin. But as the invention of a power source much lighter than the steam engine became known, innovators slowly began to design machines that would allow people to fly in a more controlled fashion.

The German pioneer Otto Lilienthal studied birds to gain more knowledge about balance and control aloft. He eventually built wings curved like a gull's, attached them to his back, and jumped off hilltops in what we would now call hang gliding. After making over two thousand flights in which he tried to steer by flinging himself from side to side, he was thrown to the ground during a sudden wind gust one day in 1896. His back broken, he died the next day. His last words were, "Sacrifices must be made."

Inspired by his quest, two young bicycle mechanics from Dayton, Ohio–Orville and Wilbur Wright–obtained Lilienthal's books and data. Soon they, too, were watching birds. By 1899 Wilbur had made a crucial discovery: Buzzards "regain their lateral balance . . . by a torsion at the tips of their wings." In their shop one day Wilbur tore off the ends of an empty inner-tube carton so that the upper and lower surfaces of the box represented the flat wings of a biplane. Then he twisted the opposing corners of the box in opposite directions. That, he told Orville, was how the buzzard contrived to hold steady in gusts aloft. With wires manipulated by an operator lying prone between the wings, Wilbur reasoned that a flier could twist the opposing wing tips of the glider to hold it steady—even in the conditions that claimed the life of their German hero.

From this breakthrough the Wrights went on to build the first great invention of the early 1900s—airframe, engine, propellers, and all. Even more amazing is that the brothers achieved this feat of engineering in their spare time, and at their own expense—about $2,000. They capped their achievement by carrying out the first powered, sustained, and controlled air flight.

Charles Lindbergh's solo flight from New York to Paris in 1927 holds equal importance to the Wrights in showing the world the possibilities of air travel. A lanky 25-year-old college dropout, Lindbergh was obsessed about flying from an early age. From his arrival at a small airstrip in New York, Lindbergh was an amazing figure. Although he was going alone on an incredibly dangerous journey, he had no navigating instruments except a compass; he was not able to see ahead when seated in his airplane except through a periscope; and his craft had only one engine. It was certain that if anything went wrong over the vast expanse of the Atlantic Ocean, he would be forever lost.

Eventually, the enthusiasm over Lindbergh's accomplishment crossed the border from the emotion to the pocketbook. *Aviation* magazine reported in August 1927 that on Wall Street numerous aviation stocks that had become dormant were suddenly bid up to astronomical levels. Sensing that commercial air transportation was fast becoming a reality, investors poured over a billion dollars into aviation shares in the next two years.

By the mid-1930s, there were about 360 airline companies flying in the United States. Similarly, about 300 domestic manufacturers, many of them existing on capital raised through initial public offerings, fought among themselves for a share of the airplane market. Air traffic began to thicken in some of the larger cities, and at about the same time 20 big-city airports started to use radios in their control towers. A modern industry had been born.

WHAT GOES UP . . .

A more modern snapshot of the aviation industry gives a revealing view of how a transforming industry can itself be transformed through changes in the economic landscape.

First, of the 300-plus aircraft manufacturers that existed between 1919 and 1939, only about a handful exist today. Some of them disappeared from view due to mergers with larger competitors; many more simply failed to turn a profit and vanished.

A pair of titanic economic forces similarly pared down the airline industry. In 1978, the U.S. government decided to deregulate air travel, which allowed airlines to set their own prices. The consequence was, in the words of one airline executive, a gargantuan transfer of money from the province of the airlines to the pockets of consumers.

The eventual result was a wave of consolidation, as smaller airlines were simply not able to cope with lower ticket prices. It seems that the airlines were all struggling to achieve economies of scale–a term that refers to the tendency of large firms to reduce their per-unit costs by sheer volume.

The other economic force–the recession of 1990–1991–nearly brought the industry to its knees. The combined losses of the airlines in those two years, which totaled a staggering $8 billion, wiped out the entire profit that the industry had generated since it began in the 1930s.

Today, U.S. air travel is dominated by six large airlines.

In the words of the famous investor Warren Buffett in the November 22, 1999, issue of *Fortune* magazine (see Figure 2.3):

Sizing all this up, I like to think that if I had been at Kitty Hawk in 1903 when Orville Wright took off, I would have been farsighted enough, and public spirited enough–I owe this to future capitalists–to shoot him down. I mean, Karl Marx could not have done as much damage to capitalists as Orville did.

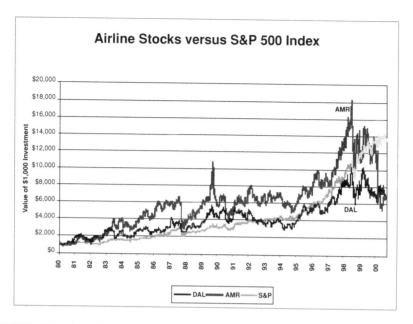

FIGURE 2.3 American Airlines (AMR) and Delta AirLines (DAL) have not kept pace with the S&P 500 index in the past 20 years.
Copyright © Stockpoint, Inc.

USING THE PAST AS A GUIDE

Having seen both the impressive upside potential and the staggering downside risks of growth investing, it is vital that we consider those screens that will maximize our returns and minimize our risks.

Maintain a Large Cap Bias

It is important in growth investing to consider the market capitalization of our portfolio. By keeping with a large cap bias, we will concentrate on those issues that are market leaders in their given industries. These stocks have the best chance of maintaining their market shares and profit margins even in the worst of times. And when the market is rising, large-cap growth stocks often surpass their smaller rivals.

Avoid Concentration

Stocks that lie in the same industry sector tend to be highly correlated (Figure 2.4). When a sector of the market falls out of favor, the best performer in the group often needs lower but not as low as the other stocks in the group. For this reason, our screen will eliminate stocks in the same or related industries.

Reevaluate Periodically

To ensure that the portfolio contains the most dynamic growth stocks, we recommend that all positions are reevaluated every six

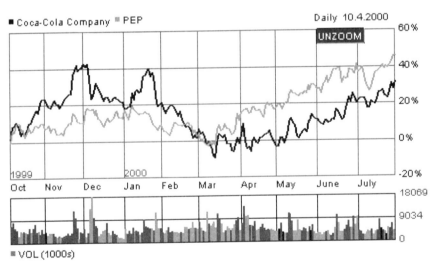

FIGURE 2.4 Like many companies in the same industry group, the stocks of PepsiCo (PEP) and Coca-Cola (KO) often trade in the same general direction. Copyright © Stockpoint, Inc.

months. To do this, simply log on to the worldlyinvestor.com web site, access the current growth stock screen (the site will update the screen monthly), and compare the previous month's holdings with those shown.

THE WORLDLYINVESTOR.COM GROWTH STOCK SCREEN

The worldlyinvestor.com growth stock screen has the following criteria:

- *Large Cap Bias.* Since we will concentrate our search on companies that are market leaders (in either established or emerging industries), we will concentrate on those companies with a market capitalization greater than $3 billion.
- *Impressive Five-Year Historic Growth.* The earnings growth of the companies must be in the top 25 percent for their respective industries.
- *Top-Tier Future Expected Growth.* The expected future growth of our companies, as measured by the consensus average of Wall Street analysts, must also fall in the top 25 percent for their respective industries.
- *Reasonable Debt Load.* To ensure that our companies are not financing their growth with expensive debt, the ratio of debt to equity must be below the industry average.

The result of this screen is shown as Figure 2.5.

The worldlyinvestor.com growth stock screen contains a lot of well-known stocks, unlike the companies that showed up on our momentum screen. There is a good reason for this: These 80-odd firms have achieved significant market share and impressive profit growth.

A more detailed examination reveals three potential growth stock winners.

Biomet (BMET, Figure 2.6) is a leading manufacturer of prod-

Company	Ticker Symbol	Market Cap ($mil)	5 Year History EPS Growth Rate (Actual)	Next 3–5 Year EPS Growth Rate (Est.)
LEISURE SERVICE				
Marriott Intl-A	MAR	$ 9,555	14.5%	16.0%
MEDIA				
Macrovision Corp	MVSN	$ 3,095	42.7%	42.5%
Viacom Inc Cl A	VIA	$ 47,376	34.4%	20.8%
Viacom Inc Cl B	VIA.B	$ 46,951	38.6%	20.3%
OTHER CONSUMER DISCRETIONARY				
Harley-Davidson	HDI	$ 12,529	22.4%	19.1%
FOOD/DRUG-RETAIL/WHOLESALE				
Cardinal Health	CAH	$ 19,806	22.8%	21.4%
Starbucks Corp	SBUX	$ 7,479	33.8%	25.3%
Walgreen Co	WAG	$ 32,881	17.8%	16.6%
NONFOOD RETAIL-WHOLESALE				
Bed Bath & Beyond	BBBY	$ 5,705	33.1%	25.7%
Best Buy	BBY	$ 15,810	72.8%	23.3%
Cdw Comptr Ctrs	CDWC	$ 6,198	45.1%	23.4%
Dollar General	DG	$ 6,963	25.8%	22.9%
Dollar Tree	DLTR	$ 4,931	47.1%	25.0%
Family Dollar	FDO	$ 3,433	28.2%	22.8%
Kohls Corp	KSS	$ 20,790	30.3%	23.0%
DRUGS				
Amgen Inc	AMGN	$ 75,339	19.1%	17.8%
Chiron Corp	CHIR	$ 9,950	34.8%	24.3%
Genentech Inc	DNA	$ 42,738	10.9%	26.6%
Genzyme-General	GENZ	$ 5,650	24.0%	17.1%

FIGURE 2.5 The worldlyinvestor.com Growth Stock Screen.

Company	Ticker Symbol	Market Cap ($mil)	5 Year History EPS Growth Rate (Actual)	Next 3–5 Year EPS Growth Rate (Est.)
Lilly Eli & Co	LLY	$112,653	18.4%	14.6%
Pfizer Inc	PFE	$185,159	16.7%	20.2%
Schering Plough	SGP	$ 70,917	18.9%	15.2%
Watson Pharma	WPI	$ 5,093	23.6%	21.0%
MEDICAL CARE				
Unitedhealth Gp	UNH	$ 14,495	10.3%	16.3%
MEDICAL PRODUCTS				
Baxter Intl	BAX	$ 21,191	14.3%	13.4%
Medtronic	MDT	$ 60,070	22.7%	18.0%
Minimed Inc	MNMD	$ 3,833	62.3%	41.3%
INDUSTRIAL PRODUCTS-SERVICES				
Cintas Corp	CTAS	$ 7,907	20.7%	20.1%
Tyco Intl Ltd	TYC	$ 81,082	37.8%	20.6%
COMPUTER-OFFICE EQUIPMENT				
Cisco Systems	CSCO	$453,429	41.0%	31.9%
Done Emc Corp-Mass	EMC	$162,744	32.7%	31.3%
Network Applian	NTAP	$ 27,411	82.9%	49.8%
Sandisk Corp	SNDK	$ 4,289	10.9%	37.3%
Sun Microsystems	SUNW	$148,131	30.5%	22.1%
Symbol Techs	SBL	$ 7,345	24.5%	21.8%
COMPUTER SOFTWARE-SERVICES				
Adobe Systems	ADBE	$ 16,822	13.5%	25.0%
Business Object	BOBJ	$ 3,151	25.4%	36.7%
Concord Efs Inc	CEFT	$ 6,134	45.9%	33.8%
I2 Technologies	ITWO	$ 23,838	64.2%	43.0%

(Continued)

FIGURE 2.5 *(Continued)*

Company	Ticker Symbol	Market Cap ($mil)	5 Year History EPS Growth Rate (Actual)	Next 3–5 Year EPS Growth Rate (Est.)
Mercury Interac	MERQ	$ 8,740	60.6%	38.8%
Oracle Corp	ORCL	$211,994	36.5%	25.4%
Paychex Inc	PAYX	$ 16,175	34.7%	28.5%
Siebel Systems	SEBL	$ 35,443	162.6%	41.5%
SunGard Data	SDS	$ 3,979	19.6%	18.8%
Veritas Software	VRTS	$ 51,628	52.1%	47.6%
ELECTRONIC-SEMICONDUCTORS				
Altera Corp	ALTR	$ 20,554	23.7%	26.9%
Burr Brown Corp	BBRC	$ 4,952	15.2%	24.8%
Intel Corp	INTC	$472,837	22.7%	20.4%
Linear Tec Corp	LLTC	$ 20,831	19.2%	26.7%
Maxim Intg Pdts	MXIM	$ 21,058	29.3%	26.9%
Micrel Semicond	MCRL	$ 4,417	48.7%	30.3%
Microchip Tech	MCHP	$ 4,788	16.2%	27.2%
Pmc-Sierra Inc	PMCS	$ 30,354	22.4%	40.8%
Rambus Inc	RMBS	$ 8,760	67.8%	62.5%
Rf Micro Device	RFMD	$ 6,991	170.5%	44.6%
Sdl Inc	SDLI	$ 25,108	37.1%	43.0%
Texas Instrs	TXN	$111,275	12.7%	25.2%
Vitesse Semicon	VTSS	$ 13,151	86.9%	38.2%
Xilinx Inc	XLNX	$ 28,633	15.7%	28.3%
ELECTRONICS				
Amer Power Conv	APCC	$ 8,735	27.5%	23.9%
Flextronic Intl	FLEX	$ 14,198	32.0%	31.3%
Jabil Circuit	JBL	$ 11,148	57.2%	31.4%

FIGURE 2.5 *(Continued)*

Company	Ticker Symbol	Market Cap ($mil)	5 Year History EPS Growth Rate (Actual)	Next 3–5 Year EPS Growth Rate (Est.)
Sanmina Corp	SANM	$ 14,161	40.0%	30.5%
Sci Sys Inc	SCI	$ 6,771	22.8%	23.0%
MISC TECHNOLOGY				
Perkin Elmer Inc	PKI	$ 3,710	13.1%	15.6%
Waters Corp	WAT	$ 9,300	38.2%	20.0%
TELECOMMUNICATIONS EQUIPMENT				
Adc Telecomm	ADCT	$ 30,124	29.5%	28.0%
Adv Fiber Comm	AFCI	$ 4,113	17.8%	28.3%
Amdocs Ltd	DOX	$ 17,732	49.1%	36.6%
Comverse Tech	CMVT	$ 15,280	43.4%	28.8%
JDS Uniphase	JDSU	$ 74,698	66.7%	47.9%
Polycom Inc	PLCM	$ 3,359	156.2%	41.4%
Scientific Atla	SFA	$ 13,457	12.0%	23.3%
Tellabs Inc	TLAB	$ 30,021	41.9%	29.2%
OIL MACHINERY-SERVICES-DRILLING				
Cooper Cameron	CAM	$ 3,535	22.0%	27.4%
Diamond Offshor	DO	$ 4,820	10.6%	19.0%
Ensco Intl Inc	ESV	$ 4,990	25.5%	20.5%
Global Marine	GLM	$ 4,924	34.2%	20.5%
Noble Drilling	NE	$ 5,694	37.3%	23.0%
Transocean Sedc	RIG	$ 11,157	40.1%	22.6%
OIL-EXPLORATION&PRODUCTION				
Devon Energy	DVN	$ 4,481	19.9%	15.4%

(Continued)

FIGURE 2.5 *(Continued)*

Company	Ticker Symbol	Market Cap ($mil)	5 Year History EPS Growth Rate (Actual)	Next 3–5 Year EPS Growth Rate (Est.)
BANKS-MAJOR				
Bank of NY Co	BK	$ 35,770	11.9%	13.5%
BANKS & THRIFTS				
State St. Corp	STT	$ 17,637	20.0%	14.1%
FINANCE				
Countrywide Cr	CCR	$ 3,865	18.3%	13.3%
INSURANCE				
Ambac Finl Inc	ABK	$ 4,089	17.8%	14.3%
Amer Intl Grp	AIG	$187,085	14.8%	13.6%
Cigna Corp	CI	$ 16,754	58.9%	13.6%
Nationwide Fin	NFS	$ 4,705	27.4%	15.4%
INVEST BKRS-MGRS				
Alliance Cap	AC	$ 8,182	24.0%	16.0%
Axa Finl Inc	AXF	$ 16,966	27.3%	14.3%
Schwab	SCH	$ 49,365	32.6%	24.3%
T Rowe Price	TROW	$ 5,373	30.8%	15.5%
TRANSPORTATION-AIR				
Southwest Air	LUV	$ 10,266	28.9%	13.1%
TRANSPORTATION				
Kansas City Sou	KSU	$ 10,447	35.2%	17.0%
BUSINESS SERVICE				
Convergys Corp	CVG	$ 8,442	14.0%	22.2%
Robt Half Intl	RHI	$ 5,560	38.9%	21.6%

FIGURE 2.5   *(Continued)*

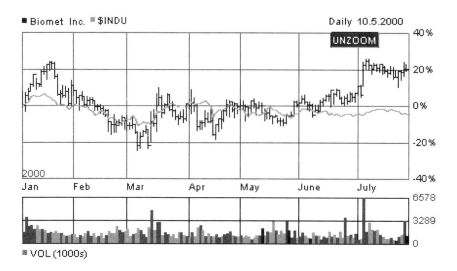

FIGURE 2.6 Biomet (BMET) stock, January to July 2000. Note the increased volume in July 2000, which indicates possible buying from momentum traders. Copyright © Stockpoint, Inc.

ucts used by orthopedic surgeons and other medical specialists. Boasting annual earnings growth of 17 percent per year and projected growth of 15 percent, the company seems like a bargain–especially when one compares its financial performance to that of its peer group.

And although BMET boasts higher earnings growth and a lower price-to-book value than the S&P 500 index, its stock is trading at only a slight premium over the S&P 500 index.

Best Buy (BBY, Figure 2.7) also seems to be a best buy. Not only does the company's growth rate exceed its price-earnings ratio by a factor of nearly 2:1, but as of July 2000 the stock has still not recovered from its downtrend in April. And with six consecutive earnings surprises, the stock can easily gather attention from momentum traders and large investors.

Finally, SunGard Data Systems (SDS, Figure 2.8) offers the best of both worlds: an established growth stock at a reasonable price.

Our focus list of the top growth stocks is shown as Figure 2.9.

FIGURE 2.7   Best Buy (BBY), October 1999 to July 2000.
Copyright © Stockpoint, Inc.

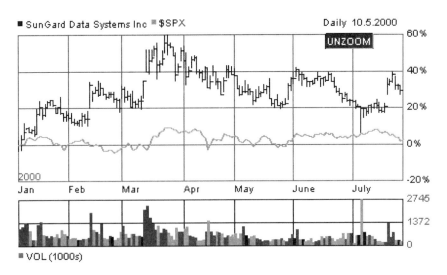

FIGURE 2.8   SunGard Data Systems (SDS).
Copyright © Stockpoint, Inc.

Stock	Ticker Symbol	P/E Ratio	Earning Growth	Long-Term Debt	Return on Equity
Biomet	BMET	28.7	17%	9%	20.9%
Best Buy	BBY	43.2	73%	1%	32.7%
SunGard	SDS	21.9	20%	1%	15.1%
S&P 500		28.0	12%		

FIGURE 2.9   The worldlyinvestor.com Growth Stock Focus List.

WorldlyInvestor Quick Summary

1. What are growth stocks?
- Stocks of companies whose sales and earnings have grown faster than the norm and are expected to continue to do so.
- Often these firms have a competitive advantage that justifies their higher-than-average price-to-earnings ratios.
- These stocks are not cheap, but investors are willing to purchase them due to their expected high-octane growth and competitive advantage.
- Growth stocks generally do not pay dividends; profits are reinvested in the companies.

2. When historically have growth stocks done well?
- In the early 1970s the Nifty Fifty were often called one-decision stocks—buy and never sell. After losing 80 percent of their value in the bear market in 1973–1974, they bounced back strongly and have outperformed the S&P 500 ever since.
- From 1989 to 1999 the Nasdaq appreciated eightfold versus a gain of less than fourfold in the Dow, an index comprised of more established companies.

3. Beware of being too early in trying to catch growth industries. Many look promising early on, with apparently significant potential, but never reach their potential. The airline industry is a good case in point.

4. WorldlyInvestor growth stock screen:
- Large-capitalization stocks—over $3 billion—that are market leaders.
- Impressive five-year growth—must be in the top 25 percent within their industries.
- Top-tier future expected growth—once again in the top 25 percent of their industries.
- Debt load below industry average.

CHAPTER

3

Uncovering the Value in Value Stocks

It's called the "Fosbury flop," but the creator of today's standard high-jump technique says a more accurate description might be the "Fosbury fluke."

Like many other high jumpers in the United States, Dick Fosbury learned the method of high jumping taught to him by his coaches and modeled after the usual straddle method. His jumps, though, were mediocre at best. Fosbury preferred to use more of a scissors-type method, akin to jumping hurdles. He eventually refined this technique and actually started to jump backward from the point of takeoff.

By the time of the 1968 Olympic Games in Mexico City, Fosbury had perfected his technique. Still, stepping out on the field, he felt like he was "marching to the lions." The stadium fell silent during his winning jump of 7′4¼″. "I knew I had it once it was past my hips," he recalls. "My eyes were wide; they were spinning. I was ecstatic."

Imitators quickly appeared, intent on capturing a piece of Fosbury's success. "Kids took up the flop almost immediately, because it was on television, I won the gold medal using it, and they said, 'That looks fun. I want to do that,'" Fosbury says. "The elite athletes, though, were not interested in dropping 12 years of dedication and practice to switch over to something that was unproved."

Then along came Dwight Stones in 1972, and a wave of young

jumpers using Fosbury's style. By 1976, all three Olympic medalists were floppers. By the 1980s, the straddle was virtually extinct.

THE DAWN OF VALUE INVESTING

Like today's "flopping" style of high jumping, value investing–which is the art of buying stocks that trade below their true value and selling them after a price run-up–was not created. Rather, it slowly gained acceptance in the investment community as large market players incorporated the technique into their methodologies.

The first well-known value investor was John Maynard Keynes. Perhaps the most famous economist of all time, he was definitely not the stereotypical economist of people's assumptions. Keynes married a Russian ballerina and was a member of the Bloomsbury Group, a cadre of intellectuals whose ranks included such avant-garde authors as Virginia Woolf, E. M. Forster, and Bertrand Russell. He was also a highly successful stock picker, and as bursar of King's College was able to increase the school's endowment significantly with his investment acumen.

In his 1936 book *The General Theory of Employment, Interest, and Money*, Keynes reasoned that professional investors should focus their energies on analyzing how the crowd will value a security "three months or a year hence." Keynes, in other words, applied psychological principles rather than financial evaluation to the study of the stock market. He saw the market as a beauty contest where the only thing that mattered was the opinion of the judges. In this

---

John Burr Williams

The Theory of Investment Value was written by Williams as his Ph.D. thesis at Harvard in 1937. The book is a favorite of investing legend Warren Buffett.

instance, it was much more sensible to choose the contestant that the judges will pick, rather than one's personal favorite. Likewise, an investment should be selected based on what someone else is willing to pay. This approach has been commonly referred to as the "Greater Fool Theory."

Although Keynes liked to emphasize the more qualitative aspects of the investing approach, John Burr Williams was considerably more left-brained. Williams's model for valuing a security calls for the investor to make a long-run projection of a company's future dividend payments. In his *Theory of Investment Value*, he showed how to combine this estimate with the expected degree of accuracy of that forecast to arrive at the intrinsic value of the stock. Only if the stock's traded price is below its intrinsic price–if it represents a good *value*– is it deemed worthy of purchase.

A less rigorous version of the value approached had been introduced by Benjamin Graham in the mid-1930s, and has long been a popular approach to stock investing. *Security Analysis*, written with David Dodd of Columbia University, quickly became one of the most influential texts of all time. Graham's more popular version of that book, *The Intelligent Investor* (published in 1949), is still widely read by nonprofessionals intent on managing their own affairs. Graham's most famous student is Warren Buffett, who used Graham's fundamental philosophy to become one of the most successful investors in the world.

Even though Graham did more than anyone to further refine the value approach, he was no iconoclast. Graham regularly retested his theories and experimented with modifications. Even when he had reached his eighties, he put aside an hour every day to study stocks and their performance, continually digging for a simpler and even more straightforward way to achieve superior investment results.

Yet, there are plenty of common attributes shared by all value investors. First, the process is company-specific; the intent is to uncover the "true value" of the company, which consists of the sum of its assets (i.e., land, equipment, patents) and the present value of ex-

Bernard Baruch

Bernard M. Baruch rose from a Depression-Era clerk earning $3 a week to become a financial leader and economic adviser to presidents. His financial acumen made him a millionaire by the age of 30!

pected future profits. Once the value of the company is determined, it is compared to its share price. The difference between the market value and the intrinsic value is often viewed by value investors as a safety margin. An investment is made only when this margin is judged to be sufficient to offer both a reasonable guarantee against a loss of capital and an attractive rate of return.

VALUE INVESTING LEGENDS

Graham's work was so influential in the investment community that, prior to the big growth stock boom of the past decade, virtually all of investing superstars were value oriented. Bernard Baruch, John Templeton, Gerald Loeb, Philip Fischer—the list of famous value investors goes on and on. Perhaps the reason for the popularity of the value approach is its link to the one financial measure that can be quantified—book value (the total value of a firm's fixed assets). It is quite comforting to have an investment philosophy that can be defended quantitatively. "Why did I buy GE? Because it trades below its true value!"

The "True Value" of a Stock

No one knows exactly how to calculate an accurate per-share value for any company. But many value investors use a stock's book value as a proxy. *Book value* is defined as the total value of a company's assets (land, cash on hand, factories, etc.) minus its total liabilities (short-term and long-term debt).

Undoubtedly, the best-known proponent of the value investing approach is Warren Buffett, who was a student of Ben Graham at Columbia University. Buffett has managed to generate market-beating returns by adhering to a strict but simple approach to investing. His method concentrates on reasonably priced issues whose price-earnings (P/E) ratios are exceeded by the companies' growth rates. Further, he believes in holding positions for a decade or longer. By choosing such companies as Coca-Cola (KO), Gillette, and Dairy Queen, Buffett's holding company Berkshire Hathaway has managed to beat the return of the S&P 500 index handily (Figure 3.1).

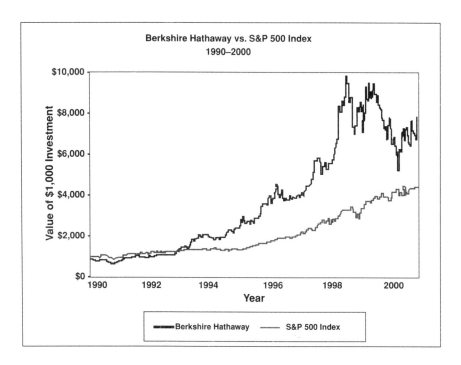

FIGURE 3.1 Even in the growth stock–dominated 1990s, Warren Buffett's Berkshire Hathaway (BRKA) managed to generate market-beating returns through a value investing approach.
Copyright © Stockpoint, Inc.

In Buffett's words:

> Our managers have produced extraordinary results by doing rather ordinary things—but doing them exceptionally well. Our managers protect their franchises, they control costs, they search for new products and markets that build on their existing strengths, and they don't get diverted. They work exceptionally hard at the details of their businesses, and it shows.

There is one more reason the value approach continues to hold favor, especially with more experienced investors: over long periods of time, it historically has knocked the socks off a strategy of buying and holding growth stocks (see Figure 3.2).

As Figure 3.2 shows, a $1,000 investment in the S&P 500/BARRA value index (a proxy for large-cap stocks with low price-to-

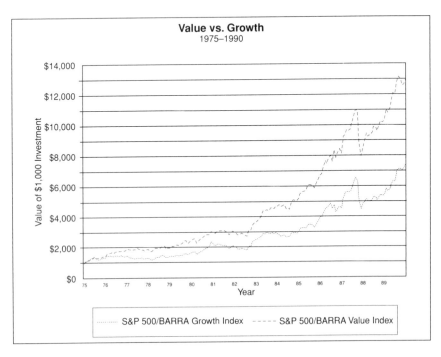

FIGURE 3.2 Value stocks vastly outperformed growth stocks from the mid-1970s to the end of the 1980s.

book-value ratios) in January 1975 would be worth $12,971 15 years later—a return over 75 percent higher than the return of the S&P 500/BARRA growth index.

Similar results have been found in foreign stock markets as well. The value players seemed to have it all—history, logic, and raw performance.

But as we shall see, their edge would not last indefinitely.

THE NEW PARADIGM 1990s

Growth investors' day in the sun began in the early 1990s. The decade witnessed incredible appreciation in technology stocks, as shown in Figure 3.3.

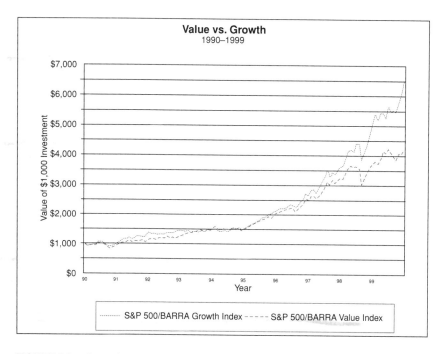

FIGURE 3.3 Growth stocks trounced value stocks in the late 1990s by a huge margin. Especially noteworthy was the growth stock rally in the fourth quarter of 1999.

Some believe that, with the advent of the Internet and continued advances in computing power, the stock market is vastly different than it was even a decade ago.

Ed Yardeni, the chief economist at Deutsche Bank Alex. Brown, coined the phrase *New Competitive Economy* (NCE) to describe the changes brought on by increased technology. He lists a number of ways that the New Economy differs from the Old Economy:

1. *Low consumer inflation.* According to Yardeni, economic booms used to lead to higher inflation, which forced the Federal Reserve to increase short-term interest rates and resulted in an economic downturn. In the NCE, global competition keeps a lid on inflation, and forces companies to cut costs and boost productivity. By offering consumers better goods and services at reasonable prices, companies expand production, sell more units, and employ more workers.

2. *Heightened competition.* Since competition tends to depress profits, firms must constantly innovate to boost profitability. The result is a high-tech revolution. In the NCE, high-tech spending now accounts for a large proportion of economic growth.

3. *Low wage inflation.* Wage inflation remains low because price inflation is moderated. Also, many employees are being compensated with stock incentives, which serves to keep a lid on salary growth.

If Yardeni's analysis is accurate, the investing world has indeed changed significantly. In his view, the true value of a company is represented more by the measure of its intellectual property, which is neither fully nor accurately measured by traditional accounting methods. As a result, the stock of companies that have little or no earnings but boast a high degree of innovation or technology could trade at a premium to the intrinsic value models used by value investors like Ben Graham.

But even if Yardeni's view does signal that the stock market has

> **The Odds of Winning**
>
> Even when presented with the fact that a person is 100 times more likely to be struck by lightning than win a lottery grand prize, people are still willing to bet. This is a perfect example of irrational behavior.

changed, that does not mean that the value approach has no merit. Indeed, the secret to the power of value investing may lie in the human psyche—and the uncontrollable, almost instinctive urge found in all of us to direct our decisions toward maximizing our short-term pleasure at the expense of everything else.

A BEHAVIORAL EXPLANATION

The fact that people act in an irrational fashion is hard to deny. People buy lottery tickets, even though the odds of winning are astronomical. A large number of educated adults smoke cigarettes, ignoring substantive evidence that the habit is deadly. It does not seem like much of a leap to suggest that our irrational tendencies exhibit themselves when we make investing decisions. Yet, the implication that investors are not consistently rational has huge consequences for the prevailing view that the future direction of stock prices is not predictable.

The most widely accepted mind-set about stock prices is encompassed in the Capital Asset Pricing Model (CAPM), which was developed in the 1960s. In essence, the CAPM suggests that the risk and the potential return of a security are inextricably linked. A high-flying biotechnology stock, for instance, should return more than a stodgy utility bond—but only because the risk associated with owning the stock is greater. That there could be other factors that might explain the return of a security other than the security's risk profile is to open a Pandora's box of possibilities—not the least of which is that a savvy stock picker armed with this knowledge could most assuredly beat the market.

The belief that the well-documented tendencies of individuals toward irrational behavior could cause tradable inefficiencies in the stock market represents what is happening on the cutting edge of finance. There are a number of reasons why many investment pros feel that human biases influence investment decisions:

- **High trading volume.** Rational investors should trade for only a few reasons: to rebalance their portfolios, to sell stocks because they need cash, or to buy them when they receive cash. Although it is difficult to say how much volume is to be expected from totally rational investors, the daily average trading volume on the New York Stock Exchange is clearly extreme.

- **Excessive volatility.** In a rational world, prices change only when news arrives. In the real world, security prices change constantly (and often dramatically) for no reason. Stock and bond prices are much more volatile than advocates of efficient market theory would predict.

- **The dividend effect.** Under U.S. tax law, dividends are taxed at a higher rate than capital gains. Companies can thus make their taxpaying shareholders better off by repurchasing shares with the revenue set aside for dividends, rather than by actually dispersing them. Why do most large companies pay cash

---

Cisco Systems

On May 15, 2000, Cisco Systems stock dropped over 7 percent in one day. The loss was attributed to a negative article in *Barron's* over the weekend. Upon examination, the article contained no information that the market did not already have! Cisco Systems lost 7 percent of its value that day for no discernible, rational, or valid reason.

---

dividends, and why do stock prices rise when dividends are initiated or increased? Neither question has any satisfactory rational answer.

NOT SO GREAT EXPECTATIONS

A field known as *behavioral finance* has evolved that attempts better to understand how emotions and cognitive errors influence investors. Many researchers believe that the study of psychology and other social sciences can shed considerable light on the efficiency of financial markets as well as explain many stock market anomalies, market bubbles, and crashes. Some believe that the historical outperformance of value investing results from investors' irrational overconfidence in exciting growth companies and from the fact that investors derive pleasure and pride from owning growth stocks. Some researchers believe that these human flaws are consistent, predictable, and can be exploited for profit.

Many proponents of behavioral finance are value investors. Why? In general, it seems that investors have the tendency to mistakenly overestimate the prospects for growth stocks while underestimating the potential of value stocks. Specifically, these investors often extrapolate past performance too far into the future. As a result, overpriced growth (or "glamour") stocks that have done well are expected to continue moving higher—while out-of-favor value stocks are seen as perpetual losers.

But pity the poor growth stock that falls short of the mark. Growth issues that disappoint are often beaten down excessively. Consider Brio Technologies (BRIO, Figure 3.4), for example. A business-to-business software company, Brio ran into trouble in December 1999 when it issued an earnings announcement that was below Wall Street expectations. After running into earnings trouble again in mid-2000, the stock continued its plunge, dropping to a two-year low.

At the same time, value stocks on the road to recovery can reward

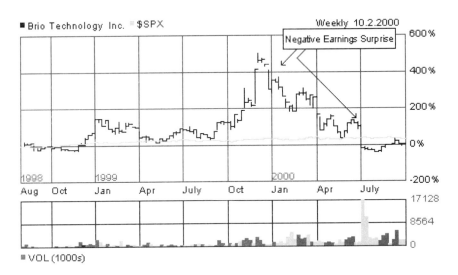

FIGURE 3.4   Brio Technologies (BRIO) was socked by negative earnings surprises in 2000.
Copyright © Stockpoint, Inc.

loyal investors with a slow but steadily increasing price as their fortunes improve.

Value stocks do not show promise only on domestic exchanges. Studies in foreign stock markets have come to similar conclusions regarding the long-run performance of value and growth stocks. Studies focusing on French, Japanese, British, German, and Korean markets found that value stocks outperformed growth stocks by about the same margins as the strategy performed in the United States.

Other studies have shown that value stocks hold up even after considering the effects of transaction costs. One study found that, after adjusted for 1 percent transaction costs and annual rebalancing, investors would have outperformed the stock market by about 5 percent per annum over the 1963–1988 period by concentrating their portfolios in value-oriented issues.

All of this evidence of the long-term efficacy of value investing might lead one to expect that a legion of professional money managers would build their portfolios based on this philosophy. This is not the case, as the recent performance of growth stocks has muddied the waters. According to investment manager and author Josef Lakonishok, the value approach "is difficult to defend and the stocks are not so pretty. People are sticking to their [growth] guns. It is how they got clients. Money managers know that they cannot afford to underperform for a long time."

One example of the investing public's aversion to bad performance is the fate of Tiger Management LLC, a leading investment firm. Founded in 1980, Tiger returned a stunning average annual return of 30 percent–until 1999. Not able to compete with other firms that were laden with technology companies, the company posted a loss of 19 percent for the year. The first quarter of 2000 was no better; after losing 13 percent, company chief Julian Robertson decided to return all assets to investors.

THE WORLDLYINVESTOR.COM VALUE STOCK SCREEN

According to many value investors, simply buying the stock of good companies cannot produce market-beating returns. Rather, big profits can be made only if those companies are much better than Wall Street, or any other investor, thinks they are. On that note, we present worldlyinvestor.com's value screen: our criteria for picking value stocks with the most potential for appreciation.

- ***Large Cap Bias.*** We will concentrate on established companies in out-of-favor industries rather than poorly run firms in more popular industries.

- ***Low Price-to-Book (P/B) Ratio.*** This ratio, which is defined as the stock price divided by the book value of the company per share, measures a stock's relative value. Many studies have shown that stocks with very low P/B ratios outperform stocks with relatively high P/Bs over long time periods.

- *Below-Average Market Performance.* Since we are looking for those stocks that are about to turn the corner, we must consider only those issues that have lagged behind the overall market for the past year. Therefore, we will screen for companies that have experienced price declines in their stock for the past six months.

- *Good Earnings Prospects.* Finally, we will focus on those stocks that, according to analysts' consensus, have a good prospect for above-average earnings growth in the next three to five years.

The result of the screen is shown as Figure 3.5.

Note that the list is dominated by a number of industry groups that have recently fallen out of favor with investors–namely the transportation and utility sectors. Many of these companies have been ignored by investors for so long that their stock prices have been stagnant or have fallen for the past few years, even though their potential for future profitability have actually improved.

In sifting through the list, three promising names come to mind:

Georgia-Pacific Group (GP, Figure 3.6) is a building products and paper company. The stock has fallen dramatically in 2000, mainly due to two consecutive earnings shortfalls. But it seems as though the market has overreacted to these short-term difficulties. The company now trades at a modest premium to its book value.

KeyCorp (KEY, Figure 3.7) is primarily engaged in commercial and retail banking. The stock is cheap for two reasons–its low price-to-earnings ratio and a modest price-to-book value ratio when compared to its peers. However, KeyCorp's projected growth rate is comparable to that of the banking industry as a whole. KeyCorp stock is slightly off for the year, which makes it even more attractive among value investors.

Finally, UAL Corporation (UAL, Figure 3.8) has suffered many of the same setbacks as other stocks in the airline industry. The most challenging dynamic faced by the industry is the greatly increased

Company	Ticker Symbol	Market Cap ($mil)	Price Book	P/E Using 12-month EPS
FOOD				
Archer Daniels	ADM	$ 6,436	1.07	22.74
LEISURE SERVICE				
Park Place Enmt	PPE	$ 3,817	1.02	20.94
Royal Caribbean	RCL	$ 3,681	1.46	9.23
NONFOOD RETAIL-WHOLESALE				
Federated Dept	FD	$ 6,043	0.93	8.03
Kmart Corp	KM	$ 3,961	0.63	6.84
JC Penney Inc	JCP	$ 4,692	0.69	10.94
Toys R Us	TOY	$ 3,743	1.13	12.02
DRUGS				
Novo-Nordisk As	NVO	$12,639	0.47	39.01
MEDICAL CARE				
Aetna Inc	AET	$ 9,936	0.99	14.87
AUTOS-TIRES-TRUCKS				
DaimlerChrysler	DCX	$54,740	0.89	8.46
Dana Corp	DCN	$ 3,466	1.27	5.58
Goodyear Tire	GT	$ 3,362	0.93	12.87
METALS-NONFERROUS				
Alcan Alum Ltd	AL	$ 7,013	1.30	14.09
STEEL				
Nucor Corp	NUE	$ 3,035	1.38	10.44
PAPER				
Georgia-Pacific Grp	GP	$ 4,914	1.27	6.24
Intl Paper	IP	$14,775	1.43	15.10
CONGLOMERATES				
Fortune Brands	FO	$ 3,830	1.46	11.52

(Continued)

FIGURE 3.5   The worldlyinvestor.com Value Stock Screen.

Company	Ticker Symbol	Market Cap ($mil)	Price Book	P/E Using 12-month EPS
AEROSPACE-DEFENSE				
Northrop Grumman	NOC	$ 4,669	1.43	8.47
Raytheon Co A	RTN.A	$ 6,647	0.61	10.36
Raytheon Co B	RTN.B	$ 6,795	0.62	10.59
OIL-EXPLORATION & PRODUCTION				
Devon Energy	DVN	$ 4,481	1.25	27.24
BANKS-MAJOR				
FleetBoston	FBF	$20,348	1.45	12.00
KeyCorp New	KEY	$ 8,451	1.36	8.24
BANKS & THRIFTS				
Southtrust Corp	SOTR	$ 4,297	1.46	9.43
Unionbancal Cp	UB	$ 3,015	1.02	5.89
FINANCE				
Cit Group Inc	CIT	$ 5,333	0.59	9.08
Countrywide Credit	CCR	$ 3,865	1.33	10.81
INSURANCE				
Ace Limited	ACL	$ 6,782	1.36	18.71
Allmerica Finl	AFC	$ 3,035	1.37	10.46
Allstate Corp	ALL	$17,871	1.16	9.45
Done Cincinnati Finl	CINF	$ 5,667	1.07	21.24
Loews Corp	LTR	$ 6,373	0.69	9.26
MBIA Inc	MBI	$ 5,184	1.49	10.98
St. Paul Cos. Inc	SPC	$ 8,217	1.37	14.85
Unumprovident	UNM	$ 5,035	1.06	7.70
XI Cap Ltd-A	XL	$ 7,267	1.34	15.88
INVEST BKRS-MGRS				
Bear Stearns	BSC	$ 5,157	1.38	7.93

FIGURE 3.5 *(Continued)*

Company	Ticker Symbol	Market Cap ($mil)	Price Book	P/E Using 12-month EPS
REAL ESTATE				
Archstone Comun.	ASN	$ 3,289	1.45	16.07
Equity Off Prpt	EOP	$ 8,611	1.17	21.73
Equity Resident	EQR	$ 6,197	1.46	20.84
Public Storage	PSA	$ 3,291	1.34	16.37
UTILITY-ELEC PWR				
Amer Elec Pwr	AEP	$ 6,357	1.27	12.89
Consol Edison	ED	$ 6,730	1.30	9.77
DTE Energy Co	DTE	$ 4,494	1.17	9.32
Edison Intl	EIX	$ 6,625	1.33	10.22
Entergy Corp	ETR	$ 6,712	0.99	11.58
Firstenergy Corp.	FE	$ 5,662	1.25	9.71
GPU Inc	GPU	$ 3,412	1.00	7.68
New Centy Enrgs	NCE	$ 3,808	1.38	10.75
Northeast Util	NU	$ 3,370	1.43	19.07
Northern St. Pwr	NSP	$ 3,299	1.27	13.64
Pg&E Corp	PCG	$ 9,922	1.44	10.06
Pinnacle West	PNW	$ 3,072	1.39	10.48
Txu Corp	TXU	$ 8,405	1.06	9.27
UTILITY-GAS DISTR				
Sempra Energy	SRE	$ 3,792	1.49	10.43
TRANSPORTATION-AIR				
AMR Corp	AMR	$ 4,584	0.66	6.49
TRANSPORTATION				
Burlington Nsf Cp	BNI	$11,058	1.47	10.59
Csx Corp	CSX	$ 5,216	0.90	17.43
Norfolk Southrn	NSC	$ 6,297	1.06	36.53
Union Pac Corp	UNP	$10,456	1.31	12.23

FIGURE 3.5 *(Continued)*

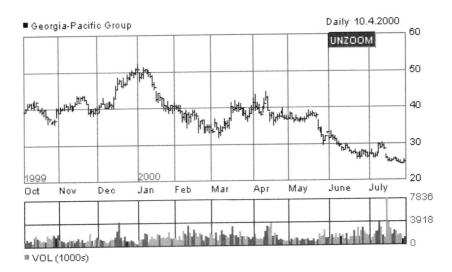

FIGURE 3.6 Georgia-Pacific Group (GP).

Copyright © Stockpoint, Inc.

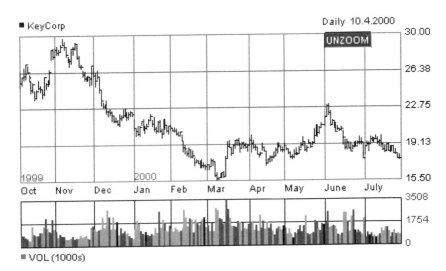

FIGURE 3.7 KeyCorp (KEY).

Copyright © Stockpoint, Inc.

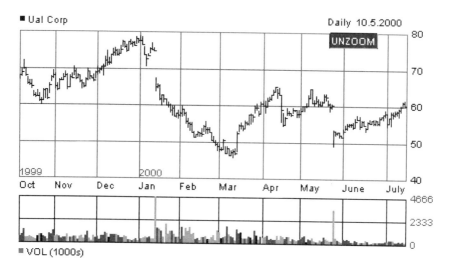

FIGURE 3.8   UAL Corporation (UAL), the parent company of United Air Lines. Copyright © Stockpoint, Inc.

price of jet fuel. But the company has an aggressive plan to hedge away its exposure to fuel costs, and the surging economy continues to experience record air travel.

As the world's largest airline, UAL will benefit from this industry growth. Yet, the stock is valued more cheaply than stocks of many of its peers, and the company is trading substantially below its book value.

Our value stock focus list is shown as Figure 3.9.

Stock	Ticker Symbol	Price/Book Ratio	P/E Ratio	Earnings Growth
Georgia-Pacific	GP	1.3	6.2	7%
KeyCorp	KEY	1.4	8.2	9%
UAL Corp.	UAL	0.6	6.1	10%
S&P 500		7.3	28.0	12%

FIGURE 3.9   The worldlyinvestor.com Value Stock Focus List.

WorldlyInvestor Quick Summary

1. What is a value stock?
   - It is a stock that is trading below its intrinsic value and therefore represents a "good" value.
   - The difference between the market value and the stock's intrinsic value is seen as a safety margin.

2. The book value of a company is equal to the sum of its assets plus the present value of its future expected profits.

3. Value stocks vastly outperformed growth stocks from the 1920s through the end of the 1980s when growth stocks came back with a vengeance.

4. It is comforting to have an investment strategy that can be defended logically.

5. WorldlyInvestor value stock screen:
   - Large-capitalization stocks in out-of-favor industries.
   - Low price-to-book-value ratio.
   - Price decline over the past six months.
   - Good earnings prospects over the next three to five years.

4

Distressed Stocks, the Dregs of the Market

It may seem counterintuitive, but some of the biggest returns can come from stocks that no one wants.

So far, we have examined strategies for selecting three distinct types of stocks. The first strategy examined the profit potential of buying the best-performing stocks–the so-called momentum issues. The second chapter showed the benefit in purchasing high-quality growth companies with steadily rising share prices and good earnings. In the third chapter, we discussed the merits of value stocks. Those companies with solid earnings growth but whose stocks were underperforming the overall market were shown to be especially promising.

We will now discuss the merit of those companies that seem not to have anything going for them–poor earnings, a slumping stock price, and general corporate malaise.

Distressed stocks are not simply those issues that are suffering a temporary slowdown. These companies have serious problems. There are a variety of reasons a company suffers a terrible change in its fortunes. Sometimes the market for its products change radically and the company cannot keep up with its competition. IBM is a good example. Although IBM created one of the first personal computers, the company was slow in reducing its reliance on mainframes to continue carrying the day. As a result, IBM's stock experienced a three-year drop of over 70 percent (Figure 4.1).

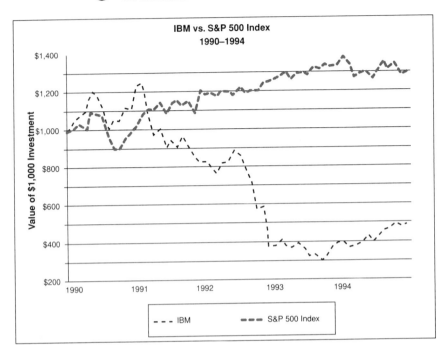

FIGURE 4.1 From 1990 to late 1993, IBM's stock lost one-half of its value. Copyright © Stockpoint, Inc.

After such a protracted pullback, few institutional investors would dare purchase shares in Big Blue. At the time it was trading near its book value, sported an extremely low P/E ratio of 7, and was a perennial loser–a company that, with no ability to keep up with new technology, seemed destined for the same trash heap as Digital Equipment Corporation (DEC), a early market leader in the computing industry.

But behind the scenes, IBM executives were intent on saving the reputation of their company. As a result of major cost cutting and the development of new technologies, IBM started mounting a comeback.

The result of IBM's efforts was astonishing. As institutional investors slowly began accumulating the stock, IBM trounced the S&P 500 index by 2:1 over the next four years (Figure 4.2).

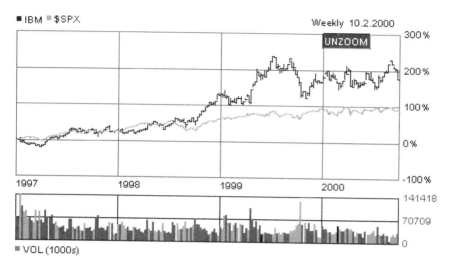

FIGURE 4.2 IBM rose from the ashes, beating the broad market by a wide margin.
Copyright © Stockpoint, Inc.

As the IBM example shows, successful investing in distressed companies requires buying them when they are at their worst, when everybody else seems to be writing them off, and analysts and TV anchors on CNBC scoff at their mention. It takes courage and conviction, but the returns can be huge. And more importantly, distressed securities can be an important element to a well-rounded stock portfolio.

THE QUEST FOR EXCELLENCE

Many investors select stocks for their personal portfolios by looking for those companies that exhibit above-average financial performance. After all, mutual fund managers generally hold stocks of "good" companies, yet the S&P 500 index outperforms the bulk of active managers, year in and year out.

As we shall see, the predilection of fund managers to pick already established, well-performing stocks is similar to a baseball team paying millions of dollars for a superstar third baseman—while ignoring potential superstars in the minor leagues.

The 1982 best-seller *In Search of Excellence: Lessons from America's Best-Run Corporations* by management gurus Thomas J. Peters and Robert H. Waterman Jr. examined 62 publicly traded companies that were considered to be innovative and excellent by leading businesspeople, consultants, members of the press, and academics. These companies were then screened by six measures of long-term financial performance for the time period 1961 through 1980.

The first two measures used were *asset growth* and *equity growth*. As a tool in selecting stocks, growth ratios are frequently compared to the inflation rate of the economy to determine whether a company is growing in real terms. Industry-wide growth rates are also used to gauge the performance of a company versus its competitors.

The third measure, *price-to-book ratio* (or *market-to-book ratio*), is a key ratio for determining the value of a stock. According to Peters and Waterman, this ratio serves as a proxy for the amount of shareholder wealth created as a result of the firm's business activities.

$$\text{Price-to-book ratio} = \frac{\text{Stock price}}{\text{Book value per share}}$$

The last three measures used were the *return on capital*, the *return on equity*, and the *return on sales*. These ratios show whether a company is consuming cash or creating assets through its continuous operations, and also indicates how efficiently the firm operates.

$$\text{Return on capital} = \frac{\text{Net income}}{\text{Total firm assets}}$$

Where:

$$\text{Assets} = \text{Total equity} + \text{Debt}$$

$$\text{Return on equity} = \frac{\text{Net income}}{\text{Total firm equity}}$$

$$\text{Return on sales} = \frac{\text{Net income}}{\text{Total Sales}}$$

In order to qualify for inclusion in the book *In Search of Excellence*, a company must have been in the top half of its industry in at least four out of the six criteria.

As a final yardstick, Peters and Waterman asked selected industry experts to rate each company's 20-year record of innovation, defined as a continuous flow of industry bellwether products and services and general speed of response to changing market dynamics.

As a result of this carefully laid out selection process, the authors culled the original list of 62 companies down to 29. And after studying the managerial processes of these remaining firms, the authors identified eight attributes that they felt best characterized an exceptionally well-managed firm:

1. *A bias toward action.* Even though decision making is an analytical process, these firms have a tendency to get things done and respond quickly to crises.

2. *Close relations with customers.* These companies offer unparalleled quality, service, and reliability.

3. *Autonomy and entrepreneurship.* These large organizations are uncharacteristically open-minded, which fosters creativity and practical risk taking.

4. *Productivity through people.* By "respecting the individual," these companies achieve a high level of output per employee.

5. *Hands-on and value-driven practice.* These companies have stated value commitments, which frequently become the ultimate drivers of important decisions.

6. ***Sticking to their knitting.*** The excellent companies successfully avoid the temptation to grow through acquisition of businesses outside their areas of expertise.

7. ***Simple form, lean staff.*** There are minimal corporate-level employees in the excellent companies, and most of these firms boast elegantly simple organizational structures.

8. ***Simultaneous loose-tight properties.*** Although the excellent companies frequently push autonomy down to the shop floor, their core values are relentlessly driven by senior management.

The authors' descriptions of the excellent companies are heart-warming, filled with tales of caring and committed executives who are fully versed in both the science and the art of management. These firms had attributes that many would be thrilled to see in their own places of employment. Due to their innovative decision-making processes, one might imagine that these companies would be perpetually ahead of their peers in virtually all measures of financial performance. And it is easy to assume that these companies boast stocks whose prices rise each year, that form the core of many professionally managed portfolios, and that were highly touted by every brokerage firm on Wall Street.

A list of the companies highlighted in the book is shown as Figure 4.3.

Curious to see how much these companies outdistanced the rest of the market, researcher Michelle Clayman studied the financial performance of the firms after the release of *In Search of Excellence*. As Figure 4.4 shows, she found that the four-year period following the selection process witnessed significant *deterioration* in the key financial variables used to identify the excellent companies.

What could possibly explain the disappointing decline in the performances of these supposedly well-run firms? Apparently the attainment of certain financial attributes in the past is simply not a good indication of what a company will be able to achieve in the future. In fact, two-thirds of the excellent firms disappeared, got acquired and

The Excellent Companies

Company	Ticker Symbol	Company	Ticker Symbol
Hewlett-Packard	HWP	Dana Corporation	DCN
IBM	IBM	Minnesota Mining	MMM
Schlumberger	SLB	Delta Air Lines	DAL
Texas Instruments	TXN	McDonald's	MCD
Data General	DGN	Disney	DIS
Intel	INTC	Kmart	KM
National Semiconductor	NSM	Boeing	BA
Wang Labs	WANB	Fluor	FLR
Eastman Kodak	EK	Dow Chemical	DOW
Johnson & Johnson	JNJ	DuPont	DD
Procter & Gamble	PG	Amoco	AN
Avon Products	AVP	Wal-Mart	WMT
Bristol-Myers	BMY	Raychem	RYC
Merck	MRK	Maytag	MYG
Caterpillar	CAT		

FIGURE 4.3 The companies highlighted in the 1982 best-seller *In Search of Excellence*.

disassembled, or went through extreme difficulties in the years following their selection.

It seems that companies with good financial ratios, lots of smart MBAs, and enviable profit growth have already been discovered by investors. By the time the Peters/Waterman book was published, there were no investors left to buy the stocks of those companies. As a result, many of the stocks on the list dropped in value.

This reasoning certainly runs counter to the lessons learned in one's youth. Once attained, excellence is assumed to become a personality trait. Great athletes are expected to stay at the top of their collective sports until illness or injury takes its toll. Popular actors are

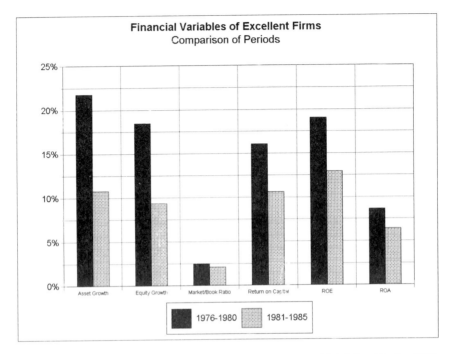

FIGURE 4.4 The financial performance of the companies highlighted in the 1982 best-seller *In Search of Excellence* seemed to deteriorate after the release of the book.

also assumed to retain their box office status until age makes it all but impossible for them to fulfill their cinematic obligations. Likewise, great companies should continue on the winning path until their most promising managers choose to retire. But in the case of companies, their dynamic, state-of-the-art training programs should continuously train the next batch of corporate executives. If anyone or anything had no excuse not to retain greatness, it must certainly be the modern organization.

The phenomenon known as *reversion to the mean* best captures this idea. Simply, mean reversion is the tendency of some naturally occurring processes to remain at, or return to, a long-run average level. For example, if one supposed that a financial measure like return on

---

Casinos Rely on Reversion to the Mean

Casinos are always eager for big winners to keep playing. They understand that even the luckiest gambler will eventually revert to the mean and the house will regain its edge. The casino knows it will win over time.

---

assets (ROA) followed a mean reverting process, a randomly selected group of firms that boasted a relatively high ROA would eventually experience below-par ROA. This would serve to reduce the long-run ROA of the group to the average of the overall market.

As Figure 4.4 shows, this seems to be the case in all of the financial measures used by Peters and Waterman. Perhaps these companies achieved a high level of excellence that was simply not possible to maintain over a long period of time.

In addition to examining the future financial performance of the excellent companies, Clayman was also interested in evaluating the widely held belief that financial ratios help to identify superior investments. Again, the results were quite disappointing.

According to Clayman, 11 of the 29 companies outperformed the S&P 500 index, while 18 (almost two-thirds) of the firms underperformed the index. She noted that the majority of the excellent companies underperformed "because the markets overestimated their future growth and future returns on equity and, as a result, their market-to-book ratios were overvalued."

What she is saying, of course, is that the stocks of excellent companies were simply too expensive. Market participants had bid up the prices of the stocks in the mistaken belief that their earnings growth would continue indefinitely. And when that perception failed to match up to reality, many of the stocks in the excellent universe likewise reverted to the mean.

It should be noted, however, that an equally weighted portfolio of all 29 excellent companies outperformed the S&P 500 index by 1.1 percent from 1981 to 1985. The biggest reason for this was the exceptional performance of three stocks in the universe–Wal-Mart (which outpaced the index by over 4:1), Maytag (over 2:1), and McDonald's (also about 2:1). However, the portfolio was almost 20 percent more volatile than the S&P 500 index. This indicates that the outperformance of the excellent portfolio was likely due to its extra risk.

THE SEARCH FOR DISASTER

The results from studying the 29 excellent companies suggest that identification of superior historical financial measures does not ensure either superior future earnings or superior investment returns.

The next logical step, then, is to reverse our view. If excellent companies fail to make the grade, how about "unexcellent" issues?

In that vein, Clayman identified a list of 39 companies that at the end of 1980 sported the worst combination of the six financial characteristics used to select the excellent firms.

The list of unexcellent companies (Figure 4.5) shows a number of companies that have become well-known financial disasters. The list also contains a number of firms mired in such slow-growing industries as textiles, iron forging, and tire manufacturing.

As Figure 4.6 shows, the unexcellent companies' financial results seemed to go from bad to worse. But interestingly, many of the companies had poor relative earnings growth, dramatically falling return on equity, and decreasing asset growth yet still enjoyed an increase in their price-to-book ratio. This implies that market participants saw in those firms something other than poor financial characteristics. Indeed, when the unexcellent firms and the excellent firms are compared, the excellent group still represents a far better selection in terms of financial performance.

It was noted earlier that top-tier financial performance does not ensure future stellar performance. If this is the case, does bottom-tier financial performance have any predictive value? When Clayman

The "Unexcellent" Companies

Company	Ticker Symbol	Company	Ticker Symbol
First Penna Corp.	FPA	J.P. Stevens	STN
American Motors	AMC	F.W. Woolworth	Z
Macmillan Inc.	MLL	Hasbro Inc.	HAS
Great Atlantic & Pacific Tea	GAP	Goodyear Tire & Rubber	GT
Massey Ferguson	MSE	Associated Dry Goods	DG
Firestone	FIR	National Intergroup	NII
Bethlehem Steel	BS	Spring Industries	SMI
Sherwin-Williams	SHW	American Can Co.	AC
Mohasco Corp.	MOH	Brunswick Corp.	BC
Singer Co.	SMF	Allis-Chalmers	AH
Interlake	IK	ITT Corp.	ITT
Bemis	BMS	Federal Paper Board	FBO
Hartmarx	HMX	Celanese Corp.	CZ
Outboard Marine	OH	Kaufman & Broad	KB
Westinghouse	WX	Owens-Illinois	OI
West Point Pepperell	WPM	Armco	AS
Burlington Industries	BUR	FMC Corp.	FMC
Chicago Pneumatic Corp.	CGG	Williams Cos.	WMB
U.S. Steel	X	Pacific Lighting	PLT
B.F. Goodrich	GR		

FIGURE 4.5 The "Unexcellent" Companies from Michelle Clayman's study.

examined the stock performance of the unexcellent firms, she was again surprised to find that 25 (almost two-thirds) of the 39 companies outperformed the S&P 500—*the exact reverse of the performance of the excellent companies.*

But the most remarkable finding of the study was that an equally weighted portfolio of the 39 unexcellent companies outperformed the

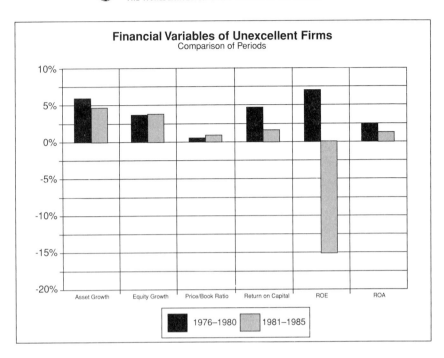

FIGURE 4.6 The financial performance of the unexcellent companies highlighted in Michelle Clayman's 1987 study generally deteriorated in the four years after these stocks were selected.

S&P 500 index by a staggering 12.4 percent per year. Despite the fact that the two portfolios were virtually identical with respect to market risk, the unexcellent portfolio beat the excellent portfolio by a staggering 64 percent in the five-year period 1981–1985 (Figure 4.7).

Clayman did not feel that picking poorly performing companies for investment was a valid conclusion to her study:

> We would by no means suggest picking stocks on the basis of poor financial characteristics, although our evidence suggests that companies with low price/book ratios are likely to see those ratios drift upward over time. The financial analyst must, instead, look beyond current and historical financial and [managerial] attributes to estimate investment returns.

FIGURE 4.7 The stock of unexcellent companies boasted a much greater average rate of return than the stock of the excellent companies according to Michelle Clayman's study.

However, she did note that corporate performance had a tendency to revert to the mean, as underlying economic forces attract new entrants to attractive markets and encourage participants to leave unattractive markets. Because of this tendency, companies that have been good performers may prove to be inferior investments–while bad performers occasionally provide superior investment returns.

PLENTIFUL CORROBORATION

There have been other studies that have confirmed Clayman's views. For example, Werner DeBondt and Richard Thaler conducted a study of the 35 best- and worst-performing stocks on the New York Stock Exchange from 1932 through 1977. They studied the best and worst performers over the preceding three- and five-year periods. They found that the best performers over the previous periods subsequently underperformed, while the poor performers from the prior periods subsequently produced significantly greater returns than the NYSE index.

THE WORLDLYINVESTOR.COM DISTRESSED STOCK SCREEN

The philosophy behind the worldlyinvestor.com distressed stock screen is quite simple—companies that have nothing going for them seem to have only one way to move—higher! As stated earlier in the chapter, we will focus on stocks that are distinctly unexcellent, with the following unexcellent qualities:

- Below-average asset growth.
- Below-average equity growth.
- Low price-to-book ratio.
- Below-average return on capital, return on equity, and return on sales.

We will further supplement our search with a two more criteria.

First, we will require that our stocks post a dividend. Why? Since we may have to wait a while before our companies are noticed by Wall Street, it's wise to have something to show for our efforts if things do not go as planned.

And finally, to increase the chance that our stocks have not yet been identified by large institutional investors, we will divert our attention away from stocks with market capitalizations above $2 billion.

The result of the screen is shown as Figure 4.8. As the size of the table shows, there is no shortage of distressed companies—even in bull markets like this one.

Whereas insurance and utility stocks dominate the value screen in Chapter 3, the distressed screen is dominated by the real estate and banking industries. The typical real estate stock on the list sports such a small market capitalization that the risk involved in owning any of them is extremely high (that might have something to do with why they are so cheap in the first place). And our value screen has already chosen a stock from the banking group (Key-Corp).

Company	Ticker Symbol	Market Cap ($mil)	Price/ Book	Dividend Yield	Return on Assets
APPAREL					
Brown Shoe Co	BWS	$ 246	0.99	2.96	5.22
Kellwood	KWD	$ 536	1.13	2.85	6.31
Oxford Inds Inc	OXM	$ 132	0.90	4.89	6.83
Stride Rite Corp	SRR	$ 289	1.24	2.99	0.03
FOOD					
Earthgrains Co	EGR	$ 817	1.25	1.04	3.30
Intl Multifoods	IMC	$ 334	1.31	4.49	3.43
Sanderson Farms	SAFM	$ 106	0.82	2.60	−0.08
Smucker Jm Cl A	SJM.A	$ 523	1.66	3.47	7.15
PUBLISHING					
Pulitzer Inc	PTZ	$ 963	0.43	1.45	4.34
HOME FURNISHING-APPLIANCE					
Bassett Furnitr	BSET	$ 155	0.64	6.10	5.45
Interface Inc A	IFSIA	$ 233	0.61	4.00	2.24
Virco Mfg	VIR	$ 129	1.40	0.64	5.13
LEISURE SERVICE					
Marcus Corp	MCS	$ 366	1.18	1.78	3.11
OTHER CONSUMER DISCRETIONARY					
Huffy Corp	HUF	$ 47	1.25	7.35	−6.56
FOOD/DRUG-RETAIL/WHOLESALE					
Bergen Brunswig	BBC	$1,244	0.83	0.43	1.21
Blue Square-Isr	BSI	$ 189	0.66	1.63	3.41
Bob Evans Farms	BOBE	$ 606	1.37	2.29	8.85
Cke Restaurants	CKR	$ 170	0.32	2.37	−0.10
Longs Drug Stores	LDG	$ 862	1.28	2.46	5.30
Nash Finch Co	NAFC	$ 97	0.54	4.24	1.19

(Continued)

FIGURE 4.8 The worldlyinvestor.com Distressed Stock Screen.

Company	Ticker Symbol	Market Cap ($mil)	Price/ Book	Dividend Yield	Return on Assets
NONFOOD RETAIL-WHOLESALE					
Dillards Inc-A	DDS	$1,410	0.56	1.06	2.40
Univl Fst Prods	UFPI	$ 324	1.56	0.50	6.64
AUTOS-TIRES-TRUCKS					
Detroit Diesel	DDC	$ 391	1.06	2.96	3.71
Wabash National	WNC	$ 282	0.74	1.31	4.95
CHEMICALS & FERTILIZER					
Arch Chemicals	ARJ	$ 476	1.10	3.72	5.15
Chemfirst Inc	CEM	$ 384	1.59	1.66	5.76
Fuller(Hb) Co	FULL	$ 626	1.66	1.88	5.89
Lubrizol Corp	LZ	$1,285	1.66	4.35	7.34
Miss Chemical	GRO	$ 106	0.25	2.95	−2.95
Schulman(A) Inc	SHLM	$ 372	1.09	4.36	7.90
Done Stepan Co	SCL	$ 228	1.70	2.69	6.40
METALS-NONFERROUS					
Amcast Inds	AIZ	$ 91	0.54	5.50	0.94
Century Alum Co	CENX	$ 273	1.51	1.49	0.56
Southern Peru	PCU	$ 173	0.15	1.63	3.30
STEEL					
Ak Steel Hldg	AKS	$1,007	0.43	5.52	2.69
Commercial Metl	CMC	$ 389	0.98	1.83	4.39
Quanex Corp	NX	$ 226	0.78	3.88	5.58
Ryerson Tull	RT	$ 255	0.37	1.94	2.97
PAPER					
Boise Cascd Cp	BCC	$1,638	1.07	2.10	3.31
Republic Group	RGC	$ 143	1.37	2.98	6.72

FIGURE 4.8 *(Continued)*

Company	Ticker Symbol	Market Cap ($mil)	Price/ Book	Dividend Yield	Return on Assets
CONTAINERS & GLASS					
Ball Corp	BLL	$1,005	1.56	1.77	3.83
INDUSTRIAL PRODUCTS-SERVICES					
Cadmus Comm	CDMS	$ 87	0.56	2.05	2.12
Champion Inds	CHMP	$ 40	0.86	4.85	3.33
Insteel Inds	III	$ 51	0.66	3.96	3.94
MACHINERY					
Primesource Cp	PSRC	$ 35	0.60	3.47	2.70
POLLUTION CONTROL					
Calgon Carbon	CCC	$ 315	1.74	2.46	2.23
BUILDING PRODUCTS					
Pope & Talbot	POP	$ 261	1.30	2.45	5.42
Rayonier Inc	RYN	$1,117	1.74	3.53	3.84
Rpm Inc	RPM	$1,078	1.51	4.78	4.72
Texas Inds	TXI	$ 660	1.04	0.96	4.00
CONSTRUCTION-BUILDING SERVICES					
Centex Corp	CTX	$1,411	1.00	0.67	5.87
D R Horton Inc	DHI	$ 912	1.19	1.09	7.29
K&B Home Corp	KBH	$ 851	1.46	1.45	6.08
Lennar Corp	LEN	$1,427	1.53	0.22	7.69
Pitt Des Moines	PDM	$ 208	1.19	2.84	8.33
CONGLOMERATES					
Kaman Corp A	KAMNA	$ 269	0.87	3.79	5.96
Whitman Corp	WH	$1,764	1.61	0.54	2.60
COMPUTER-OFFICE EQUIPMENT					
Data Research	DRAI	$ 33	1.00	1.68	6.57

(Continued)

FIGURE 4.8 *(Continued)*

Company	Ticker Symbol	Market Cap ($mil)	Price/ Book	Dividend Yield	Return on Assets
ELECTRONICS					
Pioneer Standrd	PIOS	$ 477	1.26	0.79	3.67
MISC TECHNOLOGY					
Watts Inds A	WTS	$ 343	1.57	1.85	5.77
Woodward Govnr	WGOV	$ 336	1.39	3.11	6.72
AEROSPACE-DEFENSE					
Engineered Supp	EASI	$ 104	1.62	0.24	4.77
Heico Corp	HEI	$ 140	1.01	0.30	6.75
COAL					
Arch Coal Inc	ACI	$ 320	1.33	2.75	−0.71
OIL-MISC					
Cornerstone Pp	CNO	$ 245	0.60	14.83	0.38
Star Gas Ptnrs	SGU	$ 260	1.43	14.21	2.23
OIL & GAS PRODUCTION-PIPELINE					
Lakehead Pipe	LHP	$1,037	1.58	8.43	5.44
Northern Border	NBP	$ 847	1.47	9.00	4.17
BANKS & THRIFTS					
Andover Bcp Inc	ANDB	$ 189	1.48	3.25	1.19
Capitol Fedl Fn	CFFN	$1,011	1.01	3.63	1.05
Cfs Bancorp	CITZ	$ 166	0.88	3.95	0.79
Colonial Bncgrp	CNB	$1,161	1.69	4.19	1.12
Columbia Bcp-Or	CBBO	$ 50	1.34	4.32	1.43
Commercial Fed	CFB	$ 981	1.09	1.61	0.83
Commun Trust Bc	CTBI	$ 188	1.10	4.90	1.01
Covest Bcshs	COVB	$ 48	1.05	2.91	0.76
F&M Bancorp/Md	FMBN	$ 230	1.33	5.17	1.02

FIGURE 4.8 *(Continued)*

Distressed Stocks, the Dregs of the Market

Company	Ticker Symbol	Market Cap ($mil)	Price/ Book	Dividend Yield	Return on Assets
Flag Finl Corp	FLAG	$ 42	0.63	4.68	0.11
Flagstar Bancp	FLGS	$ 145	0.88	3.35	0.78
Iberiabank Corp	IBKC	$ 102	0.87	4.10	0.71
Jacksonvill Bcp	JXVL	$ 26	0.87	3.81	1.25
Mid-America Bcp	MAB	$ 293	1.73	3.35	1.42
Oceanfirst Finl	OCFC	$ 224	1.55	4.05	1.04
Park Bancorp	PFED	$ 21	0.98	3.82	0.87
Republic Bcp-A	RBCAA	$ 116	1.12	1.69	0.96
Seacoast Finl	SCFS	$ 252	0.97	2.21	1.12
St Francis Cap	STFR	$ 145	1.12	2.48	0.74
Staten Isl Bc	SIB	$ 671	1.27	2.52	1.20
Timberland Banc	TSBK	$ 53	0.81	3.03	1.59
Unionbancorp	UBCD	$ 43	0.80	2.18	0.78
FINANCE					
Finova Group	FNV	$ 981	0.59	4.50	1.33
Municipal Mtg	MMA	$ 364	1.03	7.90	4.95
INSURANCE					
Alfa Corp	ALFA	$ 686	1.70	2.97	4.73
Enhance Fin Svs	EFS	$ 601	0.82	1.52	6.18
Fbl Finl Grp-A	FFG	$ 495	1.01	2.26	1.65
Fidelity Natl	FNF	$1,216	1.19	2.21	6.39
Fremont Genl	FMT	$ 357	0.49	6.28	−0.18
Great Amer Finl	GFR	$ 803	1.53	0.53	1.03
Harleysville Gp	HGIC	$ 521	1.01	2.98	1.40
Liberty Finl Co	L	$1,142	0.95	1.68	0.71
Midland Co	MLAN	$ 236	0.92	1.20	3.49
Stancorp Fnl Cp	SFG	$1,079	1.37	0.74	1.50

(Continued)

FIGURE 4.8   (Continued)

Company	Ticker Symbol	Market Cap ($mil)	Price/ Book	Dividend Yield	Return on Assets
INVEST BKRS-MGRS					
Jefferies Gp-Nw	JEF	$ 562	1.45	0.87	1.43
Sw Secs Group	SWS	$ 562	1.75	0.82	0.84
INVESTMENT FUND					
Pmc Capital Inc	PMC	$ 118	1.64	10.00	8.25
REAL ESTATE					
Agree Rlty Corp	ADC	$ 74	1.42	10.86	4.43
Arden Realty	ARI	$1,543	1.12	7.63	3.77
Brandywine Rt	BDN	$ 709	1.06	8.15	2.08
Burnham Pacific	BPP	$ 236	0.59	14.36	1.13
Captec Net Leas	CRRR	$ 107	0.79	13.51	5.82
Carramer Realty	CRE	$1,902	1.12	6.52	2.82
Corr Pptys Trst	CPV	$ 80	0.61	12.98	4.26
Crown Amer Rlty	CWN	$ 138	0.77	15.81	1.15
Dev Diverfd Rlt	DDR	$ 968	1.72	9.14	4.26
Entmnt Ppty Tr	EPR	$ 219	0.82	11.81	4.66
First Wash Rlty	FRW	$ 220	0.84	8.94	4.30
Franchise Fin	FFA	$1,401	1.54	8.52	9.09
Glenborogh Reit	GLB	$ 523	0.71	9.43	2.26
Glimcher Realty	GRT	$ 343	1.44	13.32	2.60
Home Pptys Ny	HME	$ 597	1.39	7.14	2.61
Hospitality Prp	HPT	$1,408	0.97	11.07	5.33
Irt Property	IRT	$ 281	1.14	10.67	5.52
Istar Finl Inc	SFI	$1,796	1.14	11.11	6.73
Jameson Inns	JAMS	$ 89	0.64	12.65	3.47
Jdn Realty Corp	JDN	$ 377	0.69	10.79	6.05

FIGURE 4.8 *(Continued)*

Distressed Stocks, the Dregs of the Market

Company	Ticker Symbol	Market Cap ($mil)	Price/ Book	Dividend Yield	Return on Assets
Kilroy Realty	KRC	$ 688	1.55	6.63	3.09
Lexington Ppty	LXP	$ 209	1.19	9.85	3.29
Meditrust Paird	MT	$ 410	0.15	64.00	1.07
Natl Health Inv	NHI	$ 261	0.70	23.95	6.43
Natl Health Rty	NHR	$ 80	0.63	15.88	3.46
Ntwde Health Pr	NHP	$ 676	1.39	12.58	4.89
Omega Hlthcare	OHI	$ 108	0.31	37.21	3.74
Pac Gulf Prop	PAG	$ 525	1.21	6.94	3.89
Ps Business Pks	PSB	$ 594	1.20	3.94	4.90
Regency Rlty Cp	REG	$1,265	0.64	8.58	3.71
Shurgard Storag	SHU	$ 691	1.26	8.61	4.35
Sovran Slf Stor	SSS	$ 278	1.10	9.94	4.81
UTILITY-ELEC PWR					
Conectiv Inc	CIV	$1,445	1.40	5.16	2.49
Western Resour	WR	$1,167	0.61	7.06	0.89
UTILITY-GAS DISTR					
Atmos Energy Cp	ATO	$ 644	1.68	5.60	1.39
South Jersey In	SJI	$ 308	1.61	5.38	3.11
TRANSPORTATION-AIR					
Cnf Transport	CNF	$1,334	1.43	1.46	5.91
TRANSPORTATION					
Overseas Shipho	OSG	$ 843	1.27	2.41	0.09
Usfreightways	USFC	$ 740	1.32	1.34	9.20
Werner Entrprs	WERN	$ 624	1.27	0.76	6.59
BUSINESS SERVICE					
Kelly Svcs A	KELYA	$ 908	1.57	3.93	8.34

FIGURE 4.8   *(Continued)*

Our distressed stock focus list, then, contains stocks from some of the remaining market sectors.

Cooper Tire (CTB, Figure 4.9) manufactures automotive products, including tires and sealants. The company trades at a modest discount to book value, has an attractive 3.4 percent dividend yield, and, as the graph shows, is decidedly out of favor. However, considering its impressive potential ability to better analysts' expectations, it should not be long before the stock begins to enjoy renewed favor on Wall Street.

Bob Evans Farms (BOBE, Figure 4.10) operates in one of the least admired market sectors, restaurants and foods. It trades at its industry average in terms of price-to-earnings and price-to-book-value ratios, but the company seems to be better suited for a rally when the restaurant sector comes back into favor.

Pulitzer Inc. (PTZ, Figure 4.11), the media publisher, trades at an astonishing discount to book value. However, the company is starting to show evidence of a turnaround with impressive short-term earnings.

Our focus list of distressed companies is shown as Figure 4.12.

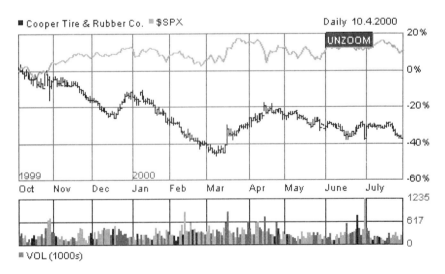

FIGURE 4.9 Cooper Tire (CTB).
Copyright © Stockpoint, Inc.

FIGURE 4.10 Bob Evans Farms (BOBE).
Copyright © Stockpoint, Inc.

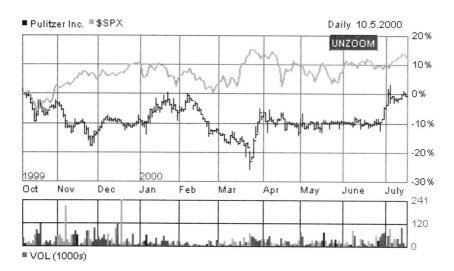

FIGURE 4.11 Pulitzer, Inc. (PTZ).
Copyright © Stockpoint, Inc.

Stock	Ticker Symbol	Price/Book Ratio	Industry Price/Book Ratio	Dividend Yield
Cooper Tire	CTB	0.9	1.1	3.4%
Bob Evans Farms	BOBE	1.4	1.4	2.3%
Pulitzer Inc.	PTZ	0.4	2.9	1.4%
S&P 500		7.3		1.1%

FIGURE 4.12   The worldlyinvestor.com Distressed Stock Focus List.

WorldlyInvestor Quick Summary

1. Distressed companies are those that have serious problems. They differ from value plays in that they are not simply undervalued; they are generally close to some form of reorganization, or their stock price has suffered greatly.

2. Investors in this arena must be willing to be highly contrarian. Distressed stocks are usually shunned by most, especially the so-called experts.

3. While the outlook may not dramatically improve for these stocks, the price often does rise due to a phenomenon known as *reversion to the mean*. Just as high-flying stocks tend to come down to earth over time, distressed stocks tend to rise toward the average return of the market.

4. Identifying prospects—finding "unexcellent" companies:
   - Below-average asset growth.
   - Below-average equity growth.
   - Low price-to-book ratio.
   - Below-average return on capital, return on equity, and return on sales.
   - Must post a dividend.
   - Market capitalization less than $2 billion to help ensure the stock is below the institutional investors' radar screens.

PART TWO

Index Trading with Exchange-Traded Funds and Mutual Funds

Investors have heard a lot about market indexes in the past few years. As indexes have made all-time highs, only to succumb to mind-numbing volatility and huge price breaks, following the fortunes of such broad market measures as the Dow Jones Industrial Average, the Standard & Poor's 500 index, and the Nasdaq index have become popular pastimes.

What many investors may not know, however, is that it is possible to profit handsomely by trading broad market indexes instead of individual stocks.

Chapter 5 explains the various investment vehicles that can be used to trade the market as a whole. The list includes exchange-traded funds, index mutual funds, and derivatives (options and futures). The chapter also describes the Quant View Portfolio, a set of index strategies that are discussed in worldlyinvestor.com's "Market View" column. Since its inception in late October 1999, the portfolio has handily beaten the return of the S&P 500 index.

Chapter 6 explains how investors can profit from market movements associated with the release of economic information. These reports include the monthly employment, inflation, and production data that are followed closely by the news media.

Chapter 7 shows how savvy traders can profitably exploit the market's tendency to rise around holidays, at the end of the month, and at the end of the year. These simple strategies will show how to take advantage of these market tendencies during these periods—and when to sit on the sidelines.

Finally, Chapter 8 describes one of the most closely guarded secrets in investment management—how to exploit the pricing errors in mutual funds.

5

Exchange-Traded Funds— The Next Generation of Indexed Investing

The previous section of *The WorldlyInvestor Guide to Beating the Market* dealt with trading individual stocks. But there are many strategies that can be much more effectively exploited by trading the broad market as a whole.

As an active trader for many years, I can attest that it is often simpler to catch wide swings in the overall market by trading indexed-based securities rather than individual stocks. One reason for this is the often dramatic effect company-specific information (earnings, new product introductions, etc.) can have on individual issues. For example, during the various phases of the Microsoft antitrust trial, tech stocks exhibited enormous volatility. At one point in mid-2000, Microsoft stock lost more than 40 percent of its value. However, the Dow Jones Industrial Average–an index that includes such blue-chip tech names as Cisco and IBM–did not experience such wide price swings (Figure 5.1).

As Figure 5.1 shows, a profitable buy signal in the Dow would have resulted in a loss if the trade were initiated in one of the biggest components of that index–Microsoft.

There are other reasons to believe that it is easier to trade indexes

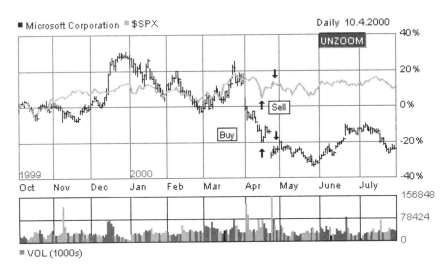

FIGURE 5.1 A buy signal in a broad market index like the Dow cannot easily be exploited in an individual stock like Microsoft.
Copyright © Stockpoint, Inc.

than individual stocks. Macroeconomic information such as changes in interest rates, employment reports, and inflation gauges tend to run in trends. For example, between July 1989 and January 1994 the Federal Reserve Board progressively lowered interest rates without interruption. Lower rates are usually good for the market, because in such an environment the rates on bank accounts and fixed-income securities like bonds are so low that investors prefer to place their money in the stock market, causing stock prices to increase. Between July 1989 and January 1994, the S&P 500 index boasted an average annual return of 13.03 percent. But during this profitable period, nearly 40 percent of stocks in the index actually lost value!

The period 1989–1994 is no exception. During the Nasdaq index's record run of 1999, which saw the index soar over 80 percent for the year, over one-half of the stocks in the index ended the year lower than where they began.

It is for these reasons that the Quant View Portfolio was designed around the trading of market indexes. To date, all of the trades in the portfolio have been in the Standard & Poor's 500, an index of the 500 largest stocks in terms of market capitalization. As shown in Figure 5.2, the portfolio has been a success from the start. Initiated at the end of October 1999, the Quant View Portfolio has beaten the overall market on an absolute return basis by more than 2:1. Even more amazing is that this return was earned in only 54 trading days.

Quant View Track Record

Dates Entry	Exit	Trading Days	Type of Trade	Point Gain/Loss	Percent Gain/Loss
10/28/99	11/02/99	4	End-of-month	12.49	0.93%
11/23/99	11/29/99	3	Holiday trade	3.17	0.23%
12/10/99	12/15/99	3	PPI report	(3.39)	−0.24%
12/22/99	12/28/99	3	Holiday trade	21.67	1.51%
01/28/00	02/03/00	4	End-of-month	64.80	4.76%
02/28/00	03/03/00	4	End-of-month	61.12	4.53%
03/03/00	03/08/00	3	Employment short	42.47	3.01%
03/30/00	04/05/00	4	End-of-month	(0.55)	−0.04%
04/07/00	04/10/00	3	Employment short	49.16	3.24%
05/07/00	05/10/00	3	Employment short	49.58	3.46%
06/02/00	06/07/00	3	Employment short	6.11	0.42%
06/09/00	06/14/00	3	PPI report	13.59	0.93%
06/29/00	07/06/00	4	End-of-month	14.28	0.99%
07/07/00	07/12/00	3	Employment short	(14.02)	−0.95%
07/28/00	08/03/00	4	End-of-month	34.30	2.42%
08/04/00	08/09/00	3	Employment short	(9.94)	−0.68%
Totals		54		344.84	24.53%

FIGURE 5.2 The Quant View Portfolio consists of a number of highly profitable short-term strategies. The trades are based on calendar-based anomalies and the market's reaction to government releases. All positions are executed in the S&P 500 index.

In other words, the portfolio has doubled the return of the S&P 500 index by being invested on average only one day per week!

Further, the Quant View Portfolio has shown its ability to make money in either rising or falling markets. Nearly one-half of its return has been generated from its short sales in the S&P 500 index (such positions seek to profit in a falling market by selling the index at a given price, and then buying it back at a lower price in the future).

Nearly all investment portfolios are totally dependent on the continuing rise of the stock market for profits. The Quant View Portfolio's ability to cash in on market downtrends places it in a unique and opportunistic category.

One of the most often asked questions from visitors to the worldlyinvestor.com web site refers to the best way to execute Quant View Portfolio trades. There are three ways that an individual investor can exploit the market anomalies described in worldlyinvestor.com's "Market View" column: index mutual funds, exchange-traded funds (ETFs), and derivatives (options and futures).

As we shall see, the advent of exchange-traded funds offers Quant View traders an opportunity to exploit the portfolio's strategies with unparalleled flexibility, low cost, and simplicity.

INDEX MUTUAL FUNDS

Traditional mutual funds are by far the most popular investment vehicle in the world. Many individual investors utilize funds for their diversification and ease of use. Mutual funds are commonly available in many 401(k) plans, and no-load funds can be purchased through a variety of discount brokerage firms such as Schwab, E*Trade, and TD Waterhouse.

Index mutual funds are one of the fastest-growing sectors of the mutual fund industry, and for some very good reasons. First, the performance of index funds is hard to beat. Even the most experienced professional mutual fund managers, who attempt to pick the best-

Mutual Funds and Benchmarks

In order to evaluate the performance of mutual fund managers, their returns are often compared to a number of market benchmarks. For example, a fund such as Fidelity Magellan (FMAGX) that focuses on large-cap stocks is usually compared to the S&P 500 index. A technology fund, however, is more likely to be benchmarked to the Nasdaq.

performing stocks for their portfolios, have an extremely difficult time exceeding the return of the market as a whole. In the past 10 years, less than 7 percent of all actively managed funds were able to exceed the return of the S&P 500 index.

Second, index funds have relatively modest fee structures. Although actively managed funds charge an annual management fee of 1.4 percent per year, index funds often levy fees that are only one-tenth that amount.

Finally, size works as a detriment to actively managed funds. As actively managed funds grow, it becomes increasingly more difficult for the portfolio manager to generate market-beating returns. Most of these problems are related to increased transaction costs. But an index fund manager may actually find it easier to equal the return on the fund's benchmark as the client list grows, because the increased assets allow for a more complete replication of all of the stocks in the index.

As Figure 5.3 shows, the Vanguard 500 Index Fund (VFINX) not only is the largest fund, but it also does an excellent job of tracking the index.

Even though index mutual funds make good long-term investments, their use as a short-term trading vehicle is suspect. One reason is that such funds often discourage short-term investors, because frequent additions and redemptions to the fund force the portfolio manager to buy and sell stock in order to stay fully invested. This activity is bad for the other investors in the fund, because it triggers

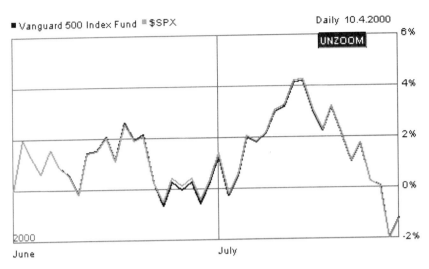

FIGURE 5.3 The Vanguard 500 Index Fund (VFINX) closely tracked its benchmark, the S&P 500 index, in the two-month period shown (June–July 2000). Savvy trading and rock-bottom expenses have allowed the fund to exceed the return of the index over a multiyear period.
Copyright © Stockpoint, Inc.

capital gains and generates increased commissions and other transaction costs. Vanguard, for example, allows its clients to switch in and out of its index funds only a few times per year.

In response to the demand for an easy-to-access, short-term indexed trading vehicle, two firms have developed funds for short-term traders. ProFunds and Rydex offer investors a number of index funds that are based on the Nasdaq, the S&P 500 index, and a few foreign stock markets. There are no transaction charges on any of the funds offered by the companies. Funds can be bought and sold with no restrictions.

As Figure 5.4 shows, these index funds do a good job of tracking the S&P 500 index on a day-by-day basis. However, the relatively high expense ratios of these funds (their fees are closer to those of the average actively managed fund than to those of an index fund) tend to drag down their performance over longer periods of time.

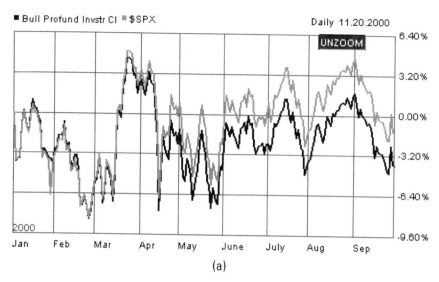

(a)

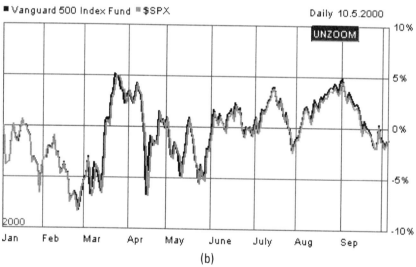

(b)

FIGURE 5.4 Although (a) ProFunds' Bull Fund (BLPIX) does a good job of tracking the day-to-day changes in the S&P 500 index, the (b) Vanguard 500 Index Fund (VFINX) manages to capture the long-run returns of the index more accurately.

Copyright © Stockpoint, Inc.

The real benefit of the ProFunds and Rydex offerings is the ease with which traders can employ leverage and short selling. ProFunds' UltraBull (ULPIX), for example, has an objective of returning twice that of the S&P 500 index. Similarly, the Rydex Nova Fund (RYNBX) seeks to capture 1.5 times the daily price movement of the S&P 500 (the company has also recently created a fund with the same leverage as UltraBull). These funds might be of interest to an investor wishing to leverage the returns of the Quant View Portfolio. Since a typical strategy in the portfolio has a holding period of only three days, many readers have expressed an interest in multiplying their returns using a leveraged investment vehicle.

Finally, both companies also offer funds that are designed to profit when the S&P 500 index drops in value. How do these funds work? Simply, they maintain positions in a number of derivative securities that gain when the market declines, and lose money if the market rallies.

ProFunds' short offerings include Bear (BRPIX) and its leveraged cousin, UltraBear (URPIX), shown in Figure 5.5. Rydex's funds include Ursa (RYURX) and Tempest, which does not yet have a symbol.

By using these funds, traders don't have to worry about opening a margin account or the headaches associated with short sales. And since the fund companies do not charge transaction costs, traders save on commissions.

But this convenience comes with one disadvantage. Like all other traditional open-ended mutual funds, these indexed products are priced only at the end of the trading day. Intraday trading is not permitted.

EXCHANGE-TRADED FUNDS

Exchange-traded funds (ETFs) are considered by many to be the next evolutionary stage of index investing. They are a hybrid of traditional funds, closed-end funds, and common stocks.

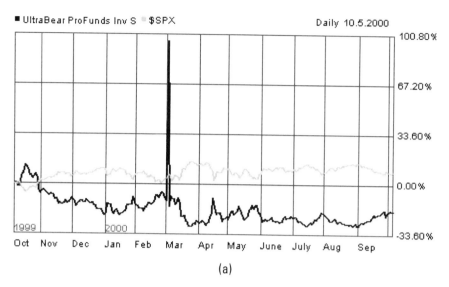

(a)

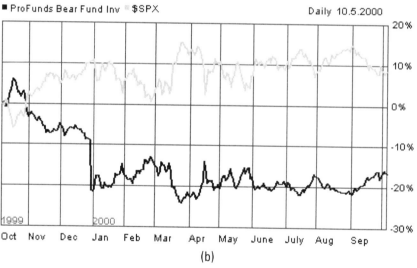

(b)

FIGURE 5.5 ProFunds also offers several vehicles that profit when the market drops. However, (a) double-levered UltraBear (URPIX) and (b) Bear ProFunds (BRPIX), do not exactly mirror the returns of their benchmark, the S&P 500 index.

Copyright © Stockpoint, Inc.

ETFs resemble traditional, open-ended index funds in many ways. Both investments are managed to match the return of a stated index, such as the S&P 500 or the Nasdaq. But unlike mutual funds, which are priced only at the close of each session, investors are able to buy and sell ETFs throughout the trading day at the then-prevailing price.

In other words, ETFs allow investors to trade indexes as easily as they trade individual stocks.

Exchange-traded funds are also much less expensive than the typical index mutual fund. The popular Spider (SPY: AMEX), which is managed by State Street Advisors, is one of the oldest ETFs in existence. It boasts an annual management fee of only 0.12 percent, which is 0.06 percent lower than even the cheapest traditional index fund offered by Vanguard.

And with the new entrants in the exchange-traded fund arena, fees are headed even lower. Barclay Investor's Services S&P 500 Index ETF (IVY: AMEX), which was launched on May 19, 2000, levies an annual management fee of just 0.0945 percent. Vanguard's proposed ETFs will carry even lower fees.

What does this mean to investors? Simply that ETFs should track their respective equity benchmarks much more closely than do traditional index mutual funds.

Further, ETFs are a bit more tax efficient than are mutual funds. Since investors wishing to buy and sell shares do so on the open market, the portfolio manager is not forced to sell the fund's position and incur capital gains taxes for the existing shareholders.

Do not be surprised if some of the benefits of exchange-traded funds sound familiar. Closed-end funds (CEFs), which have existed for decades, are very similar to ETFs. CEFs are exchange-traded vehicles that can be bought and sold at any time during the trading day, and can often have the same desirable tax efficiencies as ETFs. But that is where the similarities end.

One of the biggest differences between CEFs and ETFs relates to the pricing of the two funds. CEFs can frequently trade at a discount or premium to their net asset value (NAV). For instance, the German Fund, which trades a basket of German-based companies, has traded at as much as a 30 percent discount to the intrinsic value of its holdings. The reason? There is no mechanism that allows investors to buy a discounted fund and sell the stocks that it owns, which would force the two prices to converge. This type of trading is called *arbitrage.*

So many CEFs trade at a discount that investors are wary of buying them. There is little worse than buying a CEF at a discount with the anticipation of big profits when it returns to par—and it never happens. This has been the situation for countless CEF investors, and things seem to be actually getting worse rather than better. As a group, CEFs are trading at their widest discounts in 20 years.

Investor apathy toward CEFs is the main reason that there are only 517 of them trading on U.S. exchanges. Closed-end funds have just $123 billion in assets, compared to the $4.6 trillion that is tucked away in traditional mutual funds.

As opposed to the discount dilemma common to CEFs, ETFs trade at or extremely close to their net asset value almost all of the time. The reason? ETFs have a built-in mechanism for ensuring that the fund and the underlying index track each other very closely.

Similar to a CEF, an ETF begins its life with a fixed number of shares. Most investors in exchange-traded funds, like closed-end funds, buy and sell shares on an exchange. As opposed to investor money flowing in and out as investors buy and sell shares as in traditional mutual funds, both CEFs and ETFs are exchange-traded. Shares flow from buyer to seller without affecting the underlying portfolio. The price of an exchange-traded fund partially reflects the shares' reception in the marketplace.

But unlike CEFs, ETFs have a nifty feature that ensures that its NAV is always close to its trading level. Institutional investors have the option of creating new ETF shares by delivering stock to the fund in return. This is called a PIK (payment in kind), and is allowed only in 50,000-share blocks. Although most individual investors will never participate in a PIK transaction, this feature of ETFs allows large investors the opportunity to arbitrage any substantial price differences between the fund's NAV and share price until the difference goes away.

All of these features of ETFs allow them to offer virtually an exact replicate of the performance of their underlying equity index. Figure 5.6 shows the performance of the Spider ETF (SPY: AMEX) versus its benchmark, the S&P 500 index.

Finally, exchange-traded funds share an attribute with the heavily traded common stocks–vast liquidity. It is not unusual for the ETF based on the Nasdaq 100 index (QQQ: AMEX) to trade 10 million shares per day. For this reason, it is quite easy to profit from anticipated market drops by selling these shares short. *Short selling* involves the sale of a stock not previously owned by the seller in the expecta-

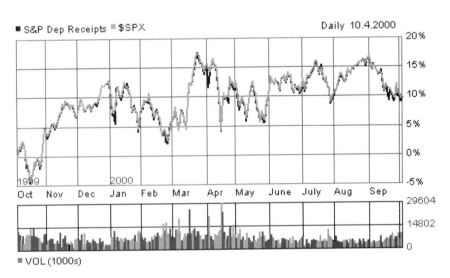

FIGURE 5.6 The returns of State Street's SPY exchange-traded fund almost exactly mirrors that of its benchmark, the S&P 500 index.
Copyright © Stockpoint, Inc.

tion that it will be possible to repurchase the stock at a lower price at some time in the future.

The process of short selling begins by placing a sell order with a brokerage firm. The broker then attempts to borrow the shares to be shorted from the firm's stock loan or margin department. Assuming that the stock is available to loan, the broker accepts the order and the client is now short the chosen security.

So what happens to the money that was raised by the sale of the borrowed shares? Initially, 50 percent of it must remain in the trading account in which the investor shorted the stocks. This is called *margin*, and it must reflect no less than 35 percent of the shorted stock's value at any given time.

When the holding period of the trade has run its course, a buy order is placed with the broker. This locks in the lower price and offsets the short position in the account. The profit would be based on the difference between the price at which the stock was shorted, less the later purchase price, less commissions and interest (remember, shorted stock is borrowed—so there are interest costs involved).

Although shorting highly liquid issues such as QQQ and SPY is relatively straightforward, short selling individual stocks is often quite difficult. For one thing, these individual securities are sometimes not available for loaning, because so many traders are short the stocks already. A market statistic called *short interest* is commonly used to measure the amount of common stock sold short and not yet repurchased.

One of the other risks in a strategy that shorts individual stocks is the danger of a *short squeeze*. In this situation, a high-volume buying wave drives prices higher. As the stock's price continues upward, it pressures existing shorts to cover their positions, which serves to accelerate the price increase. This event is often triggered by an unusually positive earnings announcement by the company.

Finally, it should be noted that when a stock is purchased, the maximum allowable loss is 100 percent (if the stock goes to $0). However, when a stock is sold short, the 100 percent loss level is hit when the stock doubles in price. If the stock's price continues even higher, one's potential loss could exceed 100 percent.

A short squeeze is much more likely in an individual stock. It is highly unlikely to occur in an indexed ETF because the ETF's price is based on a large basket of securities.

Further, it should be noted that the trades in the Quant View Portfolio are limited in duration, and typically last three to four days. This further lessens the risk that a short squeeze could happen during one of these holding periods.

Exchange-Traded Funds and Margin

Finally, it is also possible to establish a leveraged position in the market using ETFs. To do this, one must set up a margin account. This type of brokerage account allows investors to buy shares with funds borrowed from the brokerage firm.

For example, suppose one wants to buy 200 shares of a $20 stock. Normally, one would need $4,000 (plus commissions) to make the purchase. But if the security is bought on margin, $2,000 (or up to 50 percent of the purchase price) can be borrowed from the brokerage firm. If the stock appreciates in value, all of the gains on the trade would have been made on only one-hald of the initial investment.

Of course, if the stock falls the loss would proportionally increase. And, because the money is borrowed from the brokerage firm, margin transactions incur interest costs. But again, since the Quant View holding periods are so short, the interest incurred would be negligble.

OPTIONS AND FUTURES

Index options offer investors the opportunity to implement the Quant View strategies in an efficient manner. But due to the inherent leverage involved in options trading, and the time value deterioration of option prices, most traders should consider using index mutual funds and ETFs as their primary trading vehicles.

However, this book would not be complete without addressing the topic. So here goes—but trader beware.

The Options Market

Index options began trading in earnest in the early 1980s as a direct offshoot of the financial futures markets. Options can be separated into two categories—*call options* (which rise in value with the market) and *put options* (which rise when the market drops).

At this point, it should be obvious that options can be used to profit in either a rising or a falling market. This is a key requirement for any investment vehicle, since the Quant View Portfolio goes both long and short.

The purchaser of a call option has the right but not the obligation to purchase the underlying stock or index at a specified "strike" price prior to the preset expiration of the options contract. Similarly, the purchaser of a put option has the right, but not the obligation to sell the underlying stock or index at the strike price prior to expiration.

In order to purchase a put or a call you have to pay what is called a "premium." The premium is *not* a performance deposit or margin. It goes directly to the person who sold the option to you. The premium is basically the market price of the option. It is determined primarily by how far the current price of the underlying instrument is from the strike price of the option and by the time to expiration.

If the price of the underlying index (i.e., the S&P 500) is greater than the call strike price the option is said to be "in the money." It has intrinsic value because the call could be exercised for an immediate profit. The reverse would be true for a put.

Another attribute unique to options relates to the time value of money. The greater the number of days until an option expires, the greater its *time value*. This reason is simple—with more time, there is a greater probability that the underlying price will move in your favor.

The Value of Options

There are a number of criteria that determine the value of a given options contract:

Strike price. The closer the strike price is to the stock's price, the greater the value of the option.

Time until expiration. Options with more time until expiration have a greater value.

Stock volatility. The higher the volatility of the underlying stock, the greater the value of the option.

Let's suppose that an S&P 500 index call option that expires in September with a strike price of 1,500 currently trades at 54. A similar option that expires in October trades at 74. The difference is due to the greater time value of the October contract.

But with that increased premium comes a higher *beta*. Beta is calculated by dividing the price movement in the option by the price movement in the underlying index. If our option moves 2 points and the index moves 3 points, for example, the option's beta is $^2/_3$ or 0.67. The cheaper September option might have a beta of 0.50, which means that the profit from holding the September option will be smaller than if one used the more expensive October contract.

So, like all other things, you get what you pay for when purchasing options.

A Quant View Example

Options exist for many market indexes. One of the most popular contracts is the OEX, which tracks the S&P 100 index. There are also options on the S&P 500, the Nasdaq, and the Dow Jones Industrial Average. All of these options trade on the Chicago Board Options Exchange.

Since we confine our trades in the Quant View Portfolio to the S&P 500 index, we will cite an example from that market.

It is July 2000, the S&P 500 is trading at 1,501, and the Quant View Portfolio issues a buy signal on Tuesday's close in the S&P 500. The specified holding period for the trade is through Friday's close.

Buy 1 September 2000 1,500 call option on the S&P 500 (SPX) at 52⅜.

This means that a 100-share option will cost $100 \times 52\frac{3}{8} = \$5,237.50$. Commission costs for both buying and selling the option will run about $30, plus a $1.75 per contract exchange fee. Thus, the total cost of our position is $5,269.25.

Over the course of the next three days the stock market rallies to 1,575 (a gain of 5 percent in the index), and as a disciplined, systematic Quant View trader you exit on Friday's close. The call is now worth 97, making the position worth $9,700.

The bottom line is as follows:

Call premium sale price	$9,700.00
Less: purchase price	$5,269.25
Total gain	$4,430.75

The trade represents a gain of $4,430.75 divided by $5,269.25 = 84 percent.

Sounds great, doesn't it? But remember—options traders lose as quickly as they profit.

In other words, it is best to trade options only if you have deep pockets.

The Futures Markets

A futures contract is simply a standardized, exchange-traded agreement to buy or sell a particular financial instrument, index, or commodity for delivery at an agreed-upon price and time in the future.

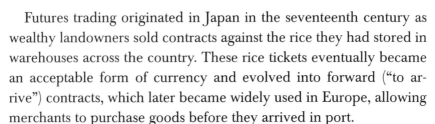

Futures trading originated in Japan in the seventeenth century as wealthy landowners sold contracts against the rice they had stored in warehouses across the country. These rice tickets eventually became an acceptable form of currency and evolved into forward ("to arrive") contracts, which later became widely used in Europe, allowing merchants to purchase goods before they arrived in port.

Forward contracts were used extensively in the U.S. grain trade by farmers and grain merchants to hedge the wild swings in price caused by fluctuations in supply and demand around harvest time. Forward contracts are generally written between two parties and are not transferable. The popularity of these contracts allowed for standardization of delivery date and grade of grain. Once standardized, the contracts could be traded on an organized exchange between market participants, and the futures markets came into being.

As the economy has grown, the need for hedging in the financial and currency markets has driven the development of many contracts outside of the agrarian commodities. In fact, trading in the stock index, currency, and financial futures now dwarfs the traditional commodity markets.

Futures contracts offer some distinct advantages to the index trader over the conventional index mutual fund. The primary advantage offered by these instruments is the leverage inherent in each contract. When used correctly, leverage can make for very efficient trading. However, when used unwisely leverage will significantly shorten one's trading career.

Trading a stock or mutual fund on margin allows one to borrow up to 50 percent of the value of the instrument. For example, you could buy $10,000 worth of stock by putting up $5,000 and borrowing $5,000 in a margin account. You would have to pay interest on the money that you borrowed. The futures markets are quite different. The exchanges require that both the buyer and the seller post an initial security deposit called margin. This deposit requirement is quite low, typically less than 5 percent of the value of the contract. And since there is no loan involved, there is no cost for the leverage.

Not only are you able to trade with significantly more leverage than you can in the stock market, but also the margin utilized has no cost. No-cost leverage is the key benefit of futures trading.

Initiating a short trade on a stock can be somewhat cumbersome, and as a result many traders are reluctant to go short. This is not the case in the futures markets. The mechanics of shorting a contract are exactly the same as buying a contract. A simple sell order is all that is required. When a trader exits a short position, a buy order is entered and the two positions automatically offset each other.

A Quant View Example

Like options, futures contracts are available for many market indexes. The most active is the S&P 500 index contract, which trades on the Chicago Mercantile Exchange (CME). Other contracts include the Nasdaq 100, the Dow Jones Industrial Average, the S&P Midcap 400, and the Russell 2000. As the underlying equity markets have appreciated, so have the sizes of the respective futures contracts, making them less accessible to smaller traders. In response to this problem the Chicago Mercantile Exchange created two smaller contracts, the Mini S&P 500 contract and the Mini Nasdaq 100. Both of the mini contracts are exact replicas of their larger brethren, except they are only one-fifth the size and sport much lower margin requirements.

As all the strategies in the Quant View Portfolio are based on the S&P 500 index, we will once again use an example from that market. However, this time we will use an example on the short side.

Once again it is July 2000, but now the S&P 500 is trading at 1,490, and the Quant View Portfolio issues a sell signal on Friday's close. The specified holding period for the trade is through the following Wednesday's close.

Sell 1 September 2000 Mini S&P 500 contract on the close at 1,490.

The current margin requirement for the mini contract is set by the exchange at $7,032 per contract. Since futures do not require the posting of margin, all that is required from the brokerage firm is that the client's capital not fall below the margin level stated. Thus, the only cost for the position is the commission, which averages around $20 per contract.

Right on cue, the market drops precipitously into Wednesday's close, losing 90 points on the S&P 500, or 6 percent. The position is duly closed out by buying one September Mini S&P 500 contract on the close. The gain in the short position is:

90 points × $50 per point	$4,500
Less: commission	$20
Total gain	$4,480

Assuming that the trader's account maintained a cash level equal to twice the broker margin requirement of $7,032, the trade represents a gain of $4,480 divided by $14,064 = 32 percent.

Remember—leverage works both ways! Had the index rallied 6 percent in this example, the trader would have *lost 32 percent.* It is also important to remember that if the market goes against your position prior to the exit, you will have to post additional margin.

In other words, potential futures traders should have even deeper pockets than those traders considering options to implement the Quant View Portfolio.

WorldlyInvestor Quick Summary

1. Broad market indexes are generally easier to trade than individual stocks for the following reasons:
   - They are not subject to the dramatic and volatile effects of company-specific news.
   - Macroeconomic factors tend to run in trends—changes in interest rates are one example. It is this type of information that drives the trending behavior and performance of the broad market indexes.

2. Execution vehicles for index-based strategies:
   - Index mutual funds:

     Accurately track the underlying index.

     Have low fees.

     Some offer leverage and short selling.

     Downside—they are priced daily, not allowing for intraday execution.
   - Exchange-traded funds:

     Accurately track the underlying index.

     Have lower fees than index mutual funds.

     Can be more tax efficient than index mutual funds.

     Margin and short selling readily available—less likely to succumb to a short squeeze.

     Priced intraday—more trading flexibility and greater risk control.
   - Derivatives —options:

     Use only if well capitalized.

     Only purchasing options is recommended, never writing them. This limits the maximum loss to the premium paid.

     Purchase "at the money" calls for bull strategies and "at the money" puts for bearish strategies.

     The upside on calls is unlimited while the upside on puts is limited only by how low the underlying price can fall, making for a great trading vehicle.

     Inherent leverage, when used prudently, can allow for very efficient trading.

- Derivatives—futures:

  Use only if well capitalized.

  Like options, the ease of shorting and inherent leverage make for a very efficient trading vehicle if used prudently.

  Unlike options, your losses can be virtually unlimited if the strategy is not properly executed.

6

Trading ETFs with Publicly Available Information

Though trading strategies may often differ in style, time frame, and other factors, they do have one thing in common: a reliance on other traders' mistakes for their success. Unless other traders collectively misprice the securities that we trade—by driving prices either too high in a period of overoptimism or too low in a fit of depression—trading ideas cannot achieve the edge necessary for market-beating returns.

Even though the academic community was the first to insist that investors act rationally and do not make mistakes in valuing stocks, one of the most often cited examples of stock mispricing can be found in (of all places) a scholarly journal. In a February 2000 *Journal of Finance* article titled "Contagious Speculation and a Cure for Cancer," Gur Huberman and Tomer Regev discuss the market action of EntreMed (ENMD), a biotech stock that received favorable mention in the Sunday, May 3, 1998, edition of the *New York Times*. The news story caused EntreMed's stock to rocket threefold during the next trading session.

The *Times* story reported on ENMD's breakthrough technology in cancer research. If the investing public had not been aware of the information contained in the article, the stock run-up could be attributed to traders assimilating this new information into the value of the company.

Even the Best Make Mistakes!

Everyone makes mistakes. Nowhere is this more apparent than in the world of sports. For example, the Russian military rifle team failed to appear for competition at the 1908 Olympic Games because they were operating on the Julian calendar instead of the customary Gregorian calendar. The team showed up 12 days late for their event! In more modern times, golfer Andy Bean was penalized two strokes for using the grip of his putter to sink a two-inch putt at the 1983 Canadian Open. He finished the tournament two strokes behind the leader.

Source: "Boneheads and Dingbats: Classic Sports Mistakes" (www.letsfindout.com).

But surprisingly, the information had been reported in the popular press (including the *Times*) *five months earlier.*

According to Figure 6.1, it seems that the trading community collectively overestimated the impact of the May 1998 story on the company. A savvy trader with knowledge that the information had

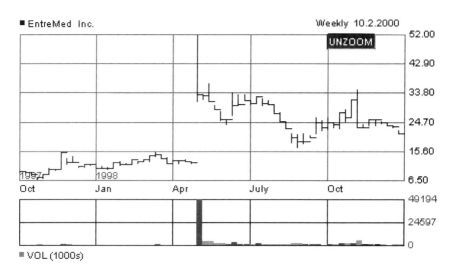

FIGURE 6.1   EntreMed (ENMD: Nasdaq), October 1997 through December 1998. Copyright © Stockpoint, Inc.

been reported five months earlier could have established a short position on May 4, and profited as other traders drove the stock's price lower.

Even considering the EntreMed incident, many question the extent of securities mispricings. The topic has spawned a raging debate in the financial community. It even caused the development of a new investment theory–the efficient market hypothesis (EMH)–that forms the foundation for today's asset management industry.

The basic tenet behind the EMH is that competition in the capital markets will drive security prices to a level that reflects all available information. In other words, simply knowing something about company's stock is not enough to produce market-beating returns. Rather, one must be able to analyze the information in a way that others cannot.

For example, most investors could easily obtain the most recent earnings report of Microsoft. But how many could take that data and analyze it to discover something about the company that other traders have not yet figured out yet?

FUNDAMENTAL AND TECHNICAL DATA

As it turns out, there are two distinct types of information used by investors. The first type, *fundamental data*, includes market share, profit margins, and other company-specific information.

Fundamental analysis is the main tool used by Wall Street equity analysts, whose job is to find out as much about the companies that they cover as possible. The analysts then translate this data into trading recommendations, which are communicated to their brokerage clients.

Wall Street analysts face stiff competition from their peers at other firms. They typically work extremely long hours, and have access to every shred of publicly available data on the companies that they cover. Some of the most well known analysts have the ability to move the market with their comments. It is not unusual for a cadre of analysts to act in unison after a company issues important information on its fortunes. That can *really* move a stock's price.

One might assume that with significant resources at their disposal, these highly paid professionals could easily discern which stocks will earn the largest returns. But that does not seem to be the case. Numerous studies have shown that the stocks most highly regarded by financial analysts often do no better than a randomly composed equity portfolio. Does this mean that the analysts as a group are in unintelligent lot?

This is certainly not the case. The simple fact that there are such a large number of talented, discerning analysts underscores the inherent difficulty in selecting which stocks will generate market-beating returns. This brings us back to the principle of competition—with so many analysts competing to gain an edge over their peers, any new information that becomes available is almost instantaneously gobbled up, scrutinized, and incorporated in the stock's price.

But even with all of this competition, there are always those that fare better than the crowd. These superstars seem to be a bit more flexible in their techniques, and rarely limit themselves solely to company-specific fundamental information.

The second type of information is known as *technical data*. Technical analysts concern themselves solely with past price and volume information to discern the future direction of stocks.

A pure technician believes that all available information about a stock is reflected in the current price, so that all one needs to do is study past price data to get an accurate picture of the stock's supply and demand.

The main tool of the technician is the price chart, which many believe can hold important clues about the future direction of a security. As Figure 6.2 shows, technicians use a variety of methods to determine which stocks have the best chance of beating the market.

Although many forms of technical analysis are based on nothing but anecdotal evidence and have been shown to have no value in predicting the future direction of stocks, there are a number of tech-

FIGURE 6.2 The S&P 500 index, July 1998 to June 2000. Technical analysts use a variety of methods, including moving averages to determine the market's direction and trendlines to find areas of support (levels the market is not likely to drop below) or resistance (levels that the market might have a hard time penetrating to the upside).

Source: Chart created using TradeStation 4.0 by Omega Research, Inc.

nical approaches that are often mentioned in worldlyinvestor.com's "Market View" column. One of the most common is support areas.

Support areas are often caused by the "round number" effect. This is the tendency for markets to trade near psychologically important levels. Occasionally, such levels are quite obvious, like 10,000 in the case of the Dow Jones Industrial Average. But in many instances the number may be less round.

During April and May 2000, for example, the market seemed fixated by the 1,375 level in the S&P 500 index. The S&P 500 index bounced off this level six times. In the May 26, 2000, "Market View" column, I made the following comments:

If we are indeed at a short-term bottom—an opinion we have reiterated several times this week—there will probably be only a select few traders brave enough to establish long positions near this level. Why? Market psychology. After Thursday's attempt at a rally failed miserably, investor sentiment sank to the basement. It was as if your football team came within a field goal of winning a crucial game, only to fumble the ball on the opponent's five-yard line. The gloom and doom among traders must have reached new highs on yesterday's close.

A cursory glance at a daily chart of the S&P 500 index shows a different story.

[Figure 6.3] shows the optical illusion that all traders with perfect hindsight can attest to—the seemingly unpenetrable support line. If the market does indeed manage to rally out of its slump, in a month's time a plethora of talking heads on CNBC will point to this support, declare victory, and move on to the next caller.

Oh, if it was only that easy!

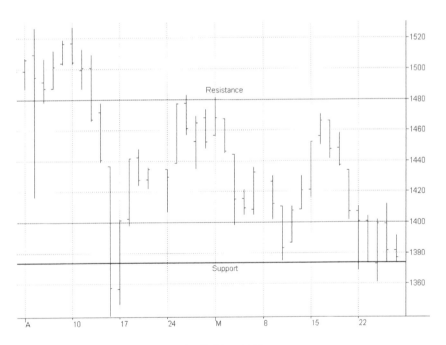

FIGURE 6.3   The S&P 500 index, April–May 2000.

Source: Chart created using TradeStation 4.0 by Omega Research, Inc.

The next trading session–May 30th–witnessed a huge rally in stocks. Five days later, the S&P 500 index was sitting 7 percent higher. The Nasdaq had its best week in history, gaining 19 percent!

Like many technical tools, support and resistance lines must be used in concert with other methods. In this instance, there were a number of other factors that led me to believe that the 1,375 level would hold yet again. First, we were approaching Memorial Day, and markets have a tendency to rally around three-day holidays. We were also trading close to the end of May, and end-of-month (EOM) periods also have a tendency to be bullish.

A NEW APPROACH

By now, it should be obvious that neither a purely technical nor a purely fundamental approach is the best way to detect market opportunities. Rather, a combination of the two styles offers the most flexibility in determining when prices have been incorrectly pushed too low or too high.

One way that the Quant View Portfolio combines technical and fundamental data is through the use of *event studies*. These studies try to discern tradable patterns that emerge from the release of information (i.e., fundamental information), and then use price action (i.e., technical information) to give us an indication of the next probable move in the market. There are three steps in constructing an event study.

The first step is to decide what type of market-moving information should be evaluated. The Quant View Portfolio has concentrated its efforts on government reports, but as we shall see, event studies can also determine if company-specific news such as earnings announcements or the addition of the company to an important market index (like the S&P 500) can create profitable trading opportunities.

Next, the data that we need to do our study must be collected. We will need all of the release dates for important economic reports for at least the past five years. Although this was once an arduous task, the Internet makes this part of the process a breeze. Most government release dates can be downloaded for free at the Labor Department web site (stats.bls.gov/blshome.htm).

Finally, the release dates must be used in concert with daily price data. Market data can be obtained from many sites on the World Wide Web, including Telescan (www.telescan.com), which charges $29.95 per month for their data downloading services. This pricing information can then be integrated into a third-party analytical software program. My favorite is TradeStation by Omega Research, Inc. (www.omegaresearch.com). TradeStation is not cheap—a site license runs about $2,400 annually—but the program offers a lot of flexibility and can be custom-tailored to suit any trader's needs.

Alternatively, those traders interested in event-based trading could simply follow the strategies in the Quant View Portfolio, which can be found on the worldlyinvestor.com web site.

Regardless of software vendor or data source, event studies all work the same way. As shown in Figure 6.4, the technique focuses on the market's reaction immediately following the release of fundamental data.

Day 0 is the "event day"—the day of the release of data. By using event studies, we can determine if the market systematically underreacts or overreacts to the release of certain kinds of key information. If this is the case, we can design a profitable trading strategy around this tendency.

In the specific release illustrated in Figure 6.3, the market shows some evidence of underreaction. Why? *Even though the S&P 500 index rose on day 0 due to the release of bullish data, the market continues going higher for three more days.* If the stock market were perfectly efficient—in other words, if prices instantaneously reflected all information—the price graph would resemble Figure 6.5.

Besides a tendency for underreaction and no reaction, there is a third possibility—market overreaction. In this instance, market partic-

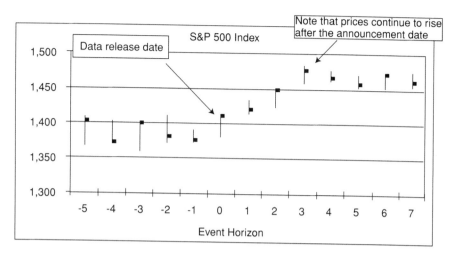

FIGURE 6.4 The S&P 500 index before and after a major economic release. Day 0 denotes the "event day"—the day of the release. The price bars show the high, low, and close (denoted by the hash mark to the right of the vertical bar). Since stocks continued to rise in the days following the announcement, the market exhibited an underreaction tendency.

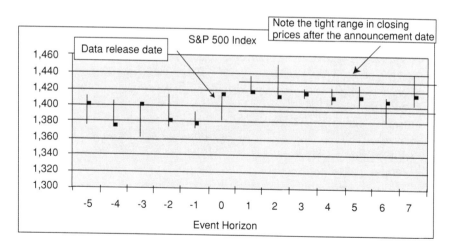

FIGURE 6.5. Note that although the S&P 500 index rose on day 0 in response to bullish news, the following sessions seemed to fluctuate only randomly. In this instance, the market seemed to nearly instantaneously assimilate the news (i.e., the market exhibited efficient behavior).

ipants initially overweight the importance of a particular news release and drive prices either too high or too low. Subsequent trading
sessions then witness a *reversion to the mean*, where stocks return to the
previous levels of before the announcement occurred. An example
of a market overreaction can be seen in Figure 6.6.

Of course, if we observe market over- and underreactions only occasionally, it is unlikely that such a tendency could be exploited for
profit. To create a profitable trading strategy, the market's tendency
to overshoot or partially ignore information must be persistent.
There are a number of statistical techniques that one can use to determine this, but the level of technical sophistication required is beyond the scope of this book. For more information, please consult
the worldlyinvestor.com web site.

After performing hundreds of event studies over the years, I have
noticed a recurring pattern in the behavior of the stock market.
Macroeconomic events (major government releases) are often met with trader

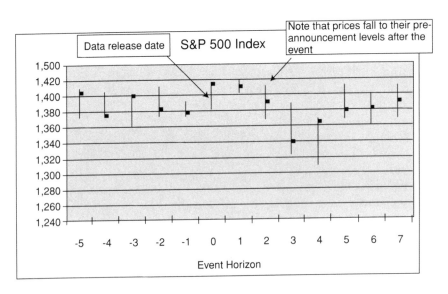

FIGURE 6.6 In an example of a market overreaction, the S&P 500 index rallies
on the day of a bullish economic report, only to fall back to (and in this case,
below) its preannouncement level.

overreaction. However, company-specific events are generally met with trader underreaction. We will examine each instance in detail, and create a trading strategy to exploit these tendencies.

TRADING AROUND MACROECONOMIC EVENTS

Economic reports are often blamed for causing excessive volatility in the markets. Indeed, as this crucial data filters into the capital markets it is common to see large price swings as the new information is assimilated by traders and other market participants. In fact, a study performed by the Federal Reserve Board found that the 25 largest price moves in the government bond market were due to the release of macroeconomic reports. The two reports most associated with large moves in the stock market are the monthly employment report and the producer price index report. Considering the importance placed on these releases by the press, economists, and other groups, it is no surprise that these events are frequently met with trader overreaction.

Macroeconomic Events of Importance

The following economic releases are known to be associated with investor overreaction:

Monthly employment. Released on the first Friday of each month, this report details changes in unemployment rates.

Producer Price Index. Usually released at midmonth, PPI measures changes in raw materials prices. PPI is a widely used inflation gauge.

Federal Reserve interest rate changes. The Fed is responsible for keeping the economy growing at a reasonable rate. It accomplishes this mission by increasing interest rates to prevent the economy from expanding too fast, or reducing short-term rates in order to stimulate demand and economic growth.

EVENT-DRIVEN QUANT VIEW STRATEGIES

The following trading strategies are currently utilized in worldly investor.com's Quant View Portfolio. Since these trades are based on movements in the broad stock market and are not stock-specific, they can be utilized using an S&P 500 index fund, an exchange-traded fund, or a broadly diversified closed-end fund. Since the characteristics of these trades change over time, it is important to refer to the worldlyinvestor.com web site as frequently as possible.

Employment Release Long Trade

This strategy initiates a long position in the S&P 500 on the day of the employment release if the index closes lower *and in the bottom 20 percent of the day's range.* This range can be calculated as follows:

$$\text{Range} = \frac{(\text{Close} - \text{Low})}{(\text{High} - \text{Low})}$$

The trade is exited on the close after it has been held for three days.

Employment Release Short Trade

This strategy initiates a short position in the S&P 500 if the market closes higher on the day of the employment release *and in the upper 20 percent of the day's range.* This range can be calculated as follows:

$$\text{Range} = \frac{(\text{High} - \text{Close})}{(\text{High} - \text{Low})}$$

PPI Release Long Trade

This strategy initiates a long position in the S&P 500 on the day of the Producer Price Index release if the index closes lower *and in the bottom 20 percent of the day's range.* This range can be calculated as follows:

$$\text{Range} = \frac{(\text{Close} - \text{Low})}{(\text{High} - \text{Low})}$$

The trade is exited on the close after it has been held for three days. The historical returns of the strategies are shown in Figure 6.7.

TRADING AROUND COMPANY-SPECIFIC NEWS

As opposed to macroeconomic releases, which are generally associated with trader overreaction, company-specific news is more commonly associated with investor underreaction. The two types of news that follow this tendency are stock split announcements and the S&P 500 effect.

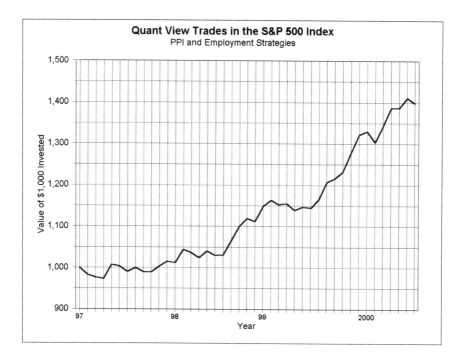

FIGURE 6.7 The employment and Producer Price Index strategies used in the Quant View Portfolio have produced handsome returns with minimal risk.

Stock Splits

Generally, stocks split because companies want to lower their stock prices. For example, if a stock has traded at $20 per share and is split 2-for-1, existing investors will own twice the number of shares at one-half the price ($10 per share) after the split takes effect.

History has shown that stock split announcements are followed by rallies. Why? Even though the company is worth exactly the same presplit as postsplit, investors still seem to be attracted by the idea that they now own twice as many shares as they did before.

But many analysts believe that splits are a signal to the capital markets. Splits are often seen as a sign of positive price momentum, probably because stocks that split tend to have experienced price appreciation prior to the announcement. Studies have shown that stocks that split tend to outperform the overall market for about a year after the fact.

Further, there is some behavioral logic to the stock split process. Many companies decide to split because their share price has become too high for many investors. Since most traders prefer to trade in 100-share increments, for example, it is considered by some better to buy 100 shares of a $50 stock than 50 shares of a $100 stock. Some research has shown that share marketability is enhanced when the price is lowered.

According to recent studies, in the three-day period following a split announcement stocks deliver an excess return of about 4 percent. Postsplit trading, however, is usually associated with falling share prices on the short-term.

If you want to exploit stock splits for the short term—owning them when they are most likely to deliver a return in excess of the underlying market—you would buy them immediately prior to the split announcement, with an exit of approximately three days.

This three-day holding period is so unusually profitable for these issues that it accounts for a big chunk of the one-year excess return period mentioned earlier.

As Figure 6.8 shows, the first trading day following the split announcement witnessed a $5 rally in the stock's price. This rather immediate reaction (up arrow) is the reason why so many sites now try to predict which stocks will split, rather than simply report split announcements.

Right on target, Hispanic Broadcasting's run-up peaked on the third day (down arrow).

Since most of the short-term gain in stock splits occurs immediately following the announcement, the best way to profit from the tendency is to find a way to predict which stocks will split. In the past few years a number of web sites have been created for just that purpose.

There are several web sites that specialize in predicting stock

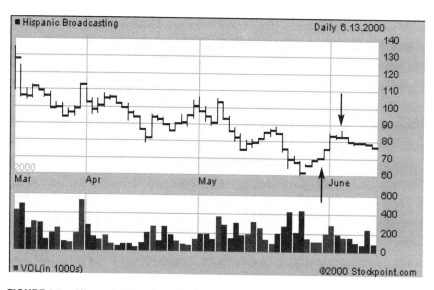

FIGURE 6.8 Hispanic Broadcasting's 2:1 stock split announcement in June 2000 caused the stock to appreciate significantly in the short term.
Copyright © Stockpoint, Inc.

splits. I prefer www.splittrader.com, which is a free site. Other sites to consider:

splitmaster.com

123stock.net/splitwatch/splitdebate.htm

www.splitpredict.com

Some of these sites may charge a subscription fee.

Incidentally, companies with low-priced stocks can announce a "reverse split." In a 1-for-2 reverse, for example, an investor holding 100 shares of a $20 stock would eventually have 50 shares of a $40 stock.

Reverse splits are usually associated with stocks whose price is less than $5 per share. Stock drops usually accompany these announcements. In the three-day period following such an announcement, the average stock loses about 7 percent of its value.

The S&P Effect

It is quite common for stocks that are added to the S&P 500 to appreciate dramatically between the announcement and their actual inclusion in the index. According to Standard & Poor's, the S&P effect has historically generated a monstrous 3 percent to 6 percent rise in a stock's price in the few days following the announcement of its addition to the index.

The reason for the increase: Index funds and other investors seeking to mirror the S&P 500's performance must purchase these new entrants.

Sometimes the effect can have market-wide implications. On December 7, 1999, Yahoo! (YHOO) gained over $67 per share, or 24 percent, when it was added to the S&P 500 index. Since Yahoo! replaced a smaller company, other positions in the index had to be sold to buy the stock. As a result, both the S&P 500 index and the

Dow posted losses on the session, while the Nasdaq (which contains Yahoo!) enjoyed big gains.

Like stock splits, the best way to profit from the S&P effect is to buy stocks before they are actually included in the index. How? By searching for firms that meet its guidelines for market capitalization (members currently have a market cap over $300 million), liquidity, and industry group classification (companies from the utilities, financial, transportation, and industrial sectors are included), one might get a leg up on potential candidates.

Plus, traders need to keep an eye out on potential and current mergers. These account for the bulk of index additions and deletions.

WorldlyInvestor Quick Summary

1. All trading strategies rely on being able to accurately interpret data in such a way as to be able to take advantage of other market participants mispricing securities.

2. Two types of data used by investors:
   - Fundamental data—company-specific information such as market share, profit margin, earnings expectations—the type of information used and generated by Wall Street analysts.
   - Technical data—historical price and volume information. Users often rely heavily on price charts to determine future direction of markets. Much is based on anecdotal evidence; however, there is some academic support for certain technical indicators.

3. New approach combines both fundamental and technical analysis.
   - Event studies:
   Determine the market-moving event to be studied—the monthly employment report, for example.
   Collect the historical dates of past occurrence of the event in question.
   Test price data around the event dates to determine if any predictable price movement occurs either before or after the event.
   Macro events such as government reports tend to be met with trader overreaction. Company-specific events tend to be met with trader underreaction.

4. Quant View strategies:
   - Macro events:
   Employment release long trade.
   Employment release short trade.
   Producer Price Index release long trade.
   - Company-specific events:
   Stock Splits
   The S&P 500 effect.

7

Exploiting Calendar Effects with Exchange-Traded Funds

In all of its forms, the modern calendar is one of the most useful devices created in the history of civilization. People consult their calendars on when to plant crops, when anniversaries or holidays fall, and when to harvest. The earliest calendars were crude devices that were strongly influenced by the geographical location of the people who made them. In the Scandinavian countries, for example, where the seasons are pronounced, the concept of a year was determined by the end of winter. But in warmer climates, the moon became the basic unit for the measurement of time. According to Jewish tradition, "the moon was created for the counting of days."

The Importance of the Calendar

The *Farmer's Almanac* is the oldest continuously published periodical in the United States. Under the guiding hand of its first editor, Robert B. Thomas, the first issue of the almanac was published in 1792, during George Washington's second term as president.

Source: www.almanac.com.

Many believe that a full moon affects people's moods. Hospital workers occasionally report that more accidents and personal assaults occur during full moons than at other times. The effect is commonly blamed on the gravitational pull of the moon on our bodies. But in fact, the moon's gravity on humans is quite negligible due to its distance from Earth (about 400,000 miles). Its slight gravitational pull is nearly completely overwhelmed by the gravitational attraction of nearby objects (buildings, bodies of water, etc.). No one has yet proven the existence of "moon madness."

Although the effect on the moon's phases on humans is open to interpretation, a more predictable relationship seems to exist between the calendar and the stock market. The tendencies of stocks to be affected by seasonal forces are known as *calendar anomalies*. While the existence of these anomalies is generally accepted, it is less clear whether investors can actually use them to earn excess returns. Investors evaluating anomalies should keep in mind that although they may have existed historically, there is no guarantee they will persist in the future. And if they do persist, transaction costs and tax effects may eliminate their efficacy.

Due to the spurious nature of these trades, we will focus on the three most consistent winners: the January effect trade, the end-of-month (EOM) trade, and the holiday trade. And to minimize the tax effects of these trades, it is suggested that these strategies be executed in individual retirement accounts (IRAs) and other sheltered accounts.

THE JANUARY EFFECT: TWO TRADES IN ONE

The January effect is the best-known market anomaly of all time. The effect is based on the tendency of small-cap stock investors to sell losing positions at year-end to take advantage of realizing their capital losses. The prices of these issues become depressed due to this selling pressure. Once the year-end selling subsides, those investors tend to put their cash back to work in the small-cap arena, causing these stocks to outperform large-cap issues.

How well known has the January effect become? At last count, over one hundred academic articles have been written on the subject. It has also spawned a book, *The Incredible January Effect*, written by Robert Haugen and Josef Lakonishok (Dow Jones Irwin, 1988). And a number of mutual funds have actually changed their accounting year so they could take optimal advantage of January's stock rally.

The United States is not the only country where the January effect has been observed. In fact, in the largest foreign stock markets in the world—including those in Japan, Germany, and Great Britain—small stocks show a tendency to rise more in January than in any other month of the year.

In fact, so many traders have sought to exploit the January effect that the strategy has changed significantly throughout the years. It has also been affected by recent changes in U.S. tax law, which has been shown to accentuate the effect. It has now morphed into two distinct opportunities—one at the end of the year, and the other at the beginning of December.

The January Value Stock Strategy (VSS)

This version of the strategy takes into consideration the recent popularity of the January effect. As a plethora of savvy market participants have discovered the anomaly, which typically involves buying small stocks around Christmas and selling them at the end of January, the optimum holding period has changed. Indeed, as Figure 7.1 shows, from 1995 through 1999 small stocks have actually underperformed large stocks during this time frame.

Therefore, our VSS strategy includes two criteria: an early holding period and a focus on value stocks.

Start Early

The past five years have failed to produce any January effect profits. But if the holding period is shifted from mid-December to mid-January, small stocks take the crown, beating out large stocks handily.

And if the trade is shifted back even farther, from the beginning of December to the first few days of the New Year, recent results are even more impressive. For this time period, the Russell 2000 index of small company stocks has outperformed the S&P 500 index for the past four consecutive years.

Why has the January effect started earlier and earlier? As more traders have implemented the strategy, they try to beat their competitors to the punch by entering and exiting the trade before everyone else. Thus, it is a good idea to look for appropriate purchases early in December, rather than waiting until the end of the month.

Focus on Value Stocks

Although market capitalization has been the historic catalyst for the January effect, recent academic research has shown that value stocks tend to rise more in the month than do growth stocks. As a result, it is more appropriate to look to small stocks with low price-to-earnings ratios, rather than high-flying Internet issues with no earnings.

Implementing the VSS

Worldlyinvestor.com begins its coverage of both January effect trades in the middle part of the fourth quarter. Our stock selections are typically held from the last day in November until the end of December.

The End-of-Year (EOY) January Effect

The EOY is the classic form of the January effect. This strategy attempts to directly exploit the tendency of small-cap stocks to outperform large-cap stocks during the first month of the year. But as noted earlier, this tendency is quite different now than its historic profile would suggest.

To see how small stocks have done relative to large-cap issues in

January, we subtracted the returns of the S&P 500 (an index of the 500 largest companies in the United States) from the Value Line Index (an index of about 1,700 stocks). As Figure 7.1 shows, what was once a slam-dunk way to start the year has now become a moving target.

Before 1994, 12 of 16 years generated profits in January. But large-cap stocks have outpaced their small-cap rivals every year since.

Obviously, the rules of this game have changed. There are three things to consider when implementing a January effect strategy:

1. *Small cap* does not always mean *high tech.*

2. Focus on what's wounded.

3. Remember to diversify.

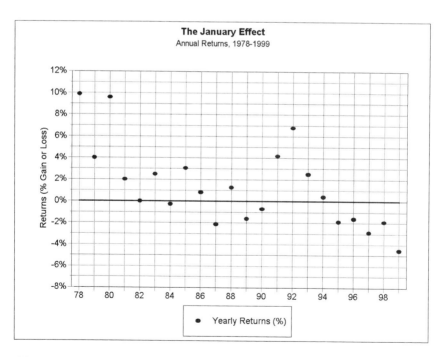

FIGURE 7.1   The returns of small stocks notably lagged those of large stocks during the month of January from 1995 to 1999.

Small Cap Does Not Always Mean *High Tech*

One might think that investors have a clear idea of what constitutes a small-cap stock. But the definition seems to vary by user. For instance, many "small stock" mutual funds boast holdings in companies with market capitalizations of up to $25 billion! There is no law to stop them. But one thing is certain: Using the Nasdaq index as a proxy for small stocks simply doesn't make sense anymore.

Consider Yahoo! (YHOO: Nasdaq). Not so long ago–1998, to be exact–many considered Yahoo! a small-company stock. But in 1999, the company was added to the Standard & Poor's 500–the index of the 500 largest companies in the United States. It now boasts a market capitalization of over $100 billion.

The Nasdaq also includes such behemoths as Intel (INTC), Cisco (CSCO) and Microsoft (MSFT), which collectively make up one-quarter of the index. The bulk of 1999's stupendous returns were due to the rise in these issues.

A more precise definition is that small-cap stocks are those companies that make up the bottom 20 percent of issues in terms of market capitalization (i.e., the number of shares outstanding times the price per share). If this rule is used, stocks with market caps up to about $1 billion can be included. This definition does not exclude any exchange–even a stock listed on the NYSE can be purchased as part of the January effect strategy, as long as its market cap is sufficiently small.

Focus on What's Wounded

Just a few years ago, focusing exclusively on stocks that make up the bottom 20 percent of market capitalization was all that was required to cash in on the January EOY effect. But now, the trade is a bit more selective. In order to maximize the effectiveness of the trade, the focus must be on those issues that have suffered the most tax-loss selling during the month of December.

Considering the number of stocks that trade, there are always an ample number that fail to rise in December—even during a raging bull market. For example, even though the Nasdaq soared over 80 percent in 1999, about one-half of all over-the-counter issues lost money during the last month of the year.

To aid in finding proper candidates, we ran a simple screen for issues in the low 20 percent of market capitalization that experienced decreasing stock prices in December 1999. To further separate the wheat from the chaff, we tagged those stocks whose *Zacks rating*—a proprietary measure of positive changes in earnings estimates calculated by Zacks Investment Research—is in the top 25 percent. Our choices are shown as Figure 7.2.

GC Companies (GCX: NYSE) operates motion picture theaters in the United States under the name General Cinema.

National RV Holdings (NVH: NYSE) designs, manufactures, and markets motor homes and travel trailers.

Travel Services International (TRVL: Nasdaq) is a distributor of cruise vacations, domestic and international airline tickets, and European auto rentals and a provider of electronic hotel reservation service, to both travel agents and travelers.

January Effect Portfolio, Selected on December 28, 1999

Company	Ticker Symbol	P/E Ratio	Market Capitalization	Earnings per Share
GC Companies	GCX	N/A	$200 million	$(5.39)
National RV Holdings	NVH	6.3	$182 million	$2.11
Travel Services	TRVL	16.9	$136 million	$0.99
New Horizons Worldwide	NEWH	13.6	$114 million	$0.61

FIGURE 7.2 The January EOY stock portfolio, as chosen in wordlyinvestor.com "Market View" column on December 28, 1999.

New Horizons Worldwide (NEWH: Nasdaq) owns and franchises computer training centers, offering a variety of training choices including instructor-led classes and Web-based learning.

As it turned out, our portfolio trounced all of the market averages with an astonishing 22.9 percent gain for the month of January 2000 (Figure 7.3).

January 2000 was not a case of a raging bull market causing all stocks to rise. In fact, the stock market was generally lower for the month. With that being the case, what is the source of our EOY portfolio returns?

As Figure 7.4 shows, nearly all stocks–from large cap to small cap, and from value stocks to growth stocks–lost a fair amount of money during January. The only characteristic that made our EOY portfolio different from the rest of the market was the requirement that our stocks lost significant ground in the prior month. Without that one factor, we would have posted results as paltry as the overall market's.

Remember to Diversify

It should be noted that although the 1999 EOY portfolio handily beat the market, one stock in the group–National RV Holdings–lost

Company	Ticker Symbol	12/28/99 Closing Share Price	01/31/00 Closing Share Price	Percent Gain/Loss
GC Companies	GCX	$25.500	$28.625	12.25%
National RV Holdings	NVH	$17.375	$16.375	−5.76%
Travel Services	TRVL	$ 9.750	$15.688	60.90%
New Horizons Worldwide	NEWH	$11.875	$14.750	24.21%
Portfolio Return				22.90%

FIGURE 7.3 January EOY Portfolio Results.

Index	Return
S&P 500 Index	−4.97%
S&P 500 Growth Index	−6.54%
S&P 500 Value Index	−3.20%
S&P Small Cap Index	−3.09%
S&P/BARRA Small Cap Growth	−1.38%
S&P/BARRA Small Cap Value	−5.09%
Dow Jones Industrials	−4.90%
Nasdaq Composite	−3.17%
worldlyinvestor.com EOY Portfolio	22.90%

FIGURE 7.4   Performance Comparison, January 2000.

money. If all of our EOY stocks had been in the transportation industry, the strategy would have yielded similar results. Thus, it is crucial to consider diversification as a critical input in the selection of EOY candidates.

Diversification is always important to investors—even for strategies with relatively short holding periods. On that note, the portfolio will always consist of at least four stocks. And these issues will always be chosen from dissimilar industries to prevent overreliance on a particular segment of the market.

The addition of the tax-selling criterion actually adds to the diversification of the EOY portfolio. In some years, the stocks will consist of issues that have risen significantly throughout the year, only to experience rough waters in December. Other stocks might have lost value steadily all year long.

So besides adding value as an effective screening criterion, the tax-selling filter also adds diversification.

January 2000 showed that the EOY can beat the market when stocks are weak. But what about when stocks post gains for the month? Only time will tell. Please consult the worldlyinvestor.com web site for updates on the current year's EOY portfolio.

THE END-OF-MONTH (EOM) TRADE

The EOM stock trade is a well-documented strategy that has produced attractive long-term profits. Specifically, the trade involves initiating a long position taken on the close two business days before month's end and held until the third day of the next month.

I first became cognizant of the EOM in 1992 while reading the 1976 investment classic *Stock Market Logic* by Norm Fosback. The book details a number of quantitative investment strategies, including the EOM. According to Fosback:

> To document the month-end concept, we have analyzed every trading day starting with the end of December 1927. Let us hypothesize two investors. The first, the Seasonal Investor, buys stocks (as represented by the Standard & Poor's 500 index) at the beginning of each month-end period, sells out at the end of the period, and holds cash until the next month-end period. The second investor, the Non-Seasonal Investor, does precisely the opposite—he holds cash during the month-end period and is long stocks during the rest of the period. Assuming no particular significance to the month-end phenomenon, the Non-Seasonal Investor actually has a tremendous advantage—for over the very long term stock prices generally advance and he is invested in stocks at least three-fourths of the time, while the Seasonal Investor is invested only one-fourth of the time.

Astonishingly, between 1927 and 1975 Fosback showed the Seasonal Investor's account grew from $10,000 to $572,020—while the Non-Seasonal Investor's shrank from $10,000 to a minuscule $899!

Although the study did not include commissions, the results are telling. There must be something special about stocks at the end of each month.

Of course, the EOM strategy would be much less attractive if, for some reason, the end-of-month period was considerably more risky than the rest of the month. This would also go far in answering the question of why such a trading opportunity exists. Everyone knows that risky strategies can be more profitable than less risky ones. That is why Internet stocks tend to rise more than utility stocks.

By using a measure of market volatility called the *standard deviation*, one can easily compare the risk incurred during the EOM period and other similar holding periods in the market. In this case, the standard deviation of a randomly selected four-day holding in the S&P 500 index is about 4 index points. This implies that the index will return between −10.3 points and +13.7 points for a non-EOM, randomly selected four-day holding period.

And what about the EOM holding period? It turns out that the standard deviation during our trade is actually a bit *lower* than during other periods (the EOM's standard deviation is around 3.5 index points). So, even though the EOM gives larger than normal profits, the volatility that investors have to stomach during the trade is actually a bit *less* than during other four-day holding periods, which typically yield much smaller profits. Thus, the risk-based explanation for the trade has little merit.

The tendency for stocks to rise at the end of the month has perplexed both individual investors and professional money managers. But confusion over why the trade has persisted should not hamper traders from taking advantage of this well-known market predilection. Unfortunately, neither Fosback nor Martin Zweig, another proponent of the method, can explain the existence of the EOM. Both recommend minimizing transaction costs when executing the strategy, since commissions can potentially eat up a large chunk of potential gains.

I first started capitalizing on the EOM trade using Value Line futures at the Kansas City Board of Trade. Due to the liquidity constraints of that market, I was forced to switch to S&P 500 index futures in Chicago in 1995. But in short order I found that the strategy was so well known among traders that it had become quite difficult to exploit in the ultra-efficient futures market. However, the trade still works well with mutual funds and individual stocks.

Since that time, I have witnessed significant changes in the strategy through the years. For example, recent studies have shown that the EOM effect is much more pronounced in large-cap stocks. The optimum holding period has also shifted slightly.

One of the most significant changes in the strategy's efficacy concerns EOM profits and the market's direction. Our analysis shows that when the S&P 500 index is in a downtrend at month's end, the EOM is a terrific way to catch a short-term move to the upside. However, when markets are trending higher going into the EOM holding period the trade is much less profitable. Therefore, the Quant View Portfolio introduced the filter that the S&P 500 index must be trading below its 10-day moving average in order to signal a trade (Figure 7.5).

Like all of our strategies, any changes to the EOM will be tracked on the worldlyinvestor.com web site.

Between 1988 and mid-2000, there were 26 occasions when stocks have faced month-end in a downtrend. The average gain in the S&P 500 index during the trade has been about seven points. Considering that the average four-day gain in the index is about two points, the odds that these results were due to chance is about one in 100. As Figure 7.6 shows, chance favors the bold.

Trading the EOM with Individual Stocks

As opposed to utilizing indexed mutual funds to play the EOM trade, many "Market View" readers prefer to exploit the strategy using a small number of stocks. To review, the EOM exists because the stock market has the tendency to rally at month's end if current market conditions early in the month are weak. From statistically analyzing daily stock market returns for the past two decades, we know that this market inclination tends to last about four days. In essence, the

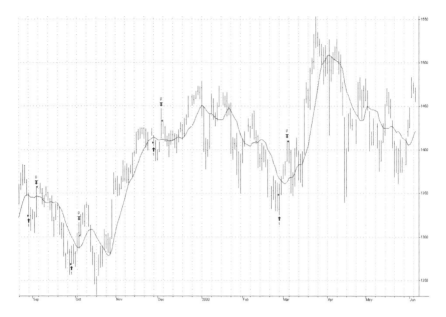

FIGURE 7.5 The S&P 500 index, September 1999 to June 2000. In order to trigger an EOM buy signal, the market must be trading below its 10-day moving average at month's end. The up arrows show entry points, while the down arrows show exit points.
Source: Chart created using TradeStation 4.0 by Omega Research, Inc.

EOM is a swing-trading method of identifying a short-term market low late in the month and a short-term market high at the beginning of the next month.

A trader interested in trading individual stocks around month's end would focus on those issues that underperformed the overall market earlier in the month. The stock should also boast large market capitalization, since the EOM trade works best for the S&P 500 index. And finally, we recommend those issues that have a Zacks rank–a proprietary measure of positive changes in earnings estimates–in the top 25 percent.

Our screen resulted in four stocks (Figure 7.7). An equally

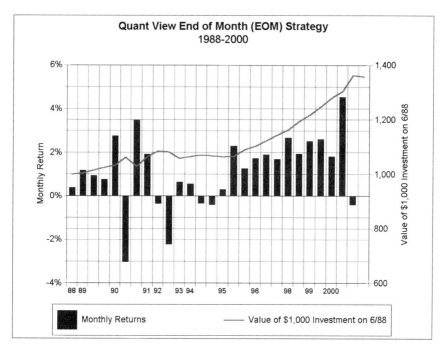

FIGURE 7.6 The end-of-month (EOM) strategy produced impressed profits from 1988 to 2000. Even though the strategy was in the market for only about 100 days during the 12-year period, a $1,000 investment at the beginning of the period would be worth nearly $1,400 in May 2000.

Company	Ticker Symbol	2/28/2000 Share Price	3/3/2000 Share Price	Percent Gain/Loss
Cox Communications	COX	$44.875	$45.44	1.3%
Wal-Mart Stores	WMT	$47.875	$52.63	9.9%
Emerson Electric	EMR	$48.438	$43.63	−9.9%
Bell South	BLS	$36.313	$46.00	26.7%
Average				7.0%
S&P 500 index	SPY	1,348.05	1,408.87	4.5%

FIGURE 7.7 February 2000 EOM Stock Portfolio.

weighted portfolio consisting of our four selections not only profited during the February 2000 EOM time frame, but actually beat the return of the S&P 500 index. This should not come as a surprise. Since our small portfolio is probably much less diversified than an investment in the S&P 500 index, it should produce more profit.

Worldlyinvestor.com regularly posts its current month EOM portfolio for its readers.

THE HOLIDAY TRADE

The stock market has long been known to rise around holidays. One of the first studies into this phenomenon was done in 1934, when it was found that the Dow Jones Industrial Average (DJIA) rose significantly on the trading days prior to Thanksgiving and Christmas. Fifty years later, another study found that an equally weighted index of stocks returned an average of 0.59 percent the day before holidays, compared to 0.056 percent for other days, a ratio greater than 9 to 1. And according to the book *The Winner's Curse* by economist and money manager Richard H. Thaler, *51 percent of the capital gains realized by the DJIA in the past 90 years have occurred on approximately 10 "preholidays" per year*–one of the most amazing market statistics I have ever seen.

My research in the past 10 years has shown the so-called holiday effect to be alive and well–especially during Thanksgiving and Christmas. In both cases, a long position initiated on the close two days before the blessed event, and held for three trading days, yields an average trade increase of nearly five index points in the S&P 500–compared to about one index point for other three-day holding periods.

Why does such an anomalous trade exist? There have been many explanations offered as to why a hole this size in the efficient market hypothesis exists, but I think the reason is twofold. In the case of Thanksgiving, holding the trade during three market days requires one to hold the trade for six calendar days, Wednesday through Mon-

FIGURE 7.8 The holiday trading strategy has produced healthy profits for over 90 years.

day, because the markets do not trade on Thanksgiving day (or the following weekend). In effect, you may be receiving six days' worth of return in only three days–an efficient way to invest (Figure 7.8).

Many market pros, of course, decry any supposed hole in efficient markets as either a statistical anomaly or just pure nonsense. But with over 90 years of impressive returns, I'm usually a buyer just before the turkey is served.

WorldlyInvestor Quick Summary

1. The January effect:
   - Works best with small-cap stocks (i.e., market capitalization less than $1 billion).
   - Value stocks (i.e., those with low price-to-earnings ratios) are more suitable than growth stocks.
   - Stocks must lose ground prior to entry.
   - Enter long position in early December before the crowd, and exit in the first few days of the new year.

   Part I of the January effect takes place in December; Part II is exploited in January.

2. The end-of-month trade:
   - Best implemented using mutual funds or large-cap stocks.
   - The S&P 500 must be under its 10-day moving average.
   - Enter a long position on the close two trading days before the end of the month, and exit on the third trading day of the new month.

3. The holiday effect:
   - Use an S&P 500 index fund or exchange-traded fund.
   - Buy on the close two days prior to either Thanksgiving or Christmas, and exit after three trading days.

8

The Strategy Your Mutual Fund Manager Doesn't Want You to Know About

Market timing is a privilege, not a right.
—Daniel Pollock,
Attorney for AIM Fund Services

In what was certainly one of the least exciting moments in the history of recorded music, the eight-track tape player was invented in the early 1960s. Its developer, William Lear, created the device to give drivers an alternative to simply listening to radio stations. In 1966, all Ford-model cars offered factory-installed in-dash eight-track tape players. Chrysler and General Motors joined in two years later.

When the major car manufacturers jumped on the eight-track bandwagon, major recording labels rushed to put their artists on the new format. Madonna's early albums and Michael Jackson's *Thriller* were among the more popular works available on 8-track tapes. Eight-track tapes were the preeminent portable audio format of the 1970s and the early 1980s.

Eight-Track Tapes: Still Breathing, but on Life Support

Check out www.8trackheaven.com for info on collecting eight-track tapes.

Although the format had a strong initial start, several major limitations pointed toward its demise. First of all, eight-track cartridges could not be moved forward or backward, forcing their users to listen to entire tracks in the order in which they were placed on the tape. The cheap components of eight-tracks also caused them to fray and break, which reduced their useful life spans. But most importantly, the audio performance of the tapes was vastly inferior to that of cassettes or record albums. As a result of these drawbacks, eight-tracks became merely a fad in the societal landscape.

It may come as a surprise, but the story of the eight-track tape has a lot in common with one of the most popular financial trends of the modern era–the "buy 'em and hold 'em" mentality of many long-term investors toward actively managed mutual funds. Although both fill a need, there are plenty of better mousetraps available.

POPULAR, BUT DISAPPOINTING

Of all the financial innovations of the past century, the advent of the modern mutual fund has been by far the most successful. The oldest

---

Passive and Active Investing

An index fund (also known as a passively managed fund) seeks to match the investment performance of a specific stock or bond benchmark index. Instead of actively trading securities in an effort to beat the market, an index fund manager simply holds all—or a representative sample—of the securities in the index. In contrast, an active fund manager buys and sells securities regularly in pursuit of maximum gain.

About 65 percent of the assets in mutual funds are actively managed.

---

mutual funds in existence today are more than 70 years old, having survived the Great Depression, World War II, and other turbulent economic and political events. At the end of 1999, mutual funds managed over $7 trillion in client assets. One in three Americans own shares in at least one fund.

Few industries have been as flamboyantly successful as the fund management business. The notion of a professional investment manager overseeing a large pool of money, which from its sheer size can achieve a level of diversification not attainable by individuals, has proven to be an almost irresistible product for long-term investors.

Intent on differentiating their funds from the competition's, marketing-savvy mutual fund companies offer many services deemed valuable by individual investors. Toll-free telephone access to account information, check-writing privileges, and dividend reinvestment are just a few of the many burdens that mutual fund organizations are willing to shoulder—just for the privilege of managing client assets.

But like an all-American college quarterback who fails to live up to expectations in the National Football League, the performance of mutual funds has been less than stellar compared to many broad market gauges. There are many factors responsible for the disappointing results of actively managed funds, but perhaps the most important is the huge amount of client assets that the typical mutual fund manager is responsible for investing. The average manager (who typically is responsible for overseeing a number of different funds) runs approximately $1.8 billion in capital—an increase of 65 percent since 1994. Although the increased size of mutual funds has done wonders for the profitability of the mutual fund industry, it has had the opposite effect on the investment performance of their client base. The reason is simple: The challenges to managing large sums of money can become so daunting that it can be nearly impossible to even match the return of the market, let alone exceed it. These challenges are represented by four distinct costs—*market impact, delay cost, opportunity cost,* and *commissions.*

Not an Inspirational Performance

According to Lipper, 91 percent of all actively managed large-cap mutual funds failed to match the return of the S&P 500 index from 1988 to 1998.

First of all, purchasing shares in large quantities is not as simple as buying cereal or beef jerky in bulk at a grocery warehouse. In fact, executing large orders for stocks is quite difficult, and can often drive the price of the stock up before the order is even filled. This type of cost is commonly referred to as *market impact.*

Market impact might occur if a well-known fund manager is buying a block of stock and copycat traders rush in to execute before the manager's entire order is filled, thus causing a short-term run-up in the stock's price. Or, in the case of a less liquid stock—for example, an Internet issue that trades on the Nasdaq—a broker may increase the bid-ask spread due to the principal risk the brokerage firm must take in order to fill the order.

Mutual fund pros sometimes divide large stocks orders into a number of smaller pieces if trading conditions are especially dicey. However, this method of trading is often accompanied by *delay costs,* which arise from the disadvantageous change in a security's price that can occur while waiting to execute an order. Viewed in isolation, delay costs can generally be reduced with more aggressive trading. However, such costs run counter to market impact; as one goes up,

Hedge Funds: The Stealth Fighters of the Markets

Hedge funds, which are private investment partnerships available only to wealthy individuals and institutional investors, often go to great lengths to hide their activity in the markets. A legend such as George Soros must be careful not to tip his hand. If other traders find out what he is doing, they might front-run his trades—which would make the price of the securities he is trying to buy increase before his order is filled.

the other goes down. Implicit in the decision to delay the implementation of a large order is whether the associated delay costs will be less than the potential market impact savings.

A situation might also arise when a mutual fund manager identifies a promising stock, but simply cannot buy it because the costs associated with its purchase are so high that it is not economically feasible to do so. This is referred to as *opportunity cost*. In many of these occasions, the stock is simply too illiquid. This is the case with many small-cap technology issues. The more assets that managers are responsible for investing, the higher the probability that they will encounter this dilemma.

And like all investors, mutual funds must also pay *commissions* to their brokers. But due to the advent of Internet trading and basket trading (an electronic order method for large investors), commissions are typically a small part of the transaction cost puzzle.

As shown in Figure 8.1, the impact of trading costs on the performance of mutual funds can be quite significant. This is especially true when one considers that the average stock mutual fund underperforms the S&P 500 index by approximately 1.3 percent per year—which, noncoincidentally, is about what the typical stock fund manager incurs in transaction costs per annum.

The transaction costs problem only gets worse as mutual funds in-

Transaction Costs for Mutual Funds

	Delay Costs	Market Impact	Opportunity Costs	Commissions	Total
Large-Cap Stock Funds	0.64%	0.15%	0.21%	0.13%	1.12%
Small-Cap Stock Funds	1.38%	0.49%	0.31%	0.19%	2.36%

FIGURE 8.1 Transaction costs by fund type. The relatively low trading volume of small-capitalization stocks makes them more expensive to buy and sell. Hence, mutual funds that specialize in small-cap stocks will always incur higher costs than large-cap funds.

Source: Table adapted from Wagner and Glass, 1999.

Mutual Funds and Fees

Even though actively managed mutual funds have failed to keep up with unmanaged index funds, the fees they charge their clients continue to increase. The average annual expenses charged by stock funds have doubled in the past 40 years and increased 65 percent over the past 20 years (the average yearly fee stands at 1.58 percent).

Even the cheapest 10 percent of funds continue to get more costly—their fees have risen 27 percent since 1980.

Source: Wall Street Journal, May 16, 2000.

---

crease in size. This helps to explain why mutual funds with a relatively low amount of client assets under management often post higher returns than larger funds do.

Most private traders never have to face the dilemma of transaction costs, because their asset base is small enough to allow them to enter and exit the stock market without much difficulty. But for those investors who rely on mutual funds, fund investors would do well to monitor the size of the mutual funds that they are holding, keeping in mind that as funds increase in popularity they often decrease in efficacy.

Although some individual mutual funds may be poor long-term investments, many funds are excellent tools for short-term traders. Our Time Zone trading strategy allows for cost-free transactions, and offers individual investors access to a potentially profitable market anomaly that is not available to fund managers. *And even more tantalizing is that the mechanism behind the strategy is not the underlying market, but the daily pricing procedure of mutual fund companies.*

THE WORLDLYINVESTOR TIME ZONE TRADING STRATEGY

To understand the strategy, it is necessary to examine the daily pricing procedure of domestic mutual funds.

Mutual funds are required by Securities and Exchange Commission mandate to determine the prices of their shares each business day. A fund's net asset value (NAV) per share is the current value of all of the fund's assets (what it owns), minus liabilities (what it owes), divided by the total number of shares outstanding. A fund's share price, or offering price, is its NAV per share plus any applicable sales charges. The offering price of a fund without a sales charge would be the same as its NAV per share.

The NAV must reflect the current market value of the fund's securities, as long as market quotations for those securities are readily available. Other assets should be priced at fair value, as determined on a good-faith basis by the fund's board of directors.

As one might imagine, mutual fund pricing is a rather intensive process that must take place in a short time frame at the end of each business day. Fund accountants internally validate each price received from the exchanges by subjecting them to various control procedures. Depending on the nature and extent of its holdings, a fund may use more than one pricing service to ensure accuracy.

The pricing process typically begins when the U.S. stock exchanges close—4:00 P.M. EST—and continues until 5:50 P.M., when the prices must be received by wire services in order for them to be posted in major newspapers.

Funds typically value exchange-traded securities using the most recent closing prices from the exchanges on which the securities are traded, even if the exchange closes before the fund's daily pricing

---

How Does a Mutual Fund Calculate Its Net Asset Value?

$$NAV = \frac{\text{Market value of fund's securities} - \text{Fund liabilities}}{\text{Number of shares outstanding}}$$

Source: Investment Company Institute.

time (which occurs with many foreign securities). For example, funds that hold positions solely in European stocks are priced six to seven hours after European exchanges close for the day.

This sets up an interesting and potentially profitable situation for buyers of European mutual funds. Let's assume that European bourses close at 10:00 A.M. EST, six hours prior to the close of the New York Stock Exchange. Further, suppose that the U.S. market was rather flat until late in the afternoon, when a huge rally propelled the domestic indexes higher.

What is the likely effect on foreign stocks of a huge rally in the U.S. stock market? Considering that global stock markets have become increasingly more correlated with each other due to the continual advancements in communications, a big rally here has an excellent chance of continuing in the other markets of the world.

Meanwhile, a potential buyer can purchase a European stock mutual fund at the market price six hours ago—before the rally in the United States even began!

To test the strategy, we constructed a system with the following characteristics:

- The S&P 500 index must rally in the last few hours of trading, and close in the upper 20 percent of the day's range.
- If this occurs, we buy the shares in a domestically priced foreign mutual fund on the close of that day. The trade is exited on the close of the next day.

As shown in Figure 8.2, the results are impressive.

The strategy averaged a 16.7 percent gain per year, compared to an 11.6 percent gain using a buy-and-hold strategy in the EAFE (Europe/Australia/Far East index). But even though the timing strategy was more profitable, it was only about one-third as risky as the buy-and-hold strategy.

Further, the superior return of the timing strategy was achieved by being in the market only one out of four business days, which means

Fund Timing versus Buy-and-Hold, 1992–1999

	Fund Timing	Buy-and-Hold
Annual return	16.7%	11.6%
Risk*	5.4%	14.6%
% up months	86.2%	63.2%
Largest equity drop	−3.5%	−15.2%

*Risk is defined as the standard deviation of returns.

FIGURE 8.2   A mutual fund timing strategy that exploits the inefficiencies related to pricing mutual fund shares. The test was performed on international mutual funds. The buy-and-hold returns were based on the performance of the EAFE (Europe/Australia/Far East) index from 1992 to 1999.

that for the majority of the time, our money was resting safely in the fund family's money market account!

Further, it did not seem to matter which mutual fund we used in our test. Our average annual return across a dozen or so funds ranged between 14 percent and 18 percent (Figure 8.3).

IS FUND TIMING ETHICAL?

There is no question that fund timing strategies work, especially those that exploit time zone differences (other fund timing strategies vary in their efficacy). But the advent of this type of trading has raised an interesting question—is fund timing ethical?

Many people believe that fund timing profits at the expense of long-term fund investors. A recent article in *Money* magazine cited a number of ways that the strategy can create problems for other shareholders, including the following:

- *Increase transaction costs.* Fund timers often buy and sell fund shares at a fast pace, creating continuous inflows and outflows of

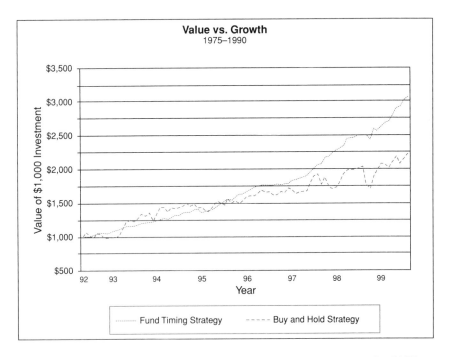

FIGURE 8.3 The WorldlyInvestor Time Zone trading strategy versus the EAFE. The occasional losses in the fund timing strategy are muted compared to those in a buy-and-hold methodology.

capital. Fund managers are forced to buy or sell securities as this money is shifted, causing higher trading costs. However, these costs are shared by all shareholders, thus reducing the return of the more long-term investors in the fund.

- *Increase taxes.* The increased volume of transactions incurred by mutual funds that allow timers tends to increase short-term capital gains, which are taxed at a higher rate than long-term capital gains.

- *Lower returns.* Investment managers claim that they are forced to keep more cash on hand, in the event that timers redeem a huge block of fund shares. "When millions of dollars can be traded out of funds at any time, the fund managers have to keep more cash on hand to cover the potential redemptions. That will lower a fund's return whenever stocks or bonds do better than cash, which is most of the time," according to *Money* columnist Jason Zweig.

- *Limit opportunities in small stocks.* Zweig also contends that fund managers are forced to forgo chances to invest in lesser-known stocks out of concern that in a sudden flurry of timer redemptions they will not be able to sell these stocks at good prices. Thus, managers tend to stick to large-cap stocks, which may reduce their returns.

Considering the potential risks posed by mutual fund timers, one might think that fund management companies would not allow such investors in their products. But ironically, many mutual funds spend millions of dollars to attract such business. Why? The money controlled by timers—about $25 billion—generates approximately $250 million in profit for fund companies.

Well-known investment manager and worldlyinvestor.com columnist Paul Merriman does not take well to Zweig's comments. First, he counters that fund management companies often seek out business from timers. The reason for this is clear—since such a firm makes more profit as its amount of client assets increases, it is in the company's best interest to gather assets from any and every source.

Of course, fund organizations are permitted to restrict market timing in their funds, and some do through redemption fees. But there is no evidence that funds with such fees actually perform better than those funds that do not charge clients for moving their money around.

A ZERO-SUM GAME

Short-term trading is often referred to as a zero-sum game, with the profits from one trader coming from the losses of another.

Suppose, for example, that I have a large position in Amazon.com. If I decide to sell all my stock at once, my order will likely pressure the market lower. That hurts all of the other shareholders in Amazon.com. Should that be an input in my decision to sell the stock? Of course not—my personal reasons to buy or sell should depend only on my circumstances and my views as to the future direction of the company.

This scenario describes my position on fund timing. Investment management companies have a fiduciary responsibility toward their shareholders. If they perceive fund timing to be a hindrance to the objectives of their clients, they should not allow the practice.

But in many cases, fund companies view timers as yet another source of client assets for which they will get paid a fee to manage. They are financially motivated to allow timers, even though their presence might reduce the funds' performance.

Long-term investors should focus on funds that do not allow such short-term trading. But even if such activity does reduce the return of other shareholders, timers will continue to operate in mutual funds.

WorldlyInvestor Quick Summary

1. Buying and holding large mutual funds often leads to underperformance relative to a benchmark primarily because of the following transaction costs:
   - Market impact.
   - Delay costs.
   - Opportunity costs.
   - . Commissions.

2. WorldlyInvestor Time Zone strategy:
   - While buy-and-hold might not lead to a market-beating strategy, many funds make excellent trading vehicles.
   - The Time Zone strategy is based on the daily pricing procedure of the fund—net asset value (NAV)—not the underlying market.
   - The NAV is usually determined by the last price traded for each security in the portfolio, even if the fund closes before the exchange pricing its holdings—for example, a fund holding foreign securities. This enables the astute trader to purchase a mutual fund at a market price that occurred several hours earlier.
   - System rules:

     The S&P 500 index must rally in the last few hours of the day and close in the upper 20 percent of the day's range.

     If this occurs, buy shares in a domestically priced foreign mutual fund on the close of the day.

     Exit on the close of the following day.
   - Not only does this methodology produce excellent returns, it does so with much less risk as it is only in the market one-third of the time. The remaining two-thirds is spent invested in a money market fund awaiting the next opportunity.
   - Remember to use funds with no redemption fees.

Topics for Online Investors

Part Three of *The WorldlyInvestor Guide to Beating the Market* explores the ways the Internet has improved the capabilities of private traders.

Chapter 9 shows how individual investors can use the World Wide Web to create a portfolio that closely mimics, and in many cases surpasses, the performance of any stock index. Many of the sites used to construct this portfolio are free or can be accessed for a modest fee.

Owning individual stocks instead of mutual fund shares offers investors some important benefits. One of the biggest advantages to this approach is more control over taxes. As we shall see, taxes have substantial effects on overall return, so an understanding of this dynamic is an important topic for any serious market participant.

Chapter 10 examines the dark side of Internet trading. First, we examine the dangers of using poorly designed trading systems. Many such systems are sold on the Web by unscrupulous operators whose only objective is to make money at the expense of others. Fortunately, there are a number of simple evaluative techniques that can be used to determine if such strategies are likely to hold up in the future as well as they did in the past.

Investing in penny stocks is another topic explored in this chapter. Although the securities industry has done a good job in cleaning up this segment of the investment industry, there are still a number of things to look out for before taking the plunge.

Chapter 10 also explores what might be the greatest danger of all–succumbing to the urge to day trade. Although there is nothing inherently wrong with the practice, traders need to be aware of the serious impediments to success that will be encountered in this endeavor.

Chapter 11 introduces a new paradigm for mutual fund investors. Since most mutual fund ratings systems depend on past performance as their main criteria, many of the most highly rated funds in the past periods are often the worst performers in the future. Worldly-Investor's mutual fund screen takes a different approach. By looking for funds with the characteristics most often associated with consistent market-beating performance–namely, small asset size and modest expenses–it takes much of the guesswork out of choosing the right mutual fund.

Finally, Chapter 12 presents a method for investing in the hottest sectors of the market–an approach that has beaten the broad market indices for 12 years running.

9

Using the Internet to Beat the S&P 500 Index

The ant is the most common creature on the earth. Every one of each ant's countless actions is specifically designed to benefit the colony as a whole. In this way, each ant is an indispensable and unique member of its community.

What is the competitive advantage of ants? The incredible success of ants in their environment can be explained by their selfless determination and devotion to their anthill. Although they are easy to eradicate in small numbers, in large numbers ants are virtually unstoppable. Army ants of the Amazon River have been known to completely consume animals thousands of times their size.

In many ways, the advantage enjoyed by the ant kingdom—which, as described, is in reality an extremely large number of very small advantages–lays the foundation for the bulk of this chapter. By using the power of the Internet and the many tools found on worldlyinvestor.com and other web sites, we will explore how an individual investor can create a portfolio that can beat nearly any market index (and virtually all actively managed mutual funds).

What advantages do individual investors have over large mutual fund managers? As we detailed in previous chapters of *The Worldly-Investor Guide to Beating the Market*, the advent of the Internet has given private traders the edge in three specific areas of the investment process:

1. *Free information.* The Internet can be used to access data on individual companies and markets that have previously been
   available only to large professional traders. Further, this data
   can be utilized with no strings attached, unlike the data typically used by the pros (who are forced to pay higher commissions to the Wall Street brokerage firms that provide it to them).

2. *Cheaper commissions.* In the past, commission costs were substantially lower for those market participants who can supply
   sufficient order flow–the large professional investment managers. Thanks to the large number of discount online brokerage
   firms, the individual investor can now enjoy lower commissions
   than those paid by mutual fund pros. And since private traders
   usually trade smaller numbers of shares at one time than mutual funds trade, their transaction (which are described in Chapter 8) are much lower than those experienced by market
   professionals.

3. *No operating expenses.* One of the most expensive areas in running a mutual fund involves investor communications. Toll-
   free fund lines, semiannual statements, customer service
   professionals, and other services offered by most mutual fund
   operators are quite expensive. These costs are largely passed
   on to fund shareholders. This partly explains why, even
   though the assets in mutual funds have soared, their average
   fees have increased 40 percent in the past 10 years. The other
   reason is likely related to greed (on the part of the fund operators) and the current bull market, which has convinced many
   investors that fund fees do not affect their long-term returns to
   a great degree.

Even with these advantages, beating a market index still involves
some effort. One must possess a fair amount of skill in navigating
through a number of financial web sites, and keep up with the latest
changes in share prices.

It is also important to recognize that all changes we make to our portfolio will have tax consequences. But as we shall see, this is where our greatest advantage lies.

KEEPING THE TAX COLLECTOR AT BAY

So what's the big advantage in maintaining a portfolio of stocks that mimics the returns of the S&P 500 index, when an indexed mutual fund can do the same thing? The answer lies in one of the few inevitabilities of modern life—taxes.

Although practitioners have spent considerable energy in creating efficient portfolios, these efforts have largely ignored the long-term effects of taxes on total return. Taxes are frequently the largest expense that many investors face—surpassing both commissions and investment management fees—but there has been little effort made to study their effects on investor wealth.

An intriguing aspect of taxes is that they are generated by the same mechanism used by investment professionals to enhance returns—active management. A money manager sells one security and buys another solely because he or she thinks such activity will result in a higher return than would be realized by simply holding a static portfolio. But the true measure of a portfolio's value is obtained only after considering the taxable consequences of capital gains realized by exiting a profitable position.

Of course, the problem does not rest entirely on the shoulders of fund managers. A fund's tax efficiency is also affected by shareholder purchases and sales. Every year, a fund has to distribute to investors all dividends and capital gains realized in the previous 12 months. If a lot of money flows into the fund from new investors, this inflow dilutes the size of the fund's year-end distribution, which makes the fund seem more tax efficient. Conversely, if investors bail out, the fund may have to sell stocks to pay off these departing shareholders, thus realizing capital gains and generating big taxable distributions for those investors who remain.

Individual investors can bypass many of these dilemmas by managing their own portfolios of stocks.

For instance, let's suppose that our portfolio has a position in Coca-Cola (KO), and the stock takes a huge hit. Although negative, the loss can be used to offset capital gains from some of the inevitable big winners that our portfolio will likely contain.

To take advantage of the loss, one might sell the Coke position and buy a similar stake in PepsiCo (PEP) or another stock in the same market sector.

And what about those big winners? As our portfolio continuously shuffles out losing stocks (like our Coca-Cola example) and buys other stocks in the same sector, it is likely that our holdings will eventually contain only appreciated stocks. At this point, some of the bigger winners can be given to children, who could sell the stock at a lower tax bracket.

And if investors die holding these winners, they can be given to heirs, who can sell them without triggering capital gains taxes.

STEPS TO BEATING A MARKET INDEX

There are four steps in creating a market-beating portfolio.

Step 1: Pick an Index

There is a myriad of market indexes, and they differ in two important ways—market capitalization and price-to-book value.

The *market capitalization* of a stock is calculated by multiplying the market price by the total number of outstanding shares. For example, a publicly traded firm with 50 million shares outstanding that trade at $20 per share would have a market capitalization of $1 billion.

The size of a company's market capitalization is used to segment the universe of stocks into various categories, including large-cap, mid-cap, and small-cap. Each type of stock tends to perform better in various stages of a market cycle, and as a result there is little consensus as to which group is preferred at any given time.

Stocks are further divided into value and growth categories according to the company's *price-to-book value.* This measure is determined by dividing the market capitalization by the book value of all of the company's assets (minus its liabilities).

The S&P 500 index has an average price-to-book ratio of 7.3. Value stocks fall below this average, and growth stocks fall above it.

The Frank Russell Company (www.russell.com) has constructed a number of market indexes that are segmented across market cap and growth-value categories. Nine of its more popular indexes are shown as Figure 9.1.

Although (as discussed in Chapter 2) large-cap growth stocks have posted superior returns, that does not necessarily mean that they will continue to do so in the future. In fact, many investors now believe that the time for small-cap value stocks to outperform is upon us.

What about the Dow?

The most followed market index is the Dow Jones Industrial Average. But that does not mean that it should be the one index an investor should attempt to replicate.

First of all, the Dow is composed only of 30 stocks. As a result, its fortunes are often a bit more volatile than those of the S&P, which is composed of 500 stocks.

Secondly, the Dow is price weighted; a stock's contribution to the changes in the index is dependent on its share price. As a result, an indexer would have to make frequent adjustments to ensure that his or her portfolio accurately followed the movements of the Dow.

In contrast, the S&P 500 is "cap weighted," which means that a stock's movement is multiplied by its market capitilization to determine the movement of the index. The S&P is thus self-adjusting; as stocks increase in value, their relative weightings within the index rise right along with the values. As a result, adjustments are rarely needed.

Because of this feature, most market indexes are cap weighted.

Index	Description	Average Market Capitalization	% of U.S. Stocks Represented
Russell 3000 Index	3,000 largest U.S. companies	$5.1 billion	98%
Russell 3000 Growth Index	Growth stocks within the Russell 3000		
Russell 3000 Value Index	Value stocks within the Russell 3000		
Russell 1000 Index	1,000 largest companies in the Russell 3000	$14.1 billion	90%
Russell 1000 Growth Index	Growth stocks within the Russell 1000		
Russell 1000 Value Index	Value stocks within the Russell 1000		
Russell Midcap Index	800 smallest companies in the Russell 1000	$4.2 billion	22%
Russell Midcap Growth Index	Growth stocks within the Russell Midcap		
Russell Midcap Value Index	Value stocks within the Russell Midcap		

FIGURE 9.1 The Russell indexes. Russell constructs its stock indexes based solely on market capitalization and style criteria (i.e., growth or value).
Source: The Frank Russell Company.

However, most large investors still prefer the S&P 500, which is referred to as a large-cap "blended" index (composed of both value and growth stocks).

The most important aspect of choosing a market index to mimic is the unique risk and reward attributes each index brings to bear. It is vital that investors be comfortable with the historic volatility and return potential of a given index before incorporating it into their portfolios. Remember, the selection of the proper index will likely account for about 90 percent of your returns, so select wisely.

For illustration's sake, we will assume that most investors will attempt to replicate the returns of the S&P 500 index. This is a logical assumption, since the bulk of actively managed mutual funds attempt to surpass this benchmark. Further, the stocks in the S&P 500 index are easily traded issues of well-known names.

Step 2: Determine the Sector Weightings of the Index

Many market indexes are composed of stocks from different industry groups. The S&P 500 index, for example, is made up of stocks from 10 distinct sectors. In order to construct our market-beating portfolio, it is essential that we know the sector weightings of our chosen index.

This is where one of WorldlyInvestor's most useful sites, LionShares.com, comes into play.

LionShares.com is the premier web site for equity ownership information. Its database contains the equity holdings for nearly 2,000 institutional money managers, representing more than $8 trillion in stocks. Up until now, the information contained in this database has been available only to Wall Street insiders and major institutions. These institutions have long considered this information invaluable in their decision-making process. Old economy suppliers of this data have gone to great lengths to maintain the status quo by making it prohibitively expensive to individuals and smaller institutions.

Fortunately for the individual investor, the Internet has changed the rules. The Securities and Exchange Commission, through its EDGAR (electronic data gathering, analysis, and retrieval) database, now requires institutional money managers to file their ownership information electronically. With its real-time connection to EDGAR, LionShares.com is able to download and parse equity ownership information in an efficient, cost-effective manner. Because of these breakthroughs, private traders can now gain access to information that was previously available only to Wall Street's "boys' club."

And for those readers that would prefer to view the data more directly, the stock components of the most popular market indexes are also available on the worldlyinvestor.com web site at no cost.

Since our index of choice is the S&P 500, I used LionShares.com to determine the asset allocation for an S&P index fund, the Vanguard 500 Index Fund (VFINX). The site shows the weightings for the 10 sectors, as shown in Figure 9.2.

If one were interested in mimicking a different index than the S&P 500, it would be necessary to determine the sector allocation for a traditional mutual fund that had the same objective. For example, those more intrigued by the Russell 2000, and index of small stocks, might reference the Vanguard Small Cap Index Fund (NAESX).

S&P 500 Index— Breakdown by Sector

Sector	% of Index
Utility	1.8
Energy	5.9
Financial	12.7
Cyclical	11.6
Durables	1.9
Staples	5.1
Services	14.0
Retail	6.3
Health	8.8
Technology	32.2
Total	100%

FIGURE 9.2 Sector weightings, S&P 500 index.
Source: LionShares.com.

Step 3: Determine the Largest Stocks in Each Sector

In order to replicate the returns of each sector (and, in turn, the index as a whole), it is necessary to know the largest stocks (by capitalization) in each sector. Again, we can use the analytical tools on LionShares.com to accomplish this objective. To illustrate, we will list the top 15 technology stocks on the site (Figure 9.3).

Using the same method for all the sectors shown in Figure 9.2, a list of the top five stocks in each of the 10 sectors is then compiled. The completed list is shown as Figure 9.4.

As Figure 9.4 shows, over one-half of the market capitalization of the S&P 500 index is composed of the top 50 stocks.

Step 4: Mirror the Weightings of the S&P 500 by Purchasing the Largest Stocks in Each Sector

To accomplish this, we must use the sector weightings from Figure 9.2 and the stock weightings from Figure 9.4.

Our objective is to replicate the return of the index as closely as possible with a relatively small number of stock positions. How is

COMPANY NAME	CAP GROUP	% OF IND	% OF PORT	POSITION	POSITION CHANGE	$ MKT VAL	$ MKT VAL CHANGE
1 MICROSOFT CORP COM	Mega	34.64	2.81	84,298,342	1,467,127	5,885,120,150	102,424,537
2 ORACLE CORP COM	Mega	20.10	1.63	45,412,096	441,749	3,414,444,674	33,214,224
3 AMERICA ONLINE INC (DEL) COM	Mega	11.62	.94	37,042,550	449,893	1,974,849,468	23,985,146
4 YAHOO INC COM	Mega	6.54	.53	8,632,331	297,975	1,110,877,412	38,345,807
5 VERITAS SOFTWARE CO COM	Large	3.28	.27	5,458,743	74,197	556,453,344	7,563,494
6 SIEBEL SYSTEMS INC COM	Large	2.74	.22	3,208,071	2,308,603	465,170,295	334,747,435
7 ADOBE SYS INC COM	Large	1.44	.12	2,138,303	-47,114	244,835,694	-5,394,553
8 COMPUTER ASSOCIATES INTL INC COM	Large	1.40	.11	9,602,450	238,716	238,265,592	5,923,260
9 VERISIGN INC COM	Large	.68	.06	726,022	101,697	115,210,979	16,138,094
10 I2 TECHNOLOGIES INC COM	Large	.54	.04	702,647	-52,593	91,168,448	-6,823,942
11 MERCURY INTERACTIVE CORP COM	Large	.52	.04	895,485	137,785	88,891,214	13,677,366
12 PEOPLESOFT INC COM	Large	.51	.04	3,943,888	-450,555	86,028,029	-9,827,956
13 ARIBA INC COM	Large	.45	.04	655,200	71,400	75,962,578	8,277,973
14 TIBCO SOFTWARE INC COM	Large	.40	.03	652,400	89,100	67,197,200	9,177,300
15 BMC SOFTWARE INC COM	Mid	.39	.03	3,533,787	-399,382	66,700,230	-7,538,335

FIGURE 9.3 The technology sector screen page from LionShares.com.
Source: LionShares.com.

Sector	Stock	Ticker Symbol	Market Capitalization ($Millions)	% of S&P 500 Index
Utility	1 Duke Energy	DUK	$ 20,853	0.17%
	2 AES	AES	$ 18,959	0.15%
	3 Williams Companies	WMB	$ 18,416	0.15%
	4 Southern	SO	$ 15,121	0.12%
	5 El Paso Energy	EPG	$ 11,780	0.09%
Energy	6 ExxonMobil	XOM	$273,268	2.17%
	7 Chevron	CHV	$ 55,377	0.44%
	8 Enron	ENE	$ 47,217	0.37%
	9 Schlumberger	SLB	$ 42,466	0.34%
	10 Texaco	TX	$ 29,431	0.23%
Financials	11 Citigroup	C	$203,325	1.61%
	12 American International Group	AIG	$181,113	1.44%
	13 Morgan Stanley Dean Witter	MWD	$ 94,224	0.75%
	14 Berkshire Hathaway B	BRKB	$ 80,229	0.64%
	15 Bank of America	BAC	$ 71,883	0.57%
Cyclicals	16 General Electric	GE	$516,932	4.17%
	17 Tyco International	TYC	$ 80,005	0.65%
	18 Corning	GLW	$ 75,001	0.61%
	19 DuPont	DD	$ 46,017	0.37%
	20 Boeing	BA	$ 37,931	0.31%
Durables	21 Ford Motor	F	$ 51,827	0.41%
	22 General Motors	GM	$ 36,029	0.29%
	23 Honeywell International	HON	$ 26,888	0.21%
	24 Harley-Davidson	HDI	$ 11,688	0.09%
	25 Nike	NKE	$ 10,887	0.09%

FIGURE 9.4 Largest Components of the S&P 500 Index by Sector.

Sector	Stock	Ticker Symbol	Market Capitalization ($Millions)	% of S&P 500 Index
Staples	26 Coca-Cola	KO	$142,164	1.13%
	27 Procter & Gamble	PG	$ 74,844	0.59%
	28 PepsiCo	PEP	$ 64,036	0.51%
	29 Philip Morris Companies	MO	$ 60,741	0.48%
	30 Gillette	G	$ 36,471	0.29%
Services	31 WorldCom	WCOM	$131,012	1.04%
	32 Time Warner	TWX	$ 99,996	0.79%
	33 AT&T	T	$ 85,526	0.68%
	34 BellSouth	BLS	$ 80,200	0.64%
	35 Bell Atlantic	BEL	$ 78,539	0.62%
Retail	36 Wal-Mart Stores	WMT	$257,289	2.04%
	37 Home Depot	HD	$115,534	0.92%
	38 Walgreen	WAG	$ 32,377	0.26%
	39 Gap	GPS	$ 26,565	0.21%
	40 Target	TGT	$ 26,390	0.21%
Health	41 Pfizer	PFE	$185,280	2.40%
	42 Merck	MRK	$179,193	2.32%
	43 Johnson & Johnson	JNJ	$141,697	1.84%
	44 Bristol-Myers Squibb	BMY	$114,903	1.49%
	45 Eli Lilly & Company	LLY	$112,794	1.46%
Technology	46 Intel	INTC	$447,721	3.56%
	47 Cisco Systems	CSCO	$446,457	3.55%
	48 Microsoft	MSFT	$420,992	3.35%
	49 Oracle	ORCL	$238,605	1.90%
	50 IBM	IBM	$194,237	1.54%
	Total			50.25%

FIGURE 9.4   *(Continued)*

Sector	Stock	Ticker Symbol	Market Capitalization ($Millions)	% of S&P 500 Index	Sector Weighting	Stock Weighting	For $100,000 Portfolio
1	Utility	Duke Energy	DUK	$ 20,853	0.17%	1.5%	0.8%	$ 776
2		AES	AES	$ 18,959	0.15%		0.7%	$ 706
3	Energy	ExxonMobil	XOM	$273,268	2.17%	5.9%	4.9%	$ 4,905
4		Chevron	CHV	$ 55,377	0.44%		1.0%	$ 994
5	Financial	Citigroup	C	$203,325	1.61%	12.7%	5.4%	$ 5,396
6		American International Group	AIG	$181,113	1.44%		4.8%	$ 4,807
7		Morgan Stanley Dean Witter	MWD	$ 94,224	0.75%		2.5%	$ 2,501
8	Cyclical	General Electric	GE	$516,932	4.17%	11.6%	8.9%	$ 8,908
9		Tyco International	TYC	$ 80,005	0.65%		1.4%	$ 1,379
10		Corning	GLW	$ 75,001	0.61%		1.3%	$ 1,292
11	Durables	Ford Motor	F	$ 51,827	0.41%	1.9%	0.9%	$ 858
12		General Motors	GM	$ 36,029	0.29%		0.6%	$ 597
13		Honeywell International	HON	$ 26,888	0.21%		0.4%	$ 445

196

14	Staples	Coca-Cola	KO	$142,164	1.13%	5.1%	3.3%	$ 3,341
15		Procter & Gamble	PG	$ 74,844	0.59%		1.8%	$ 1,759
16	Services	WorldCom	WCOM	$131,012	1.04%	14.0%	5.8%	$ 5,795
17		Time Warner	TWX	$ 99,996	0.79%		4.4%	$ 4,423
18		AT&T	T	$ 85,526	0.68%		3.8%	$ 3,783
19	Retail	Wal-Mart Stores	WMT	$257,289	2.04%	6.3%	4.3%	$ 4,348
20		Home Depot	HD	$115,534	0.92%		2.0%	$ 1,952
21	Health	Pfizer	PFE	$185,280	2.40%	8.8%	3.2%	$ 3,221
22		Merck	MRK	$179,193	2.32%		3.1%	$ 3,115
23		Johnson & Johnson	JNJ	$141,697	1.84%		2.5%	$ 2,463
24	Technology	Intel	INTC	$447,721	3.56%	32.2%	8.2%	$ 8,247
25		Cisco Systems	CSCO	$446,457	3.55%		8.2%	$ 8,224
26		Microsoft	MSFT	$420,992	3.35%		7.8%	$ 7,755
27		Oracle	ORCL	$238,605	1.90%		4.4%	$ 4,395
28		IBM	IBM	$194,237	1.54%		3.6%	$ 3,614
					100.0%	100.0%	$100,000

FIGURE 9.5 S&P 500 Portfolio Allocations for a $100,000 Account.

this possible? Almost 90 percent of a portfolio's return is due not to the stocks it contains, but rather the sector allocations within the portfolio. If we mirror the sector weightings in the S&P 500 index, our portfolio should closely track the index and will offer a number of other advantages that will be described later.

The dollar amount of stocks to purchase for a $100,000 account is shown as Figure 9.5.

How can an investor buy such a small amount of so many stocks? Fortunately, there are a number of web sites that are specifically designed just for that purpose. One of my favorites, Sharebuilder.com (www.sharebuilder.com), charges clients only a few dollars per transaction. These sites also allow small investors the chance to buy partial shares (e.g., a half-share of IBM) and dollar-cost average (invest a fixed dollar amount each month into a number of stocks).

THE BOTTOM LINE

Although it is difficult to calculate the potential savings, there are significant benefits to this tax-efficient approach to index investing. And fortunately there are plenty of web sites that will help investors keep up with the accounting requirements associated with this approach.

Many brokerages allow their clients to download their portfolios directly to some of the more popular tax programs like Microsoft Money 2000 or Quicken personal finance software. But the technology is not yet foolproof. Investors should expect to do a fair amount of setup work and tinkering to get these programs to work.

Other sites are in the process of developing features that keep a running tally of taxes owed on a Schedule D capital gains tax form. More ambitious projects are attempting to calculate the tax ramifications of portfolio changes in real time.

Worldlyinvestor.com will keep up with these developments, and periodically update readers on the web site.

WorldlyInvestor Quick Summary

Four steps to creating a market-beating portfolio:

1. Pick a market index to mimic. You must be comfortable with its historical returns and volatility. Capital-weighted indexes like the S&P 500 will require fewer adjustments than equity-weighted indexes.

2. Determine the sector weightings of the index. For example the S&P 500 is made up of 10 specific sectors. This information is readily available on web sites like www.lionshares.com.

3. Determine the largest stocks in each sector—once again using web sites such as www.lionshares.com.

4. Mirror the weightings of the index by purchasing the largest stocks in each sector. Sharebuilder.com allows small investors to purchase partial shares of stocks.

The resulting portfolio will be a tax-efficient portfolio that mirrors the index.

10

Three Rules for Investment Success

Now that we have examined a number of market-beating strategies in the first two sections of *The WorldlyInvestor Guide to Beating the Market*, and shown how to create a market-beating portfolio in Chapter 9, it is time to consider some compelling and timely investment wisdom. No matter what an investor's return goals are, these tried-and-true rules are great to have tucked away in our brains just in case temptation decides to get the best of us.

As we have seen in previous chapters, the amount of data available on the Internet and the decreasing cost of trading have transformed personal portfolio management into an increasingly lucrative venture. But with opportunity comes danger.

As we shall see, some of the danger comes from within. The temptation to "beat the Street" is so compelling among investors that they will try just about any shortcut in an attempt to boost their returns. There is the danger of falling for strategies that seem logical, but are in reality not what they seem. These strategies are frequently designed around a set of market assumptions that exist for only a short period of time. Consequently, the results obtained during the actual implementation of the system are not nearly as profitable as during the testing period.

Other dangers are external to the trader's psyche. The increasing population of unscrupulous operators who promise riches beyond the dreams of avarice through the purchase of low-priced penny stocks has risen significantly. And the lure of day trading–the rapid-fire in-and-out type of trading that has become increasingly popular in the past few years–has adversely affected many lives with its empty promises of quick and easy wealth.

Bulls and bears may debate about the next trend to hit Wall Street. But regardless of market direction, the following timeless keys to success should help investors build the prosperity that they seek–and deserve.

RULE 1: DON'T BUILD CASTLES IN THE AIR

The perception of the stock market as an investment medium has changed markedly over the years. For most of the late nineteenth and early twentieth centuries, stocks were thought of as nothing more than gambling devices. Indeed, the leading market pundit of the time was neither a portfolio manager nor an economist, but an astrologer named Evangeline Adams.

She was America's most famous fortune-teller. Since 1927, coinciding with an upsurge in the market, Evangeline had concentrated on predicting its future. Four thousand people a day wrote to her. At $20 per reading, she claimed to predict the movements of the Dow Jones Industrial Average with uncanny accuracy.

Her clients numbered some of the most famous from all walks of life. Steel tycoon Charles Schwab, banker J. P. Morgan, and even well-known entertainers such as Eddie Cantor and Mary Pickford were said to have hung on her every word.

Evangeline's own horoscope had told her to come to New York in 1899. Upon her arrival at the Windsor Hotel, she consulted the stars for the hotel's owner, Warren F. Leland. As she wrote later, "I hastened to warn him that he was under one of the worst possible combinations of planetary conditions, terrifying in their unfriendliness."

The next day the hotel burned to the ground, and Leland's family perished in the flames. Fortunately for Evangeline, he was not too distraught to tell the press about her predictions.

This was the beginning of a long and illustrious career of one of the most famous seers of all time. Having claimed to forecast Charles Lindbergh's transatlantic flight within 22 minutes of actual duration, foretold Rudolph Valentino's death, and prophesied the 1929 stock market crash 24 hours before its occurrence, Evangeline seemed to have tapped into an energy source known by few others.

Yet, not even her supposed telepathic powers could protect her from the effects of the Crash and the Great Depression that followed. Although her public forecasts steadfastly predicted better times, her personal stock holdings suffered greatly.

Burton Malkiel, author of *A Random Walk Down Wall Street*, coined the term "castle in the air theory" to describe the tendency of traders to place more emphasis on what they perceive as popular investments rather than taking a more rational approach. With few exceptions, most of the plungers that espouse this method of stock picking have experienced end results much like Evangeline's.

In modern traders' parlance, the term used to describe castle building is *curve fitting*. In its purest form, curve fitting is an attempt to discern the future direction of the market by placing too high an emphasis on past data.

Curve fitting becomes a greater issue for traders as their computing ability increases. Why? The temptation to create a profitable trading system is so great, and the data available to test such strategies is so readily available, that data tweaking inevitably occurs.

> In other words, given enough computer time, we are sure to find a set of trading rules that "work" on a set of random numbers—*provided that we are allowed to test the rule on the same set of numbers which are used to discover the rule.*

While it is not possible to avoid the curve fitting trap entirely, given the fact that trading models have to fit historical data to some degree, there are some steps to make the testing more robust. First, base the model on a sound concept, like the tendency of the market to rise toward the end of the month.

Second, the fewer rules a system has, the more likely it is to succeed in real time. The more rules employed to improve performance, the more likely the strategy will pick out historically profitable periods while failing in the future. Avoid the temptation of modifying or adding rules that conveniently keep the system out of bad periods. While this makes the statistics look great, it is more probable the actual performance will be disappointing.

Finally, develop systems on a fixed time period. For example, a trader could look for tradable tendencies using market data from 1990 to 1995, and then perform an out-of-sample test for 1996 to 2000. If the rules are robust, the results should be similar to the back-tested sample. Most curve-fitted systems will show their weaknesses at this point.

RULE 2: BEWARE OF PENNY STOCKS

At one time or another, every trader casts a furtive glance toward the penny stock arena. After all, who can resist the temptation of owning thousands of shares that could double or triple at any time? Hopefully, most readers will do no more than cast a glance.

Although technically a penny stock sells for less than a dollar, generally they are classified as stocks that trade under $5 a share and are usually listed in the over-the-counter bulletin board (OTCBB) or the Pink Sheets (an alternative listing service of illiquid penny stocks). Since penny stock companies often have few tangible assets and limited operating histories, they are usually not able to pass the listing requirements of the Nasdaq or the New York Stock Exchange.

There is scant pricing information available on these types of stocks, except for what is listed on the Pink Sheets. Given the lack of accurate pricing information, the spreads on low-priced stocks can be extremely wide, sometimes as high as 100 percent!

Traders must also contend with the *markup*. The markup is compensation to the broker-dealer for maintaining an inventory of the stock and for keeping a liquid market. A broker-dealer is allowed to charge a markup in *addition* to the spread.

Commissions tend to be much higher for penny stock transactions. Many brokers deliberately discourage their customers from trading in this arena by charging them more to do so. In any case, traders must post a very profitable trade to justify the transaction costs alone.

Penny stocks are notorious for being associated with price manipulation and fraud. With its instant information dissemination, the Internet is fueling the process. To quote a regulator: "Any scam artist that doesn't use the Internet ought to be sued for malpractice." Typically, an unscrupulous broker-dealer will buy up the majority of shares of a low-priced stock, then promote the stock through high-pressure sales and Web chat rooms. As unwary buyers are duped into purchasing the stock, its price rises, attracting more buyers. The firm actively discourages any individuals from selling. Once the inventory of stock is sold and the broker-dealer firm has made its fortune, the price begins to fall, and sadly the gullible individuals are left holding the bag. Billions of dollars are lost each year in these scams.

One recent case involved the members of the five largest crime families in the United States and the stocks of 19 companies. They managed to defraud investors of $50 million over a period of five years.

In an effort to improve its image, the OTCBB has recently begun requiring firms to file their financial statements. This has resulted in almost 60 percent of the listed stocks being delisted! Some of the major Wall Street firms are also beginning to enter the penny stock business due to the tremendous trading volumes that are being generated by online investors, which may legitimize the market making.

Interestingly enough, the very stocks that are being shunned by the OTCBB in its current sweep are showing up on the Pink Sheets. The competition between the two quotation services is beginning to heat up with the Pink Sheets offering free 15-minute-delayed quotes on its web site.

Not all penny stocks are fronts for fraudulent activity. There are many legitimate young firms struggling to build their businesses, and penny stocks offer a credible way for them to raise capital. If you want to be successful, you just have to do far more due diligence, be extremely wary, and look carefully at the transaction costs involved before executing a transaction.

RULE 3: AVOID DAY TRADING FOR THE WRONG REASONS

Society has always been fascinated by tales of traders making and losing vast fortunes on a daily basis. There are innumerable books and films on the subject that further the mystique of high-stakes traders risking all every day. Brokerage houses feed well off this myth and have long tried to find ways to cater to would-be market wizards. And the commissions generated by the high number of trades initiated by day traders are obviously highly desirable to brokerage firms.

The advent of online trading finally gave the brokerage firms what they wanted. Customers now have easy and instant access to their trading accounts 24 hours a day. They can generate commissions 24 hours a day as they trade frenetically and to their hearts' content.

Fundamentally I have no problem with day trading. In fact, the market has actually benefited from this segment of trader. Day traders add liquidity, have been a driving force behind lower costs, and have leveled the field for all. The only reason that I would discourage this activity is because the purpose of this book is to help traders make money. For reasons that will become obvious, most day traders do not fit into this category; most actually lose money. Trading is a business, and you have to take a cold, hard look at the numbers before you take the plunge.

Day trading in its purest form simply entails trading in a short-duration, intraday fashion in an attempt to make fast profits, and holding no positions overnight in order to reduce risk. The very nature of this type of trading raises a number of hurdles that need to be discussed. First, the faster you trade, the more commissions you pay and the higher your transaction costs. And although commissions have dropped dramatically in recent years, the spread between the buy (or bid price) and the ask (or sell price) has not dropped as quickly. Traders should keep this in mind as they examine their account statements; you have to overcome a much greater hurdle than simply commissions.

And the very stocks that day traders tend to favor–those with tremendous intraday volatility–tend have wider spreads. So, right out of the box you have been hit with a double whammy to overcome.

The mechanics of buying and selling must also be considered. Since the bulk of a day trader's profit often comes in the first few minutes of a trade, reliable order execution is quite important. Orders placed in volatile markets are especially vulnerable to poor execution. *Slippage* is the term used to describe the difference between the price at which you placed your order and the executed price. The more hectic the market, the greater your chances of being slipped. Worse still, it may be difficult to exit a position in a thinly traded stock at an acceptable price.

Third, operational costs further hamper your chances of being profitable. In order to compete, traders need real-time, dependable stock quotes. This additional cost must be included when examining one's performance. And if traders use margin, as many do in order to leverage their returns, interest costs are also a factor. A recent study done for the U.S. Senate concluded that a typical day trader must make over $111,000 annually from trading just to break even.

Statistics do not bode well, either–70 percent of day traders lose money! Interestingly, many people are unusually profitable *prior* to starting their day trading career. Once online, these same traders who were profitable tend to lose money due to trading much more frequently, and being overconfident in their predictive abilities.

Finally, be careful of the many trading schools and systems that offer a surefire way to riches. If anyone had a method that could produce these incredible returns, why would the originator be willing to sell it? The old adage "If it seems too good to be true it probably is" should be applied here. To add insult to injury, some of the schools are associated with brokers who are primarily interested in how often the students trade, and not in whether they are profitable. A broker's expertise lies in the execution of transactions, not in profitable trading.

Day traders compete against well-capitalized professionals with access to the best technology and research available. Not many weekend warriors would think for a minute of dropping in for a game of professional football. However, how many stop to think that they are doing the same when they enter the day-trading business?

Answer this question honestly: Are you trading for profit or entertainment? If you are trading for profit, the numbers in this game do not look good. If you are looking for entertainment, the smart thing would be to find it elsewhere. If you insist on finding your entertainment in the market, keep your account small, resist the temptation to use margin, and maintain an accurate log of your performance.

Ultimately a few will make it day trading, but not many. Be realistic about your chances; don't risk money you don't have; and don't expect to succeed immediately. Trade small and infrequently at first. Become an expert in order placement to reduce your risk and slippage. Always use stop-loss orders to keep your risk defined and under control.

It is always encouraging to see someone take an interest in one's finances. If you want to take an active management approach, it would be better to use a more balanced approach to investing–like that advocated in *The WorldlyInvestor Guide to Beating the Market.*

WorldlyInvestor Quick Summary

1. Don't build castles in the air—avoid the curve fitting trap.
   - Base trading models on a sound concept—for example, the tendency of the market to rise at the end of the month.
   - The fewer rules a system has, the more likely it is to succeed in real time.
   - Use out-of-sample testing to validate the strategy's performance and reduce the likelihood of overoptimization.

2. Beware of penny stocks.
   - Transaction costs are generally much higher for penny stocks due to wider spreads and higher commissions. Ensure that any strategy employed is actually profitable after the transaction costs.
   - Be aware of the potential for price manipulation and fraud. The exchanges that carry such stocks have minimal listing requirements. The low volume in penny stocks makes them ripe for price manipulation.
   - Read the first two points again until the urge to trade these stocks passes!

3. Avoid day trading for the wrong reasons.
   - The faster you trade, the higher your commissions and transaction costs. Keep in mind that the volatile stocks that day traders favor have wider spreads. A recent U.S. Senate report concluded that a typical day trader must make over $111,000 annually from trading just to break even.
   - Look at the stats: 70 percent of day traders lose money. These are the same people who made money before starting to day trade.
   - Look at the competition: Well-capitalized professionals with access to the best technology and research available.
   - Are you trading to make money or for entertainment?

11

The WorldlyInvestor Guide to Selecting Mutual Funds

For many of our readers, it is difficult to exploit the strategies in the first two sections of *The WorldlyInvestor Guide to Beating the Market* with the bulk of their investable assets. The reason for this is simple: Most private traders have a large proportion of their net worth invested in company-sponsored 401(k) and other retirement plans. These tax-deferred accounts generally do not allow purchases in individual equities. A variety of mutual funds are typically offered by the plan sponsor for investment.

In fact, studies have shown that over 30 percent of the average American's net worth (including homes and other fixed assets) is now invested in such plans. Since the money in these plans is tax deferred, it is insensitive to the rapid trading favored by the most successful fund pros. Retirement plan assets thus comprise the ideal pool of funds with which to utilize actively managed strategies in an attempt to exceed the returns of the market.

There is another, more important reason to address the issue of 401(k) investing. According to numerous studies, plan participants have the tendency to be either too aggressive or too conservative in their asset allocation. In the former case, many employees place nearly all of their retirement nest eggs in the stocks of their employers. This can result in a substantial windfall if the stock appreciates.

Are Mutual Funds Passé?

Investors seem to be losing their appetite for mutual funds. Adjusting for redemptions, cash inflows into mutual funds during 1999 and 2000 have dropped 30 percent below levels of just two years ago.

Several reasons for the reduction in the popularity of funds have been cited. Among them are higher fees and the confusing number of funds available for investment. But the primary reason is paltry returns. Actively managed funds, which receive about 70 percent of total fund inflows, have not performed well relative to index funds.

"Mutual funds used to be the investment of choice," according to Michael Lipper, chairman of Lipper Inc., a fund data and research company. "Now, it's more the investment people use when they have no other choice."

But the possibility of the stock dropping in value puts the hard-earned savings of many of these employees at serious risk.

Consider the employees of high-tech conglomerate Lucent Technologies, for example. A spin-off of AT&T, Lucent is the leading provider of telecom equipment and software. The company has also become a major player in the broadband (voice, data, and video) networking market through acquisitions. But neither its impressive sales growth nor its promising technological innovations have resulted in much stock price appreciation. As Figure 11.1 shows, from 1999 to 2000 Lucent lost 48 percent of its value, while the S&P 500 index returned 22 percent.

The latter case—investors being too conservative with their retirement funds—is as vexing a problem as the single-stock problem just addressed. For various reasons, including fear and lack of knowledge, many investors allocate too much of their portfolios to low-returning money market funds. Although these types of funds have minimal risk, their returns rarely keep up with the rate of inflation. As a result, investors preferring these funds must be willing to either work additional years to fund their retirement or face their golden years with fewer assets.

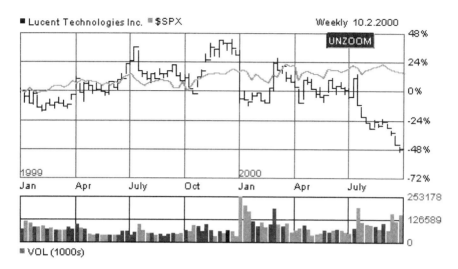

■ Lucent Technologies Inc. ■ $SPX   Weekly 10.2.2000

FIGURE 11.1 From 1999 to 2000, Lucent Technologies (LU: NYSE) lost value while the S&P 500 appreciated handsomely.
Copyright © Stockpoint, Inc.

Today, a 65-year-old retiree has an extended life span of about 20 to 25 years. The average married 65-year-old couple has an even longer second-to-die expectancy. Despite these facts, too many investors, particularly those who are dependent on interest income to meet cash flow needs, have become conservative in their asset allocation decisions. Investors need to shift their perception of risk from solely the loss of principal to include the erosion of purchasing power while they are still alive.

Clearly, the need for intelligently picking the best funds for investment is great. However, with over 10,000 mutual funds to choose from, selecting the one with the greatest odds of generating market-beating returns is challenging. Before we attempt to discern the optimal strategy for buying winning funds (and dumping losers)–which is the focus of this chapter–it is important to review previous attempts to separate the wheat from the chaff.

Studies on mutual fund returns fall into two categories. The first category has sought to determine if actively managed funds–those that are headed by an investment manager who attempts to beat the market through stock picking or other talents–are indeed capable of producing attractive returns compared to those of passively managed or index funds.

The second category seeks to determine whether the talent inherent in actively managed funds is repeatable. In other words, does a fund manager stand a better chance of beating the market in a given year if he or she was successful in doing so in the previous year?

This chapter will examine both categories in the development of a systematic method for selecting funds that have the highest probability of generating market-beating performance for the next twelve months to five years.

SERIOUS MONEY

Selecting mutual funds for investment has been a topic of serious research for a number of years. Indeed, the sheer magnitude of assets currently invested in actively managed funds is a testament to the importance of this chapter. The expense ratio of the typical actively managed fund is about 140 basis points (or 1.4 percent) per year, compared to a ratio of approximately 20 basis points per year for the largest index funds (exchange-traded funds have management fees of less than one-half this amount). Since mutual funds currently manage about $3 trillion in stock investments, the fee differential between active and passive funds of roughly 120 basis points amounts to an additional expenditure of over $36 billion per year on active fund management. In addition, actively managed funds incur much higher trading costs than do indexed funds. Given the magnitude of these costs, it is vitally important for savvy private investors to determine whether the industry as a whole (or a subset of the industry) has sufficient stock-picking talents to justify the trading costs funds incurred and the management fees that they charge.

With this much money at stake, it should come as no surprise that the performance of actively managed funds has been a hot topic for decades. Unfortunately, a vast majority of research has found that actively managed funds, on average, underperform index funds. And worse yet, many studies have shown that the net returns of actively managed funds are negatively correlated with their expense levels— the higher the fees, the lower the performance.

Many of these studies do not paint a pretty picture for active fund management. Indeed, the studies conclude that investors are better off, in the aggregate, buying low-expense index mutual funds or exchange-traded funds. But when faced with this evidence, fund management companies have not, as a whole, embraced the concept of indexing (which has proven to be a much less profitable business for fund operators). Instead, they have generally faced such accusations with denial.

Simply stated, most fund companies are unbelievably stingy when it comes to sharing investment information with their clients. Such basic information as a client's average cost per fund share, cost basis, and after-tax return are notoriously difficult to obtain from many fund companies.

Another area of discomfort for fund investors is the proper benchmark with which to compare actively managed funds. Fund companies are not required to compare their funds' performances with any benchmark, much less the proper one. Fidelity Magellan, for example, became one of the most popular funds in the world by being compared to the S&P 500; and while Peter Lynch ran the fund in the 1970s and 1980s, it trounced this popular index. But what is not generally known is that Magellan was not invested in stocks that made up the S&P 500. Rather, most of its assets were in stocks of small companies. Thus, the fact that the fund beat the S&P does not really mean anything. Its success was more closely linked to the spectacular returns of small stocks as a group than the stock-picking prowess of its star manager.

Finally, fund management companies have been notoriously opposed to disclosing the fees they charge. The U.S. General Accounting

---

Mutual Fund Benchmarks

Suppose a friend bragged that his actively managed mutual fund returned 30 percent over the past 12 months. How good was this performance?

That's where performance benchmarks come into play. The most common benchmark is the stock index that most closely resembles the types of stocks purchased by a fund. If the investment manager specializes in utility shares, for example, the best performance benchmark may be the Dow Jones Utility Index.

In general, an appropriate benchmark reflects a number of key attributes of a mutual fund portfolio, including *style*, *size*, and *sector*.

The two stock style categories, growth and value, are based on the price-to-book-value ratio of the equity mix in the portfolio. A stock fund can also be blended, meaning that it contains a mixture of growth and value stocks.

Size refers to the market capitalization (i.e., number of outstanding shares multiplied by share price) of the stocks in a portfolio. Stocks run the gamut from small-cap to mid-cap to large-cap.

Finally, a fund's sector specialization reflects the industry groups represented in the portfolio (i.e., technology, health care, financial, etc.).

Collectively, these three portfolio attributes can explain about 90 percent of the return of a mutual fund.

Office recently suggested that funds disclose, in their regular monthly statements, the dollar amount of fees that they charge—just like bank statements list their monthly charges. Fund companies have lobbied so strongly against this idea that the odds of its passage are quite slim. The best current defense for investors is to visit the Securities and Exchange Commission's mutual fund cost calculator at www.sec.gov.

THE MORNINGSTAR RATINGS SYSTEM

There have been a number of attempts by investment-oriented firms to create a rating system with which to evaluate funds. The most-well known of these is Morningstar's five-star ratings system.

Formed in the early 1980s, Morningstar's original mission was to create a balanced approach for ranking mutual funds. Their system considers both the risk and the return of a fund in calculating its final rank in its famous five-star rating system.

Morningstar Risk

Each month, Morningstar compares each fund's monthly return with the return of a risk-free investment—the 90-day U.S. government Treasury bill. The company looks at the months in which the fund trailed the T-bill and tallies up the amount by which the fund lagged the T-bill return during these months. Dividing that total by the number of months in the period—three, five, or ten years—produces the fund's average monthly underperformance.

Next, the fund's underperformance is compared to the underperformance of the most relevant of four fund groups—domestic stock, international stock, taxable bond, and municipal bond. The result is the fund's Morningstar risk score.

The risk score shows how risky a particular fund has been relative to its broad peer group. A fund with a Morningstar risk score of 1.0, for example, has been as risky as the overall group. A number lower than 1.0 denotes a less risky fund, and anything higher than 1.0 indicates a fund that has been more risky.

Morningstar Return

Morningstar then looks at the months in which the fund exceeded the return of the 90-day T-bill. The resulting figures show how much the fund exceeds the risk-free rate (after any sales charges) over three-, five-, or ten-year periods. The company then compares each fund's excess return with the average excess return produced by its broad peer group.

As with risk, a return score of 1.0 means a fund had the same excess return over the period as its peer group. A score of, say, 1.3 indicates that the fund's return was 30 percent higher than the average fund in its peer group.

Morningstar Star Ratings

To get the final star rating for a fund, Morningstar simply subtracts each fund's risk score from its return score. Then all funds are ranked in each group according to the results. Funds with scores in the top 10 percent earn five stars; the next 22.5 percent earn four stars; the middle 35 percent, three stars; the next 22.5 percent, two stars; and the bottom 10 percent, one star.

If a fund has been around for less than five years, its Morningstar rating is based entirely on its three-year rating. For a fund that has tenure of greater than five years but less than ten years, 60 percent of its Morningstar rating is based on its five-year rating and 40 percent on its three-year rating. For a fund that is more than ten years old, the star rating formula is 50 percent ten-year rating, 30 percent five-year rating, and 20 percent three-year rating.

Finally, Morningstar also offers category ratings of funds. Based on the same five-star system as the firm's overall ratings, category ratings compare funds with other funds that trade in the same sectors of the stock market.

The result of all these rather complex mathematics boils down to a simple fund rating system of one to five stars. Morningstar has enjoyed immense popularity with retail investors. In fact, one study found that 90 percent of all money flowing into stock funds in 1995 went to funds with four-star or five-star ratings!

Do funds highly rated by Morningstar tend to do well in the future? Is the popularity of Morningstar's rankings justified? According to a number of financial experts, the answer is a definite "no."

WHEN THE STARS DO NOT LINE UP

Morningstar is quick to state that its star ratings are "achievement" marks, rather than predictors of future performance. Even so, it is obvious that private investors generally shun mutual funds with the lowest ratings and choose those with the highest ratings expecting to increase their future returns.

For those many investors to whom the overall Morningstar rating is useful information in deciding which mutual funds to include in their investment portfolios, the persistence of a high rating should matter a great deal. And because the Morningstar rating is based on relative investment performance, the persistence of the rating should be related to the persistence of returns–something of great relevance to investors.

Unfortunately, there is no relationship between the Morningstar rating of a fund and its future performance. The reason is simple: The variables used by Morningstar in developing its ratings system– including information on prior returns, risks, and peer performance– are not effective indicators of future returns.

There are also several more chinks in Morningstar's well-defined armor. One faux pas, referred to as "grade inflation" by Mark Hurlbert, a *Forbes* columnist and editor of the investment performance monitoring service *Hurlbert Financial Digest*, is Morningstar's practice of giving nearly one-half of all domestic equity no-load funds (funds with no sales charge) a four- or five-star ranking.

This bias in Morningstar's system arises due to the way the company categorizes no-load funds. Instead of grading domestic equity no-loads against their peers, Morningstar puts them in a universe that also includes load funds and sector funds. Since Morningstar penalizes them for their sales commission, load funds are almost automatically excluded from receiving a high rating (as are sector funds, which can be highly volatile).

Although this bias does not improve the accuracy of Morningstar ratings, it does increase another important element—the company's bottom line. Since Morningstar licenses its star ratings for use in mutual fund advertising, its ratings practices effectively increase the number of potential customers.

Further, Morningstar has recently expanded the menu of products and services it offers to fund companies. Some allege that as Morningstar turns more of the fund companies it rates into clients, its objectivity could be compromised. Of course, the company denies these charges, stating that there is a "Chinese wall" that separates its editorial and data analysis business groups. But it does give investors a reason to pause before placing their faith blindly in the star rating system.

Further, it seems that younger funds have much better odds of getting the coveted five-star rating than older funds. With their limited operating history, newer funds have a lesser chance of having to face difficult market conditions than, say, funds that have been around for a decade or longer.

According to Hurlbert, Morningstar's top-ranked no-load stock funds have underperformed the market by an average of nearly three percentage points per year. Other studies have shown that those funds that earn a four- or five-star rating have about a 50–50 chance of repeating the feat in the next year. In other words, a fund manager rated excellent by Morningstar has no better than random odds of outperforming his or her competitors in the future.

OF ABCs AND ARROWS

Next to Morningstar, the best-known purveyors of rating mutual funds are undoubtedly financial magazines. *Forbes* entered the fray in 1955. In order to get on the *Forbes* "Honor Roll," mutual funds must have shown acumen in preserving their clients' capital during difficult periods for stocks (dubbed by the magazine as "down markets"), as well as put in an above-average performance during the boom times in between (which are referred to as "up markets"). A relatively small number of funds—usually around 20 or so—qualify in any year, compared to the dozens of funds that boast a five-star rating by Morningstar.

Still, *Forbes* cannot predict the future. According to John Bogle of the Vanguard Group, between 1973 and 1990 the *Forbes* Honor Roll underperformed the overall market by about 1 percent per year.

Another study separated *Forbes's* down market ratings from its up market ratings. The results, which are shown in Figure 11.2, reflect the findings of Bogle—namely, a lack of predictive ability.

Morningstar is not the only ratings service with a spurious

Forbes "Down Market" Rating

Fund Rating Year 1	Avg. Group Performance Year 2
A	11.2%
B	14.0%
C	15.8%

Forbes "Up Market" Rating

Fund Rating Year 1	Avg. Group Performance Year 2
A	16.2%
B	10.6%
C	12.8%
D	17.5%

FIGURE 11.2   The financial magazine *Forbes* publishes an annual list of fund ratings. The rank varies from A (the best) to F (the worst), and the rankings are performed during both down and up markets. If the rating system had predictive ability, then funds rated A would be more likely to outperform their peers in the following year. As the figure shows, this is not the case.
Source: Adapted from Fischer, 1995.

record of picking future winners. According to Hurlbert, Value Line's top-ranked no-load general equity funds have lagged the market by about four percentage points between 1994 and 1997. Considering the success of Value Line's legendary stock ranking system, which has been shown to have significant ability to discern winning stocks from losers, this result was somewhat surprising. But with so many mutual funds from which to choose—a much larger population than that of common stocks—fund ratings present a significant challenge.

The same results were obtained from examining the mutual fund ratings systems utilized by a number of other leading financial magazines, including *Money* and *Kiplinger's*. What's unfortunate about these findings is that even a cursory glance at the future performance of their most highly rated funds would show that such schemes are useless in predicting the best funds for the coming year.

Of course, the editors of these magazines are quick to point out that their ratings are not intended to be used to predict future performance. If this is the case, why are ratings assigned at all?

The answer lies in the psychological bias of many readers. Simply, people seem to be wildly attracted to the idea of ratings. Football teams, movies, and restaurants are all rated in some form or fashion. It seems intuitively logical that investments should also be on the list.

And those magazine issues that are devoted to fund ratings are often the biggest sellers. Tremendous amounts of resources are dedicated to these issues not only for the extra copies of the magazines that are sold, but also for the additional advertising revenue these issues attract.

PICKING POTENTIAL FUND WINNERS

So far, we have examined the attributes that are useless in predicting the future performance of mutual funds. How about those measures that do have predictive ability?

There turns out to be a number of characteristics that have been shown to be good indicators of future fund performance. We will break them into two groups—primary criteria and secondary criteria. We will then combine these two groups in constructing our mutual fund screening tool.

Primary Criteria

Fees

The fee load of a mutual fund, which includes the compensation paid to the investment management company and the distribution charges that pay for advertising and other sales costs, has more influence on the future performance of a fund than any other factor. When asked about the significance of the fee load, Don Phillips, the president of Morningstar, said, "If you pay the executive at Sara Lee more, it does not make the cheesecake less good. But with mutual funds, it comes directly out of the batter."

The drag of fund fees on performance is the biggest disadvantage of investing in mutual funds. The increasing fees that funds charge (Figure 11.3) are the main reason that actively managed funds as a group have lagged to overall market.

The main culprit behind rising mutual fund expenses is 12b-1 fees, which are used by fund companies to pay brokerage firms for selling shares. In many cases, investors pay more to buy their funds than they do to have them managed.

Even so, there are cadres of investment advisers who believe in the old saying "You get what you pay for." Although that may be the case when buying an automobile or a home, it does not seem to apply to the selection of mutual funds (Figure 11.4).

High fees come with another drawback—higher risks. "Fund managers are human—they want to look good." Phillips says. "Managers burdened with higher costs are more likely to take more risk to compensate for that drag."

Clearly, the more you pay to your mutual fund company, the less you get to keep for yourself. Over time, even the most talented

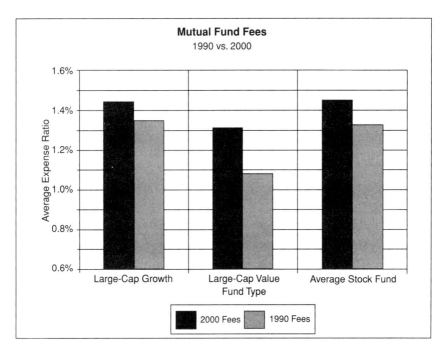

FIGURE 11.3 Mutual fund fees have climbed steadily in the past 10 years.
Source: Adapted from data obtained from Lipper Analytical Services, Inc.

fund manager will have a hard time performing well when the fund company charges an above-average fee for his or her services.

Turnover

It may seem counterintuitive, but the funds with the best performances are those that trade in and out of stocks the most.

This recent finding is the result of a study that examined the stock portfolios held by mutual fund managers. The study found that, surprisingly, the portfolios owned by fund pros outperformed the overall stock market by about 1.3 percent per year. About 60 basis points (0.6 percent) of this outperformance were due to the higher average returns associated with creating a market-beating portfolio, while the

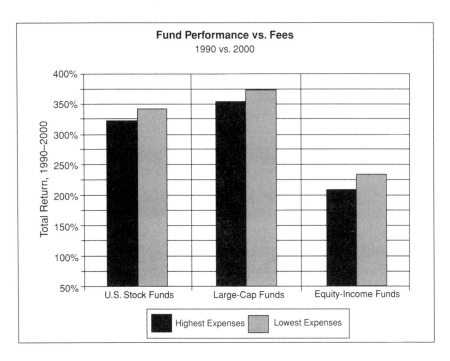

FIGURE 11.4 For the past 10 years, mutual funds with the lowest fees have earned greater returns on average than funds with the highest fees.
Source: Adapted from data obtained from Lipper Analytical Services, Inc.

remaining 70 basis points were due to the talents in picking the best-performing stocks in a given market sector.

This result was calculated with regard to transaction costs and management fees. Combined, these charges put a burden of about 2.3 percent on fund managers. As a result, the average actively managed fund lagged the overall market by 1.0 percent (2.3 percent drag minus 1.3 percent outperformance) per year.

But the group of funds with the *highest turnover* (i.e., those that held their stock positions for the shortest amount of time) were shown to add return in excess of the 2.3 percent in charges levied to shareholders.

The average portfolio turnover for stock funds is about 80 percent, which means that about 80 percent of the average fund's assets is invested in different stocks at the end of the year than at the beginning. Funds that have the highest turnover probably average above 100 percent per year.

One word of caution for taxable investors: High-turnover funds create significantly more realized capital gains than those funds with low turnover. As a result, high-turnover funds should be considered only for nontaxed accounts like IRAs and 401(k) plans.

Narrow Focus

Think that the talented manager of a large-cap growth fund you saw on CNBC can consistently beat the market? Think again.

A ton of research has shown that managers who specialize in large-cap stocks (those with a market capitalization large enough to place them in the S&P 500 index) do not stand much of a chance of exceeding the return of such index funds as the Vanguard 500 Index Trust. In fact, not a single actively managed large-cap fund outperformed the S&P 500 index in the last three- or five-year period. Only three of 94 actively managed large-cap funds managed that feat in the past decade.

Thus, the odds of selecting a superior fund in the large-cap arena are extremely small. Why? The large-cap universe is so efficiently priced that managers add no value in selecting certain stocks and ignoring others. And the high expense ratios of these funds only add to the problem.

The results are a bit more encouraging when one examines small-cap funds–those that concentrate on stocks with market capitalizations of about $1 billion and lower. As a group, small-cap funds were able to beat index funds by a small amount over the past 10 years. The same is true for mid-cap funds, which focus on stocks with a market capitalization of up to $5 billion.

The case is equally strong for sector funds. Managers who specialize in technology stocks, banks and brokerages, health care, and other narrowly defined market sectors stand a good chance of beating their respective indexes. But the portion of an investor's portfolio dedicated to large-cap stocks is best reserved for index funds, whose low fees and passive management make a hard combination to beat.

Asset Size

Funds with a relatively modest amount of client assets have a much greater probability of beating the market than fund behemoths.

The reason for this boils down to one factor: transaction costs. Larger funds have to move a lot more money around in the markets, and trading in and out of stocks affects the stock prices so much that it becomes economically burdensome to buy thinly traded issues. As a result, managers of large funds are forced to trade less often and stick to only those stocks that have sufficient trading volume.

An example of the effect of swelling assets on a mutual fund's performance is evident in the performance of the Oakmark Fund. From its inception in 1991 through 1998, its annualized return was 24.91 percent, versus 19.56 percent for the S&P 500 index. In 1992 it exceeded this benchmark by an astonishing 41.28 percent. But another story emerges when its performance and asset size is examined on a year-by-year basis (Figure 11.5).

Figure 11.5 shows an all too-familiar pattern of fund investors chasing performance, with more and more investors getting lower and lower returns. This is especially true with small-cap funds. Because of the enhanced risk of these stocks, small-cap managers can make a few lucky guesses and beat the market by a huge margin. But the enhanced publicity surrounding such a feat often results in more client assets. And since small-cap stocks are notoriously difficult to trade, performance can erode dramatically.

Oakmark Fund Performance, 1992–1998

	1992	1993	1994	1995	1996	1997	1998
Return in excess of S&P 500 index	41.3%	20.4%	2.0%	–3.1%	–6.7%	–0.8%	–24.9%
Assets ($ Millions)	328	1,214	1,626	3,301	4,194	7,301	7,667

Figure 11.5 Performance of the Oakmark Fund.
Source: Bernstein, 1999.

One caveat to this rule is that larger fund organizations–like American Funds and AIM, for example–have extensive trading operations and are thus a bit better at managing large amounts of money. All things being equal, a small fund in a large fund family is the best way to go.

Secondary Criteria

Past Performance

Choosing mutual funds based on their past performance is the albatross of the ratings game. Virtually all rankings methodologies give a high weight to this criterion, even though its value in choosing future winners is, at best, questionable.

There have been countless studies performed on the persistence of mutual fund performance. When the research focuses on stock funds in general, the result is as grim as that shown in Figure 11.6.

But the results are quite different when one ranks specialized managers with their peers. There does seem to be some performance persistence within market sectors. In other words, a top-performing manager in, say, the health-care sector stands a good chance of repeating as a top performer for the next year.

Persistence of Mutual Fund Performance, 1994–1998

	Average Annual Return	
	1990–1994	*1994–1998*
Top 30 funds of 1990–1994	18.4%	21.3%
All funds	9.4%	24.6%
S&P 500 index	8.7%	32.2%

FIGURE 11.6   Performance persistence in general equity funds.
Source: Bernstein, 1998.

Smart Money Flows

Individual investors have been shown to be pretty savvy when it comes to picking certain types of mutual funds.

Referred to as the "smart money effect," this new area of research began with the observation that funds that pick up new money inflows tend to perform better in the subsequent quarter than those funds that exhibit net money outflows.

But what makes the money smart? How do individuals choose winning funds? The funds' past performance apparently is part of the reason that people choose funds, but not all. So it's not simply the case that smart investors chase past winners—a strategy that we have shown to be ultimately unprofitable.

In the end, the researchers concluded that private investors are pretty smart when it comes to evaluating the things that count: a fund's manager, its portfolio holdings, the fund company itself, and other key data.

Further, the smart money effect is mainly concentrated in funds with a relatively modest amount of client assets. New money flowing into these funds was shown to outperform the market, as was money following the new money into small funds. When it comes to larger

Enhanced Index Funds Vary in Methodology, Returns

Apparently unsatisfied with the performance of the S&P 500 and other equity indexes, investors have of late been snapping up shares of enhanced index funds. These vehicles use the bulk of their assets to replicate the returns of a given stock market index. A small portion of the fund is actively managed in an attempt to enhance the fund's performance.

Enhanced index funds can be grouped into two broad categories. The first group attempts to add return over the stated benchmark by over- or underweighting given sectors of the market or certain individual stocks. This additional return is commonly referred to as "alpha."

The second group is a bit more quantitative. These funds buy futures contracts on a given market index (like the S&P 500) to establish the benchmark (or "beta") return. But because futures require only a nominal up-front payment, the portfolio managers of these funds are free to invest most of the funds' assets in short-term debt securities or fixed-income arbitrage strategies.

In the case of the first group, the enhanced portion of the fund's return— the "alpha"—comes from the same source as the "beta" return—namely, the stock market. As a result, one would expect the alpha and beta to be highly correlated. In other words, during bull markets both components would tend to perform well, while in bear markets both would tend to be unprofitable.

In the second group, however, alpha and beta originate from different markets. As a result, there is significant diversification potential between the two return streams, which could result in a higher risk-adjusted return.

A study by Ibbotson Associates has shown that most enhanced index funds are not worthy of their name. But the ones that are successful are more likely to fall into Group 2 than Group 1.

Does that mean that stock selection is more difficult to implement than yield enhancement strategies? Possibly. But the noncorrelation of the alpha and beta return streams is probably the biggest component in Group 2's superiority over Group 1.

Those interested might want to check out the Managers U.S. Stock Market Plus Fund or the PIMCO StockPlus Fund.

funds, the effect is negligible. Why? Perhaps because investors are more cautious when putting money in small funds and therefore try to be more sure of the prospect for gains. Plus, managers of small, nimble funds can show more skill than managers hamstrung by larger amounts of assets.

THE WORLDLYINVESTOR MUTUAL FUND SCREEN

Our WorldlyInvestor mutual fund screen seeks to find the mutual fund in a given market sector with the best chance of delivering market-beating performance for the next 12 months.

Primary screening criteria will form the basis for our fund selection methodology.

- ***Specialization.*** Since general equity funds have not been shown to deliver dependable market-beating performance, we will consider only those funds that concentrate on a given market style or sector.
- ***Low Fees.*** Total expenses must be below average for the fund's peer group.
- ***Turnover.*** The manager must trade the fund's portfolio more actively, on average, than his or her peers.
- ***Asset Size.*** We will place special emphasis on those funds with assets of less than $1 billion; if this criterion is too stringent, we will examine those funds with below-average assets.

Secondary screening criteria will be used to differentiate between those funds that score closely with the primary screens.

- ***Past Performance.*** We will consider relative peer performance in the prior 12 months and year-to-date.

- *Money Flows.* Those funds that have experienced substantial cash inflows (but have not grown too large) have been shown to follow the smart money effect.

Clearly, our screen is quite different from those available in magazines or from fund ratings services. Since we do not consider past performance as a primary criterion–the driving force behind many other selection methods–our fund choices should be markedly different from the rest of the pack. Hopefully, so will our ability to choose the best-performing funds!

An example of this difference becomes obvious when we compare one of WorldlyInvestor's small cap value selections, First American Small Cap (FSCCX), with a fund highly rated by Morningstar, Berger Small Cap Value (BSCVX).

As Figure 11.7 shows, Berger Small Cap Value clearly looks superior to First American's small cap offering–*if one considers past performance strongly indicative of future results.* But the criteria that are more important to future returns–clearly point to First American Small Cap (Figure 11.8).

The result of the WorldlyInvestor mutual fund screen for several market sectors is shown as Figure 11.9. A more complete and up-

Fund	First American Small Cap	Berger Small Cap Value
Ticker Symbol	FSCCX	BSCVX
Expense Ratio (%)	0.88%	1.37%
Assets ($Millions)	437	849
Jan.–Sept. 2000 Return	10.9%	13.6%
1-Year Return (%)	24.0%	24.3%
3-Year Return (%)	0.2%	10.4%
Morningstar Rank	1 Star	3 Stars

FIGURE 11.7   Using WorldlyInvestor's criteria to compare two mutual funds.

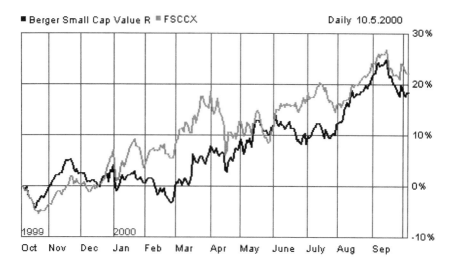

FIGURE 11.8 Based on WorldlyInvestor's Mutual Fund Screen, First American Small Cap fund (FSCCX) is poised to outperform Berger's small cap offering.

to-date list of recommended funds can be found on the worldly investor.com web site.

A FINAL QUESTION

So far, we have examined what attributes are most closely associated with mutual funds that are most likely to outperform their peers in the next 12 months. Our analysis showed that because specialized managers have much better odds of generating exceptional risk-adjusted returns, future winners can be found among given industry sectors and styles in the market.

The analysis, however, leaves one question unanswered: Which market sectors hold the best promise? That is discussed in the next chapter.

Sector	WorldlyInvestor Rank	Fund	Ticker Symbol	Expense Ratio	Assets ($Millions)	YTD Return	1-year Return
Technology	1	First American Technology	FATCX	0.90%	495	1.0%	86.0%
	2	Dresdner RCM Global	FSCCX	1.50%	495	32.3%	147.7%
		Sector Average		1.74%	838	4.07%	
Financial	1	Century Shares	CENSX	0.82%	340	22.3%	27.9%
	2	Davis Financial	DVFYX	0.86%	16	24.4%	28.8%
		Sector Average		1.73%	239	16.24%	
Utilities	1	American Century Utils	BULIX	0.69%	286	3.7%	15.0%
	2	INVESCO Utilities	FSTUX	1.26%	258	7.2%	22.8%
		Sector Average		1.42%	292	6.88%	

FIGURE 11.9 Some suggested funds based on WorldlyInvestor's selection criteria that attempt to determine the funds with the best chance of outperforming their peers in the next 12 months.

WorldlyInvestor Quick Summary

1. Studies show many 401(k) plan participants are either too aggressive or too conservative in their asset allocations.
   - Overly aggressive investors often place all their assets in one stock—that of their employer.
   - Overly conservative investors allocate too much of their assets to money market funds.

2. Studies on mutual fund performance generally fall into two categories:
   - Do actively managed funds produce more attractive returns than passively managed funds?
   - If a manager beats the market this year, is he or she likely to repeat this feat next year?

3. What has the research yielded so far on mutual funds?
   - Actively managed funds on average underperform passively managed funds.
   - Often, the higher the fees an actively managed fund charges, the lower the performance.

4. Existing performance comparisons and rankings of mutual funds:
   - Most existing ratings of funds focus on past performance and have absolutely no predictive value. In fact, a manager rated as excellent by Morningstar has no better than random odds of outperforming the competition in future years. The same is true of top funds selected by Value Line, and by *Forbes* and other leading financial publications.
   - Mutual funds are not required to compare themselves to any benchmark, much less a relevant one, in their advertising.

5. So what characteristics do have predictive value?
   - Primary criteria:

     Fee load—In general, the higher the fees, the less you get to keep for yourself. Even talented managers have difficulty overcoming the effect of above-average fees.

     Turnover—As counterintuitive as is sounds, the funds with the best performance are those that trade the most.

Narrow focus—Large-cap funds have difficulty outperforming their respective indexes. Small-cap funds also stand a better chance to deliver exceptional returns, as do sector funds.

Asset size—Smaller funds have a much greater probability of beating their larger brethren. Ideally, look for a small fund within a well-established fund family.

- Secondary criteria:

Past performance—While past performance has little predictive value on funds in general, managers in specialized sectors who perform well stand a good chance of continuing to do so.

Smart money flows—Funds (especially smaller funds) that receive net inflows in a quarter tend to perform better in the following quarter than those with net outflows.

6. WorldlyInvestor mutual fund screen:
   - Primary criteria:

Specialization—Consider only funds that concentrate on a given market style or sector.

Low fees—Total expenses must be below average for the fund's peer group.

Turnover—On average, the manager must have a higher turnover than peers have.

Asset size—Place special emphasis on funds with less than $1 billion in client assets (or at least below average for a given peer group).

   - Secondary criteria:

Past performance—Consider relative peer performance in past 12 months and year-to-date.

Money flows—Consider funds with substantial cash inflows.

CHAPTER 12

Market Timing Strategies with Mutual Funds and Exchange-Traded Funds

Of all the different trading styles available to private investors, market-timing strategies have become one of the most popular.

Market timers attempt to beat the market by identifying the market sectors with the highest returns in the next day, week, or month. Given the rather dramatic difference in returns between the most and least profitable sectors (Figure 12.1), a highly accurate timing methodology would yield tantalizing results.

A tremendous amount of information on market timing is available on the Internet. My search for data using a popular search engine (www.northernlight.com) yielded over 75,000 entries!

As an active trader, my interest in market timing is motivated purely by profit. If any of the rather outrageous claims made by firms that are marketing timing systems on the Internet have any basis in fact—claims of greater than 50 percent average annual returns are not uncommon—I would be well served to incorporate timing into my market activities.

But as a market historian, my interest in timing strategies is based more in curiosity. According to modern financial theory, beating the

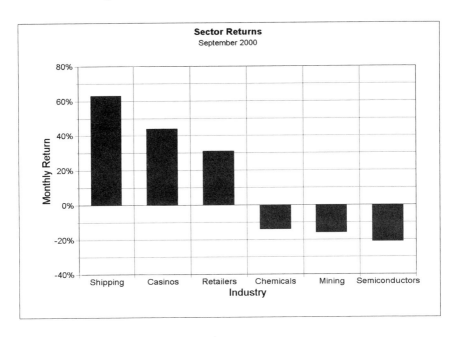

Sector Returns
September 2000

FIGURE 12.1 For a given month, the difference in returns between the best- and worst-perfoming market sectors can be huge.

market is supposed to be hard—and maybe even impossible! If relatively simple timing models can produce the types of returns their proponents claim, then the market is a lot more "stupid" than these theories would lead investors to believe. Their continued profitability would require a virtual rewriting of the laws of Modern Portfolio Theory.

As we will see, market timing can generate some surprisingly profitable results—in the right economic environment.

TIMING AND MOMENTUM

Timing strategies have long been attractive to investors as potential sources of market-beating returns. The thought of accurately buying into the hottest sectors and dumping out of the biggest losers is intriguing to both short-term traders and long-term market investors who have tired from the increasing volatility of stock returns.

Based on recent returns, a market timing system that could flawlessly switch between the best-returning market segments and asset classes would yield profits envied by even the most talented stock picker (Figure 12.2).

As Figure 12.2 shows, all of the perfect market timing systems were not only more profitable than a buy-and-hold strategy, but also considerably less risky. The strategy's return/risk measure also favors timing. Perfect timing between stocks and cash, for example, yielded nearly 50 percent per year and a return/risk ratio of almost 5:1, compared to the return of about 17 percent per year for the S&P 500 index.

Instead of switching between stocks and cash, many of today's market timers prefer a slightly different approach. The most popular of these systems attempt to identify the industry groups that exhibit the most price momentum.

Strategies that exploit momentum in market sectors work in essentially the same way as the approach discussed in Chapter 1, which

The Value of a Perfect Market Timing System

	Perfect Market Timing Stocks/Cash	Index Returns	
		Large Stocks S&P 500	Small Stocks Russell 2000
Annual return	48.2%	16.9%	15.7%
Risk measure	9.8%	14.6%	18.8%
Return/risk ratio	4.90	0.82	0.62

FIGURE 12.2 A system that could flawlessly switch between the best-performing market sectors would be more profitable and less risky than a simple buy-and-hold strategy.

Source: Adapted from Kao, 1999.

examined momentum in individual stocks. The main difference between the two is that while individual equities are used to implement the latter strategy, mutual funds or exchange-traded funds (ETFs) are used to exploit the former.

Using mutual funds to capture industry momentum has at least two advantages over stock trading. The first is that the transaction costs, consisting mainly of annual expenses and, occasionally, redemption fees, are relatively low. Second, sector mutual funds allow the investor to follow a more manageable set of investment choices. With over 200 stocks in an average industry group, sector timing using individual issues would be difficult at best.

A disadvantage of mutual funds is that all of the sector funds currently available are actively managed. As a result, these funds do not provide a "pure play" in a given sector. If the manager of a sector fund makes poor investment choices from the available stocks in a given industry group, the fund's returns may lag the returns of the sector. Because of the active nature of sector funds, significant management fees are levied to their shareholders.

Sector Funds

Sector funds are the fast-growing segment of the mutual fund industry. According to Lipper, there are about 900 sector funds, which account for to 15 percent of all domestic equity funds.

The largest sector fund family is managed by Fidelity Investments, which has 38 funds that concentrate in the health care, technology, utilities, consumer goods, financial, consumer cyclical, and natural resources industries. Fidelity designed its sector funds for active traders. The funds are priced hourly and can be traded intraday. However, the funds carry a $7.50 exchange fee and a 0.75 percent short-term trading fee on shares held 29 days or less.

Both Rydex and ProFunds also offer sector funds (each has 17 funds from which to choose). There are no charges associated with trading either family's shares.

One alternative to sector funds is exchange-traded funds (or ETFs). There are a number of sector ETFs available, and all are designed to replicate the returns of a given market sector through passive (or indexed) management. As a result, the fees associated with ETFs are much lower than those of mutual funds. However, actively trading ETF shares can result in substantial commissions for investors.

A list of sector ETFs is shown as Figure 12.3.

MORE ON MOMENTUM

Before we attempt to develop a momentum-based sector timing strategy, it is important to understand why momentum exists in stock prices.

Most market experts believe that momentum effects persist because of the tendency of investors to underreact to inputs of new information. An example of this may be the gradual increase in oil service stocks during 1999 and 2000. Even though OPEC announced production cuts relatively early in the period, these stocks continued to increase in value throughout the year (Figure 12.4).

Why did these stocks gradually increase as shown in Figure 12.4, instead of gapping higher due to the shortage of oil? Perhaps investors needed time to decide what the effect of a decreasing supply of crude oil would have on its price. This lag period thus caused prices to trend higher for a long enough period of time for momentum-savvy investors to profit.

But momentum traders do not have to estimate the future price of crude oil to benefit from market trends. Instead, they focus on those stocks (or sectors) that have experienced the largest price increase in the prior six months. They then establish a long position in these stocks with the belief that they will increase substantially in the next six-month period.

A better indication of the profit potential of momentum investing

Fund	Ticker Symbol	Fund	Ticker Symbol
HOLDRS		**iShares**	
Biotech	BBH	Utilities	IDU
Broadband	BDH	Consumer Cyclical	IYC
B2B Internet	BHH	U.S. Chemicals	IYD
Internet	HHH	U.S. Energy	IYE
Internet Architecture	IAH	U.S. Financial	IYF
Internet Infrastructure	IIH	U.S. Fin. Services	IYG
Pharmaceutical	PPH	U.S. Healthcare	IYH
Regional Bank	RKH	U.S. Industrial	IYJ
Semiconductors	SMH	Consumer Noncyclical	IYK
Telecom	TTH	Basic Materials	IYM
Utilities	UTH	U.S. Real Estate	IYR
		U.S. Internet	IYV
		U.S. Technology	IYW
Sector SPDRs		Telecommunications	IYZ
Basic Industries	XLB		
Energy	XLE		
Financial	XLF		
Industrial	XLI		
Technology	XLK		
Consumer Staples	XLP		
Utilities	XLU		
Consumer Services	XLV		
Transportation	XLY		

FIGURE 12.3 Sector-specific exchange-traded funds (ETFs), sorted by sponsor. HOLDRS are managed by Merrill Lynch; SPDRs are managed by State Street Global; and iShares are managed by Barclays Investor Services.

FIGURE 12.4 OPEC production cuts in early 1999 caused a trend to develop in oil service stocks.

Copyright © Stockpoint, Inc.

is to rank all stocks based on their returns for the past six months. If the best performers of the past six months turn out to be the star stocks of the next six months, then momentum-savvy investors could easily profit from this market tendency.

Figure 12.5 illustrates the results of such a study. The graph clearly shows that Group 1 stocks (i.e., those issues that performed best in the prior six months) performed better in the following six months than Group 2 stocks (those issues that had the next highest returns for the previous six months), and so on.

SECTOR-LEVEL MOMENTUM

A momentum strategy at the sector level is quite similar to the strategy at the stock level. The following procedure illustrates the methodology of a sector trading system with a six-month holding period that invested in the single fund with the best lag-period return:

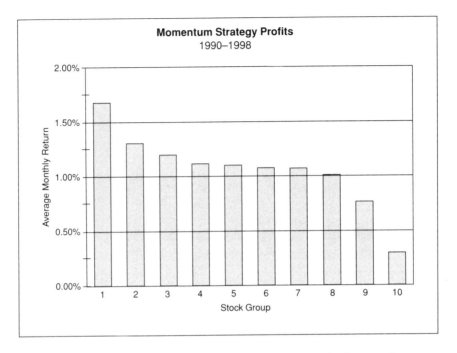

FIGURE 12.5 Stocks that experienced the highest returns in the past six months (Group 1) were shown to have the highest returns in the next six months.

Source: Adapted from Jegadeesh and Titman, 2001.

- Assuming that the first holding period was January through June 1990, the first lag period was July to December 1989.
- The sector with the best lag-period performance in the period July to December 1989 was the utilities sector, which returned 14 percent. Thus, a long position in a utilities sector fund was initiated on the first trading day in January 1990.
- Over the following six months, the utilities sector fund returned 10 percent.
- The second holding period was July 1990 through December 1990, which made the second lag period January through June 1990.

- In the second lag period, the sector with the best return was the financial sector, which returned 15 percent.
- During the second holding period, July through December 1990, the financial sector fund returned 11 percent.
- Thus, the first year of the test yielded a return of 10 percent in the first six months and 11 percent in the second six months.

This methodology was repeated from 1991 to 1999 to yield a 10-year test period return.

The result of the sector fund test confirmed the efficacy of the momentum strategy—an outcome similar to those studies that bought and sold the best-performing individual stocks. But there was a significant difference in the two tests. By using mutual funds, a trader would be fully invested in a given market sector for six months. This results in a marked lack of diversification, which only serves to increase the risk of the strategy.

For this reason, the test was changed slightly. Instead of buying the best-performing market sector, the strategy would now invest an equal amount in the three highest-performing industry groups.

The data also showed another important difference between the two trading systems. *At the sector level, momentum, although not as intense, seems to persist longer than momentum at the individual stock level.* For this reason, the sector strategy utilizes a 12-month holding period instead of the six-month holding period used for the stock-specific momentum strategy.

Figure 12.6 shows the results of the sector momentum trading system from 1990 to 1999.

Figure 12.6 makes a compelling case for sector-level momentum investing. The strategy exceeded the return of the S&P 500 index for seven years of the 10-year test period. The system is equally accurate in shorter time horizons; it beat the index over 60 percent of the time for each calendar month and quarter between 1990 and 1999.

But even though it is more accurate than a buy-and-hold strategy,

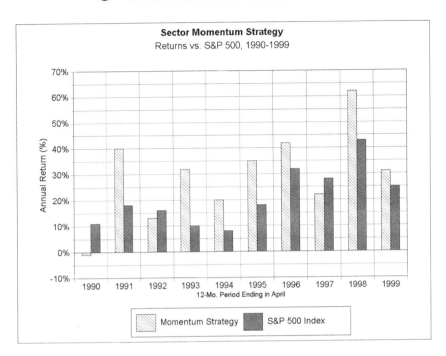

FIGURE 12.6 A simple momentum strategy using sector mutual funds outperformed the S&P 500 index in seven years of the 10-year test period. *Source:* Adapted from O'Neal, 2000.

sector timing is a bit more volatile. Again, the reason is diversification. Even though the system buys the three best-performing industry groups, the degree of diversification is much less than in a broad index like the S&P 500.

SECTOR TIMING: BETTER THAN A BUY-AND-HOLD STRATEGY?

The results from our timing strategy tell a compelling story. But does sector momentum truly offer better returns than a simple buy-and-hold strategy?

To answer this question, it is necessary to determine what causes market momentum to exist. If momentum profits are somehow linked to the health of the U.S. economy, it would signal to investors when to utilize such a strategy.

As it turns out, one economic variable is closely linked to momentum profits—the credit premium between high-yield (or "junk") bonds and U.S. government bonds. Declining default risk premiums are likely when the market perceives an upturn in the economy, which decreases the likelihood of corporate financial problems. *Thus, it seems that momentum profits are tied to the strength of the economy; when economic growth slows, momentum strategies are not as profitable as when the economy is expanding* (see Figure 12.7).

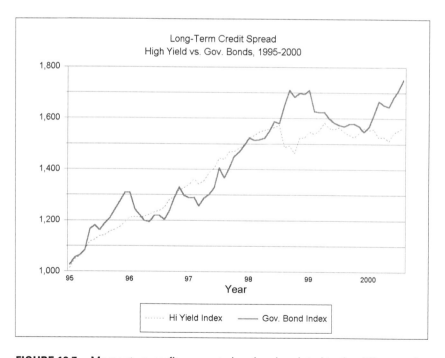

FIGURE 12.7   Momentum profits seem to be closely related to the difference in yields of high-yield (or "junk") bonds and U.S. government bonds. When government bonds perform better than high-yield bonds (as shown during 2000), momentum profits are muted.

As Figure 12.7 shows, increases in short-term interest rates by the Federal Reserve in 1999 and 2000 seemed to have caused investors to favor long-term government bonds over higher-risk corporate debt. As a result, the spread between the two investments widened considerably. Unfortunately, this economic environment is one that is not kind to sector momentum players; it may be best to consider other strategies, such as value investing, until the economy gets back on track.

As part of our continuing effort to serve our readers, look for additional information on market timing strategies on the worldlyinvestor.com web site.

WorldlyInvestor Quick Summary

1. Market timers attempt to beat the market by identifying the market sectors with the highest returns in the next day, week, or month.
   - A perfect market timing system would not only be more profitable than a buy-and-hold strategy, it would also be much less risky.
   - Historically, market timers moved between cash and stock; now, the tendency is to time between sectors using a momentum approach.

2. The most popular timing systems rely on momentum within market sectors using either mutual funds or ETFs.
   - Mutual funds offer relatively low transaction costs and a manageable universe of investment choices. However, all sector mutual funds are actively managed and so do not give a pure play in a given sector. Their management fees can be high, also.
   - Exchange-traded funds are passively managed and replicate the returns of a sector more accurately than do mutual funds. Although ETF management fees are low, active trading could generate significant transaction costs.

3. At the sector level, momentum persists longer than at the individual stock level.

3. Market timing using a momentum based methodology:
   - Rank the performance of each sector over the previous 12 months.
   - Purchase an equal amount of the three top-performing sectors and hold for 12 months.
   - At the end of the 12-month hold, rerank the sectors and purchase the three new sector leaders over the previous 12 months, again holding the trade for 12 months.
   - Repeat.

5. Momentum's failings:
   - The performance of momentum strategies declines significantly during economic recessions.
   - Due to a lack of diversification, momentum returns are more volatile than those using a buy-and-hold strategy.

Bibliography

Armstrong, Frank, "Making Sense of Mutual Fund Alphabet Soup." Brill's Interactive Mutual Fund web site (www.brill.com).

Baks, Klaas P., Andrew Metrick, and Jessica Wachter. "Should Investors Avoid All Actively Managed Mutual Funds? A Study in Bayesian Performance Evaluation." Journal of Finance web site (www.cob.ohio-state.edu/~fin/journal/jof.htm).

Barbee, Olivia. "Enhanced Mutual Funds Are Laced with Risks." *Detroit News* web site (www.detroitnews.com), January 4, 1999.

Bary, Andrew. "Today's Shifty Fifty." *Barron's*, March 15, 1999, p. 24.

Berkshire Hathaway, annual statement, 1987.

Bernstein, William. "The Grand Infatuation." Brill's Mutual Fund Interactive web site (www.fundsinteractive.com), July 1999.

Blumenthal, Robin Goldwyn. "Tried and True Approaches Win in the Long Run for Market Letters." Barron's Online web site (www.wsj.com), July 17, 2000.

Bradfield, Dave. "Chasing Winning Funds—A Worthwhile Strategy?" Cadiz Company web site (www.cadiz.co.za).

Brooks, John. *The Go-Go Years* (New York: John Wiley & Sons), 1999.

Brown, Stephen J., and William N. Goetzmann. "Mutual Fund Styles." Yale University web site (www.viking.som.yale.edu), June 6, 1996.

Buffett, Warren. "Mr. Buffett on the Stock Market." *Fortune*, November 22, 1999, pp. 212–220.

Burton, Jonathon. "Mispricings and Unrealistic Expectations." *Dow Jones Asset Management*, March/April 1999, pp. 20–28.

Buttner, Brenda. "Fund Fees Erode Returns." ABC News web site (www.abcnews.go.com).

Califano, Dave. "Why Enhanced Indexes Aren't." *Worth* Magazine web site (www.worth.com), July 1997.

"Charlie Contrarian." *The Economist*, April 8, 2000.

Christopherson, Jon A., Wayne E. Ferson, and Debra Glassman. "Conditioning Manager Alphas on Economic Information: Another Look at the Persistence of Performance." *Review of Financial Studies*, Spring 1998, pp. 111–142.

Clayman, Michelle. "In Search of Excellence: The Investor's Viewpoint." *Financial Analysts Journal*, May/June 1987, pp. 54–63.

Clements, Jonathon. "Individual Stocks' Allure: Lower Taxes." *Wall Street Journal*, June 13, 2000, p. C1.

Desai, Hemang, and Prem C. Jain. "Long-Run Common Stock Returns Following Stock Splits and Reverse Splits." *Journal of Business,* 70 (no. 3), 1997, pp. 409–433.

Dziegeleski, Marlene. "Do Mutual Fund Splits Matter?" About.com web site, (www.mutualfunds.about.com), July 21, 1999.

Easton, Thomas. "How to Judge a Fund." *Forbes* web site (www.forbes.com), February 9, 1998.

Elton, Edwin J., Martin J. Gruber, and Christopher R. Blake. "Survivorship Bias and Mutual Fund Performance." *Review of Financial Studies*, Winter 1996, pp. 1097–1120.

Fabian, Doug. "Do Enhanced Index Funds Live Up to Their Billing?" Brill's Interactive Mutual Fund web site (www.brill.com).

Fischer, Bob. "Tabloid Trash." Investment Advisory Network web site (www.ianinc.com), May 1995 (taken from *Registered Representative* Magazine).

Fleming, Michael J., and Eli Remolona. "What Moves the Bond Market?" *FRBNY Economic Policy Review*, December 1997, pp. 31–50.

Fosback, Norm. *Stock Market Logic* (New York: Institute for Econometric Research), 1976, p. 139.

Fung, William, and David Hsieh. "Performance Attribution Analysis: From Mutual Funds to Hedge Funds." Duke University Working Papers Series, February 1998.

Geisst, Charles B. *Wall Street: A History* (New York: Oxford University Press), 1999.

Graham, Benjamin. *The Intelligent Investor: A Book of Practical Counsel* (New York: HarperCollins), 1985.

Graham, Benjamin, and David L. Dodd. *Security Analysis: The Classic 1934 Edition* (New York: McGraw-Hill), 1996.

Green, Hayley. "Fund Timing: An Inalienable Right?" SmartMoney.com web site (www.smartmoney.com), May 3, 2000.

Gunter, Toddi. "Enhanced? Only the Expenses." *BusinessWeek* web site (www.businessweek.com), July 5, 1999.

Harrington, Robert, and Iqal Memon. "Do Actively Managed Funds Really Outperform the Index Funds?" University of Central Arkansas

Small Business Advancement National Center web site (www.sbanet. uca.edu).

Harvey, Campbell R. "Quantitative Performance Evaluation." Duke University web site (www.duke.edu).

Haugen, Robert, and Josef Lakonishok. *The Incredible January Effect* (Chicago: Dow Jones Irwin), 1988, pp. 88–110.

Hendricks, Darryll, Jayendu Patel, and Richard Zeckhauser. "Hot Hands in Mutual Funds: The Persistence of Performance, 1974–1987." National Bureau of Economic Research Working Paper No. 3389, June 1990.

Henig, Peter. "Qualcomm Still Hunting for Bulls." Red Herring web site (www.redherring.com), February 4, 1999.

Hong, Harrison, Terrance Lim, and Jeremy Stein. "Bad News Travels Slowly: Size, Analyst Coverage, and the Profitability of Momentum Strategies." *Journal of Finance*, 1998.

Hong, Harrison, and Jon Stein. "A Unified Theory of Underreaction, Momentum Trading and Overreaction in Asset Markets." *Journal of Finance*, 1999.

Huberman, Gur, and Tomer Regev, "Contagious Speculation and a Cure for Cancer: A Non-Event That Made Stock Prices Soar." *Journal of Finance*, February 2000.

Hurlbert, Mark. "No Stars for Morningstar." *Forbes* web site (www.forbes.com), December 29, 1997.

Indro, Daniel, Christine X. Jiang, Michael Y. Hu, and Wayne Y. Lee. "Mutual Fund Performance: Does Size Matter?" *Financial Analysts Journal*, May/June 1999, pp. 74–87.

Internet.com Corporation. "CDMA Takes Over as Top Digital Wireless Technology." www.allnetdevices.com, July 12, 1999.

Investment Company Institute. "Mutual Fund Fact Book." ICI web site (www.ici.org), 1999, pp. 11–24.

Investor Home. "Mutual Funds." Investor Home web site (www.investorhome.com), August 9, 1999.

Jegadeesh, Narasimhan, and Sheridan Titman. "Profitability of Momentum Strategies: An Evaluation of Alternative Explanations." *Journal of Finance* web site (www.afajof.org), April 2001.

Jimenez, Daniel. "A Primer on Stock Splits." TheWhiz.com (www.thewhizsnap.com), 1999.

Jubak, Jim. "Is Qualcomm Ready to Bust Out–or Just Bust?" MSN Money-Central (www.moneycentral.msn.com), March 14, 2000.

Kao, Duen–Li, and Robert D. Shumaker. "Equity Style Timing." *Financial Analysts Journal*, January/February 1999, pp. 37–48.

Knowledge Adventure, Inc. "The High Jump: Following Fosbury's Flop." (www.letsfindout.com), 1998.

Laderman, Jeffrey M. "Mutual Funds: Squeaking Past the Index Funds." *BusinessWeek* web site (www.businessweek.com), June 4, 1998.

Laderman, Jeffrey M., and Amy Barrett. "Mutual Funds: What's Wrong." *BusinessWeek* web site (www.businessweek.com), January 24, 2000.

Lee, Charles M. C., and Bhaskaran Swaminathan. "Price Momentum and Trading Volume." *Journal of Finance* web site (www.afajof.org), October 2000.

Malkiel, Burton G. *A Random Walk Down Wall Street* (New York: W. W. Norton), 1996.

McDonald, Ian. "The Big Screen: Is the Old Saw about Size True?" TheStreet.com web site (www.thestreet.com), August 5, 2000.

Middleton, Timothy. "Beware the Lure of a Winning Fund." MSN Money-Central Investor web site (www.moneycentral.msn.com), January 12, 1999.

——. "When Closed Funds Reopen, It's Time to Get In." MSN MoneyCentral Investor web site (www.moneycentral.msn.com), November 17, 1998.

Moskowitz, Tobias, and Mark Grinblatt. "Do Industries Explain Momentum?" *Journal of Finance,* 54, pp. 1249–1290.

Norton, Leslie P. "Shifty Fifty." *Barron's,* May 17, 1999, p. 41.

Odean, Terrance. 1998. "Are Investors Reluctant to Realize Their Losses?" Graduate School of Management, University of California, Davis.

——. 1999. "Do Investors Trade Too Much?" *American Economic Review.*

O'Neal, Edward S. "Industry Momentum and Sector Mutual Funds." *Financial Analysts Journal,* July/August 2000, pp. 37–49.

Oregon Live. "Fosbury Third in High Jump after 25 Years Off." www.oregonlive.com/sports/spst/sp081317.html, August 13, 1998.

Pathfinder.com. "Dick Fosbury," www.pathfinder.com/People/sp/Olympic/fos.html.

Paul A. Merriman and Associates. "Is Market Timing Ethical?" Paul A. Merriman and Associates web site (www.401khelp.com), 1999.

Peters, Thomas J., and Robert H. Waterman Jr. *In Search of Excellence: Lessons from America's Best-Run Corporations* (New York: Warner Books), 1982.

Peterson, Barbara P., and James Gloub. *Rapid Descent* (New York: Simon & Schuster), 1994, p. 224.

Pizzani, Lori. "Enhance Your Index Fund Returns." WorldlyInvestor web site (www.worldlyinvestor.com), June 27, 2000.

Raynovich, R. Scott. "Qualcomm Hurdles the Great Wall." Red Herring web site (www.redherring.com), February 2, 2000.

Riepe, Mark W., and Jennifer Zils. "Are Enhanced Index Mutual Funds Worthy of Their Name?" BARRA web site (www.barra.com), December 1997.

Robbins, Mike. "How Qualcomm Evolved into a Momentum Stock." MSN MoneyCentral (www.moneycentral.msn.com), January 26, 2000.

Rowland, Mary. "Are Mutual Fund Fees Really Going Down?" MSN MoneyCentral Investor web site (www.moneycentral.msn.com), September 29, 1999.

——. "Fight Back against Rising Mutual Fund Fees." MSN MoneyCentral Investor web site (www.moneycentral.msn.com), March 29, 2000.

——. "Five Reasons to Dislike Mutual Funds?" MSN MoneyCentral Investor web site (www.moneycentral.msn.com), August 25, 1999.

Santoni, Michael. "Do As I Say, Not As I Do." *Barron's* web site (www.wsj.com), September 25, 2000.

——. "Investment Narrowcasting." *Barron's* web site (www.wsj.com), October 2, 2000.

Sharpe, William F. "Morningstar's Risk Adjusted Ratings." *Financial Analysts Journal,* July/August 1998, pp. 21–33.

Siegel, Jeremy J. *Stocks for the Long Run* (Chicago: Irwin Professional), 1994.

SmartMoney.com. "The True Cost of Mutual Fund Fees." SmartMoney.com web site (www.smartmoney.com).

Smith, Anne Kates. "The Brains Behind Smart Money Investing." TheStreet.com web site (www.thestreet.com), June 21, 1999.

Solberg, Carl. *Conquest of the Skies* (New York: Little, Brown), 1979.

Stoll, Hans R. "Friction." Presidential Address, American Financial Association, January 8, 2000 (Boston, Massachusetts).

Teweles, Richard, Frank Jones, and Ben Warwick (eds.). *The Futures Game* (Chicago: McGraw-Hill), 1999.

Thaler, Richard H. "The End of Behavioral Finance." *Financial Analysts Journal,* November/December 1999, pp. 12–17.

——. *The Winner's Curse* (New York: Free Press), 1992.

Tobin, Isaac. "Newton's Three Laws of Motion." www.aloha.com/˜isaac/3laws.

Valenti, Catherine. "Clone Funds: Is Two a Crowd?" TheStreet.com web site (www.thestreet.com), September 19, 2000.

——. "For a Mutual Fund, How Big Is Too Big?" TheStreet.com web site (www.thestreet.com), August 21, 2000.

Waggoner, John. "Are Funds with the Highest Expenses Worth It?" *USA Today* web site (www.usatoday.com).

——. "Keep Funds Fees Down to Boost Returns." *USA Today* web site (www.usatoday.com).

Wagner, Wayne, and Steven Glass. "Analyzing Transaction Costs: Part I." *Journal of Investment Consulting,* 1, No. 2 (June 1999), p. 7.

Warshawsky, Mark, Mary DiCarlantonio, and Lisa Mullan. "The Persistence of Morningstar Ratings." *Journal of Financial Planning*, September 2000, pp. 110–126.

Warwick, Ben. *Searching for Alpha: The Quest for Exceptional Investment Performance* (New York: John Wiley & Sons), 1999.

Wermers, Russ. "Mutual Fund Performance: An Empirical Decomposition into Stock-Picking Talent, Style, Transaction Costs, and Expenses." University of Colorado Working Paper Series, February 2000.

Yankee Publishing Inc. "Who We Are." Farmer's Almanac web site (www.almanac.com/aboutofa.html), 2000.

Yardeni, Ed. "New Competitive Economy Primer." www.yardeni.com, August 14, 2000.

Zweig, Jason. "Don't Fly Blind." *Money* web site (www.money.com), October 2000.

——. "Fund Wars." *Money*, September 1, 1999, pp. 106–112.

——. "He's Not Picky–He'll Take Whatever Is Wounded." *Money* web site (www.money.com), February 1999.

Additional Recommended Reading

Atlas, Riva. 1999. "Value Addled." *Institutional Investor* 33, No. 3, March, pp. 58–68.

Banz, Rolf W. 1981. "The Relationship between Market Value and Return of Common Stocks." *Journal of Financial Economics*, November.

Beder, Tanya. 1995. "VaR: Seductive but Dangerous." *Financial Analysts Journal*, September 10, pp. 12–24.

Bernstein, Peter. 1992. *Capital Ideas*. New York: The Free Press.

———. 1996. *Against the Gods: The Remarkable Story of Risk*. New York: John Wiley & Sons.

———. 1998. "Where, Oh Where Are the .400 Hitters of Yesteryear?" *Financial Analysts Journal*, November 2, pp. 6–14.

———. 1999. "A New Look at the Efficient Market Hypothesis." *Journal of Portfolio Management* 25, Winter, p. 1.

Bogle, John. 1998. "The First Index Mutual Fund: A History of Vanguard Index Trust and the Vanguard Index Strategy." Vanguard Group web site (www.vanguard.com).

———. 1998. *Investing with Simplicity*. Keynote speech, Intelligent Investing Conference (October 3).

Briet, William, and Roger W, Spencer (eds.). 1986. *Lives of the Laureates: Seven Nobel Economists*. Cambridge, MA: MIT Press.

Brown, Ken. 1999. "The Reckoning." *SmartMoney*, February, pp. 94–102.

Butler, Jonathon. 1996. "Is Bigger Better–and for Whom?" *Worth*, August.

Chancellor, Edward. 1999. *Devil Take the Hindmost: A History of Financial Speculation*. New York: Farrar Straus Giroux.

Chow, George, Eric Jacquier, Mark Kritzman, and Kenneth Lowry. 1999. "Optimal Portfolios in Good Times and Bad." *Financial Analysts Journal*, May–June, pp. 65–73.

Clements, Jonathon. 1999. "How the Taxman Dines on Your Mutual Fund." *Wall Street Journal*, August 31, p. C1.

Clow, Robert, and Riva Atlas. 1998. "What Went Wrong." *Institutional Investor* 32, No. 12 (December), pp. 41–57.

Coy, Peter. 1997. "Mining Profits from Microdata." *Business Week*, December 1.

Ehrbar, E. F. 1976. "Indexing: An Idea Whose Time Has Come." *Fortune*, June, pp. 142–147.

Ellis, Charles. 1985. *Investment Policy*. Chicago: Dow Jones Irwin.

Elton, Edwin J., and Martin J. Gruber. 1987. *Modern Portfolio Theory and Investment Analysis*. New York: John Wiley & Sons.

Fama, Eugene F. 1998. "Rethinking Stock Market Returns." *Capital Ideas*. University of Chicago Graduate School of Business Publications, January.

Fama, Eugune F., and Kenneth French. 1996. "Multifactor Explanations of Asset Pricing Anomalies." *Journal of Finance* 51, pp. 55–84.

Fisher, Kenneth, and Meir Statman. 1999. "A Behavioral Framework for Time Diversification." *Financial Analysts Journal*, May 6, pp. 87–99.

Fritz, Michael. 1999. "Bond Index Funds Wield Better Yields." *InvestmentNews*, November 5, p. 24.

Galbraith, John Kenneth. 1961. *The Great Crash of 1929*. Cambridge: Riverside Press.

Gallacher, William R. 1994. *Winner Take All*. Chicago: Probus.

Gatev, Evan G., William N. Goetzmann, and K. Geert Rouwenhorst. 1999. *Pairs Trading: Performance of a Relative Value Arbitrage Rule*. Yale School of Management.

Gould, Carole. 1998. "Poof! For More and More Mutual Funds, a Quick Disappearing Act." *New York Times*, August 16, p. 11.

Gray, Jack. 1997. "Overquantification." *Financial Analysts Journal*, November–December, pp. 5–12.

Grossman, Sanford, and Joseph E. Stiglitz. 1980. "On the Impossibility of Informationally Efficient Markets." *American Economic Review*, June, pp. 393–408.

Haim, Larry, and Marshall Sarnat. 1984. *Portfolio and Investment Selection: Theory and Practice*. Englewood Cliffs, NJ: Prentice Hall.

Hansell, Saul. 1989. "Inside Morgan Stanley's Black Box." *Institutional Investor*, May, pp. 204–216.

Harrod, Ray. 1951. *The Life of John Maynard Keynes*. New York: W. W. Norton.

Haugen, Robert. 1990. *Modern Investment Theory*. Englewood Cliffs, NJ: Prentice Hall.

Herman, Tom. 1999. "Tax Report." *Wall Street Journal*, September 8, p. A1.

Horowitz, Donald L., and Robert J. MacKay. 1995. Derivatives: State of the Debate. Chicago Mercantile Exchange.

Institutional Investor Forum, 1999. "Mainstreaming Derivatives." *Institutional Investor*, August, p. 160.

Jegadeesh, Narashimhan, and Sheridan Titman. 1993. "Returns to Buying Winners and Selling Losers: Implications for Stock Market Efficiency." *Journal of Finance*, 48, pp.65–91.

Jeffrey, Robert H., and Robert D. Arnott. 1993. "Is Your Alpha Big Enough to Cover Its Taxes?" *Journal of Portfolio Management*, Spring, pp. 15–25.

Kahneman, Daniel, and Mark W. Riepe. 1998. "Aspects of Investor Psychology." *Journal of Portfolio Management* 24, No. 4 (Summer).

Katona, George. 1975. *Psychological Economics*. New York: Elsevier Publishing Company.

Keynes, John M. 1936. *The General Theory of Employment, Interest, and Money*. New York: Harcourt, Brace & Company.

Khin, John. 1996. "To Load or Not to Load: A Study of the Marketing and Distribution Charges of Mutual Funds." *Financial Analysts Journal*, May 6, pp. 28–36.

Lawson, Tony and Hashem Pesaran (eds.). 1985. *Keynesian Economics*. Armonk, NY: M. E. Sharpe.

LeBaron, Dean. 1998. *The Ins and Outs of Institutional Investing*. Dean LeBaron web site (www.deanlebaron.com).

Lebon, Gustave, and Charles Mackay. 1994. *The Crowd and Extraordinary Popular Delusions*. Greenville, NC: Traders Press.

Lederman, Jess, and Robert A. Klein (eds.). 1996. *Market Neutral: State of the Art Strategies for Every Market Environment*. New York: McGraw Hill.

Lewis, Michael. 1990. *Liar's Poker*. New York: Penguin Books.

——. 1999. "How the Eggheads Cracked." *New York Times Magazine*, January 24, pp. 24–42.

Lin, Po-Han. 1996. *The Beethoven Depot Website* (www.edepot.com).

Lo, Andrew, and A. Craig MacKinley. 1999. *A Non-Random Walk Down Wall Street*. Princeton, NJ: Princeton University Press.

Loeb, Gerald M. 1996. *The Battle for Investment Survival*. New York: John Wiley & Sons.

Lux, Hal. 1998. "Hedge Fund? Who, Me?" *Institutional Investor*, August, pp. 33–36.

——. 1998. "Extreme Finance." *Institutional Investor*, October, pp. 45–49.

Lux, Hal, and Jack Willoughby. 1999. "May Day II." *Institutional Investor*, January, pp. 45–46.

Maital, Shlomo. 1982. *Minds, Markets, and Money*. New York: Basic Books.

Marmer, Harry S. 1996. "Visions of the Future: The Distant Past, Yesterday, Today, and Tomorrow." *Financial Analysts Journal*, May/June, pp. 9–12.

McEnally, Richard, and Carl Ackerman. 1999. "The Returns of Hedge Funds: Risk, Return, and Incentives." *Journal of Finance*.

McQueen, Grant, and Steve Thorley. 1999. "Mining Fool's Gold." *Financial Analysts Journal*, March/April, pp. 61–71.

Miller, Jeffrey, and Peter J. Brennan. 1989. *Program Trading*. New York: J. K. Lasser.

Niederhoffer, Victor. 1997. *The Education of a Speculator*. New York: John Wiley & Sons.

Nobel Foundation. 1997. *The Nobel Foundation Website* (www.nobel.se.)

Perold, Andre F., and Robert S. Salomon Jr. 1991. "The Right Amount of Assets Under Management." *Financial Analysts Journal*, May 6, pp. 31–39.

Picerno, James. 1998. "Bull Market Blues." *Dow Jones Asset Management*, May 6, pp. 32–38.

Picerno, James. 1999. "Alarming Efficiency." *Institutional Investor*, May 6, pp. 43–48.

Pitatelli-Palmarino, Massimo. 1994. *Inevitable Illusions: How Mistakes of Reason Rule Our Minds*. New York: John Wiley & Sons.

Putnam, Bluford. 1996. "Portable Alpha and Gearing Sharpe Ratios." *Global Investor*, November.

——. 1997. "An Investment Paradigm for the New Millennium." *Global Investor*, September.

——. 1997. "The High Cost of Investment Constraints." *Global Investor*, November.

——. 1998. "What Is Market Neutral Anyway?" *Global Investor*, May.

——. 1998. "Risk Management for Banks and Funds Is Not the Same Game." *Global Investor*, September.

Rekenthaler, John. 1999. "The Long Wait." *Dow Jones Asset Management*, January, pp. 31–36.

Reltz, Michael. 1999. "Winner's Curse." *Worth*, February.

Roll, Richard, and Stephen A. Ross. 1984. "The Arbitrage Pricing Theory Approach to Strategic Portfolio Planning." *Financial Analysts Journal*, May–June, pp. 14–26.

Samuelson, Paul. 1974. "Challenge to Judgment." *Journal of Portfolio Management*, Fall.

Sharpe, William F. 1962. "A Simplified Model for Portfolio Analysis." *Management Science*, Vol. 9, pp. 277–293.

——. 1964. "Capital Asset Prices: A Theory of Market Equilibrium Under Conditions of Risk." *Journal of Finance* 19, No. 3, pp. 425–442.

Sherden, William A. 1998. *The Fortune Sellers*. New York: John Wiley & Sons.

Shleifer, Andrei and Robert W. Vishney. 1997. "The Limits of Arbitrage." *Journal of Finance* 52, No. 1 (March), pp. 35–55.

Sobel, Robert. 1968. *Wall Street: America's Financial Disasters*. New York: Macmillan.

——. 1999. "Mania Milestones." *Barron's*, February.

Sullivan, Ryan, Allan Timmermann, and Halbert White. 1998. "Data Snooping, Technical Trading Rule Performance, and the Bootstrap." *Journal of Finance.*

Taubes, Gary. 1998. "Wall Street Smarts." *Discover*, October, pp. 105–112.

Taylor, Walton, and James Yoder. 1994. "Mutual Fund Trading Activity and Investor Utility." *Financial Analysts Journal*, May 6, pp. 66–69.

Thomas, Gordon and Max Morgan-Witts. 1979. *The Day the Bubble Burst.* New York: Doubleday.

Tobin, James. 1958. "Liquidity Preference as Behavior Towards Risk." *Review of Economic Studies*, Vol. 67, pp. 65–86.

Treynor, Jack. 1999. "Zero Sum." *Financial Analysts Journal*, January/February, pp. 8–12.

Tully, Shawn. 1998. "How the Smart Money Really Invests." *Money*, July 6.

Warwick, Ben. 1996. *Event Trading.* Chicago: Irwin.

Wilford, D. Sykes, and Jose Mario Quintana. 1998. "The Unfettered Manager is the Successful Manager." *Global Investor*, October .

Williams, John B. 1938. *The Theory of Investment Value.* Cambridge: Harvard University Press.

Zweig, Jason. 1999. "Confessions of a Fund Pro." *Money*, February, pp. 73–75.

Glossary

actively managed mutual fund   A mutual fund whose portfolio manager takes an active role in security selection and risk management in an attempt to improve the portfolio's risk-adjusted return or reduce an issuer's cost of capital.

bear market   A declining market.

behavioral finance   The study and development of descriptive models of behavior in markets and organizations. These models set aside the traditional assumption of rationality, emphasizing the observed psychological factors that influence decision-making under uncertainty.

benchmark   A reference index or rate that serves as a basis for performance comparison or return calculation.

bull market   A rising market.

call option   An option that rises in value as the underlying security appreciates.

Capital Asset Pricing Model (CAPM)   An asset valuation model describing the relationship between expected risk and expected return for marketable assets.

closed-end fund (CEF)   An investment company with a fixed number of shares outstanding. Shares purchased in such a fund are purchased from another shareholder rather than issued in response to demand for new shares. In contrast to shares in an open-ended mutual fund, which can usually be redeemed at net asset value, a closed-end fund's shares can trade at a premium or a discount.

commission   A transaction fee charged by a broker for acting as an agent in a transaction.

curve fitting   Designing a trading system with the benefit of hindsight. Such systems usually lose money when utilized, even though they appear profitable using historical data.

delay costs   Lost profits that occur when large trades cannot be executed in the desired time frame.

derivative   A contract or convertible security, such as an option, future, forward, LEAPS, swap, warrant, or debt instrument that changes in value in concert with and/or obtains much of its value from price movements in a related or underlying security, future, or other instrument or index.

distressed stock   An equity that has lost or stands to lose much of its value.

dividend   Distribution to stockholders of cash or stock declared by the company's board of directors.

Dow Jones Industrial Average   A price-weighted average of 30 actively traded blue-chip stocks. Prepared and published by Dow Jones & Company, it is the oldest and most quoted of all of the market indicators.

earnings surprise   Periodic earnings of a company that exceed market expectations.

event day   The release date of an important piece of market-moving news, such as an earnings report or government inflation data.

event study   A study of the relationship between a particular event or class of events and the response of a variable of interest.

exchange-traded fund (ETF)   Mutual fund that is traded on an organized exchange.

exchange-traded securities   Securities traded on an organized exchange.

forward contract   An agreement between two parties to exchange a particular good or instrument at a set price on a future date. The buyer of the forward agrees to pay the price and take delivery of the good or instrument and is said to be long the forward, while the seller of the forward, or short, agrees to deliver the good or instrument at the agreed price on the agreed date.

fundamental analysis   Appraisal of macroeconomic data and the interaction of economic data with information from a company's financial statements and operations with the objective of predicting the company's cash flow and earnings and, ultimately, the investment value of its securities.

futures contract   An agreement, originally between two parties, a buyer and a seller, to exchange a particular good for a particular price at a date in the future. All terms are specified in a contract common to all participants in a market on an organized futures exchange.

growth investing An investment management style that emphasizes the recent past and expected future ability of a company to increase its earnings per share at an above-average rate.

holiday effect The tendency for stocks to rise immediately before and after major holidays and three-day weekends.

index mutual fund A passively managed mutual fund that tries to match the performance of a specific index by purchasing the same securities that are held by that index.

index options Calls and puts on indexes of stocks that allow investors to trade in a particular market or industry group without having to buy all of the stocks individually.

initial public offering (IPO) An issuer's first public sale of common stock, or less frequently, other securities.

January effect The tendency of small-cap stocks to outperform large-cap stocks in the first month of the year.

large-cap stocks Stocks whose respective companies' market capitalizations (stock price times total shares outstanding) are the largest in their respective markets.

leverage An investment or operating position subject to a multiplied effect on profit or position value resulting from a small change in sales quantity or price.

liquidity A market condition in which enough units of a security or other instrument are traded to allow large transactions to be absorbed by the marketplace without significant impact on price stability.

margin The required equity or other performance bond that an investor must deposit to collateralize an investment position.

market capitalization The price of a stock multiplied by the total number of shares outstanding. Also, the market's total valuation of a public company.

market impact The effect of the positions bought or sold on the price paid or received for a security.

market indexes Market indicators that represent a measure of the relative value of a combined group of stocks.

market overreaction The tendency of traders to overweight the most recent news. This is usually associated with the release of macroeconomic information.

market participants Traders, investors, and other interested parties who buy and sell securities.

market underreaction   The tendency of traders to underweight the most recent news. This is usually associated with the release of stock-specific information.

markup   A charge added to the selling price of a security by a broker-dealer when the broker-dealer is selling the security to a customer from its own account–equivalent to the commission on the sale.

mean reverting   Possessing the characteristics of having variables such as prices, rates, and volatilities that tend to return to a mean or average after reaching extremes.

Modern Portfolio Theory (MPT)   A variety of portfolio construction, asset valuation, and risk measurement concepts and models that rely on the application of statistical and quantitative techniques.

momentum   The tendency of stock prices with a strong uptrend to continue moving higher.

momentum traders   Those who participate in momentum trading.

momentum trading   Participating in market activity by increasing or reducing levels of market participation to go with the flow–increasing market exposure when the market is rising, and decreasing market exposure when the market is falling.

monthly employment report   Monthly report, released by the U.S. Department of Labor, that details the country's employment situation.

Nasdaq index   An index established by the National Association of Securities Dealers consisting of major national and international stocks.

net asset value (NAV)   The amount by which the value of an entity's assets exceeds the value of its liabilities.

news watchers   Traders who make buy and sell decisions solely on the basis of fundamental information.

opportunity cost   The value of a lost chance or a potential profit that was not realized because a course of action was taken that did not permit the investor to obtain that profit.

option   A stipulated privilege of buying or selling a stated security or commodity at a given price (strike price) within a specified time. A securities option is a negotiable contract in which the seller (writer), for a certain sum of money (option premium), gives the buyer the right to demand within a specified time the purchase (call) or sale (put) by the option seller of a specified number of securities at a fixed price or rate.

out-of-sample test   Using data not used in the estimation of a model to test the validity of a trading system.

over-the-counter bulletin board (OTCBB) A regulated quotation service that displays real-time quotes, last-sale prices, and volume information for over-the-counter (OTC) equity securities.

passively managed mutual fund A mutual fund whose portfolio manager invests assets in index portfolios or an unmanaged basket of securities and other instruments without attempting to select individual securities.

penny stock Any stock with a low price, usually less that $5 per share in the United States.

Pink Sheets Relatively inactive over-the-counter stocks not included in the Nasdaq daily listing or supplementary listings. Quotations are actually provided on pink sheets of paper, compiled daily, and distributed to dealers, investors, and pricing services.

price-to-book (P/B) Ratio A stock's current market price divided by its book value, or historical accounting value.

price-to-earnings (P/E) ratio A stock's price per share divided by a reported or forecast figure for annual earnings per share.

put option An option that increases in value as the underlying security drops in price.

Quant View Portfolio A portfolio of short-term strategies in the S&P 500 index.

quantitative trading A portfolio management or trading style that applies mathematical and statistical techniques to a single market sector (i.e., equity or debt) or to asset allocation.

relative strength Strength or performance of an asset's return measured against the return of a benchmark rather than as the absolute strength of the asset.

return on assets (ROA) Net income divided by total assets, expressed as a percent.

return on capital (ROC) Net income divided by total invested capital.

return on equity (ROE) Net income divided by net worth.

return on sales Net income divided by total sales revenue.

Russell indexes A family of market-weighted indexes created by the Frank Russell Company.

S&P effect The phenomenon associated with an increase in a stock's value due to the addition of that stock to the Standard & Poor's 500 index of stocks.

short selling Selling a security or other financial instrument not previously owned by the seller in the expectation that it will be possible to repurchase that instrument at a lower price at some time in the future.

short squeeze An upward movement in the price of an instrument stimulated by short sellers rushing to cover their positions in response to a fundamental or technical development or in response to a request from a lender for the return of a borrowed stock.

stock screen A list of stocks that meets certain criteria for price, volume, and value.

stock splits The division of outstanding shares of a company into a larger number of shares, while the proportionate equity in the company is the same before and after the split.

technical analysis An effort to forecast prices, rates, or returns in financial markets largely by analyzing data internal to a company or market, such as price or volume numbers.

time value A common reference to the difference between an option's price and its parity or intrinsic value, due to the number of days until the option expires.

transaction cost The cost of buying or selling a financial instrument measured in the context of its impact on the portfolio, including, at a minimum, any purchase or sales commission charged by the brokerage firm executing the trade and the spread between the bid and the asked prices.

value investing An investment style that emphasizes stocks that trade at or below the intrinsic value of the company.

Zacks rank A proprietary stock selection methodology of Zacks Investment Research that ranks issues by changes in the earnings estimates calculated by Wall Street analysts.

zero-sum game A game in which the profits accruing to the winner come directly from the pockets of the loser.

Index

Index

Index